Fur Trade Letters
of WILLIE TRAILL

WILLIAM EDWARD TRAILL

Editor **K. DOUGLAS MUNRO**

Fur Trade Letters

of WILLIE TRAILL

1864–1893

THE UNIVERSITY OF ALBERTA PRESS

Published by
The University of Alberta Press
Ring House 2
Edmonton, Alberta, Canada   T6G 2E1

Library and Archives Canada Cataloguing in Publication

Traill, Willie, 1844–1917
   Fur trade letters of Willie Traill, 1864–1893 / editor, K. Douglas Munro;
   foreword by Michael Peterman.

   Includes bibliographical references and index.
   ISBN 13: 978–0-88864–460–2
   ISBN 10: 0–88864–460–4

   1. Traill, Willie, 1844–1917—Correspondence. 2. Traill family. 3. Hudson's Bay
Company—History. 4. Fur trade—Canada, Western—History—19th century.
5. Northwest, Canadian—History—1870–1905. 6. Frontier and pioneer life—Canada,
Western. 7. Hudson's Bay Company—Biography. 8. Fur traders—Canada, Western—
Correspondence. I. Munro, K. Douglas, 1933– II. Title.

FC3217.1.T73A4 2006   971.2'02092   C2006–906052–5

First edition, first printing, 2006.
Printed and bound in Canada by Houghton Boston Printers, Saskatoon, Saskatchewan.
Copyediting and Indexing by Brenda Belokrinicev. Map by Wendy Johnson.

The University of Alberta Press is committed to protecting our natural environment. As part of
our efforts, this book is printed on New Leaf Paper: it contains 100% post-consumer recycled
fibres and is acid- and chlorine-free.

The University of Alberta Press gratefully acknowledges the support received for its publishing
program from The Canada Council for the Arts. The University of Alberta Press also gratefully
acknowledges the financial support of the Government of Canada through the Book Publishing
Industry Development Program (BPIDP) and from the Alberta Foundation for the Arts for its
publishing activities.

Letters are commonplace enough, yet what splendid things they are! When someone is in a distant province and one is worried about him, and then a letter suddenly arrives, one feels as though one were seeing him face to face. And it is a great comfort to have expressed one's feelings in a letter—even though one knows it cannot have arrived.

Sei Shonagon, *The Pillow of Sei Shonagon*

To T.R. "Pat" McCloy, B.A., B.L.S.

The inspiration for this book.

CONTENTS

ABBREVIATIONS

GAA   Glenbow Alberta Archives
HBCA   Hudson's Bay Company Archives
NAC   National Archives of Canada
SAB   Saskatchewan Archives Board

FOREWORD

CHILDREN'S ACCOMPLISHMENTS SEEM OFTEN TO PALE in comparison with the achievements of their parents. This has certainly been the case with the offspring of Catharine Parr Traill (1802–1899) and Susanna Moodie (1803–1885). In their books and occasional pieces, Traill and Moodie left a rich record of early settlement experience and the struggle for self-expression in Canada. They came to the new world in 1832 with their Orkney-born husbands and had not only a first-hand experience of life in the backwoods (or bush, or forest) but also a close association with the development of Canada from colony to fledgling nation. Both women had been writers in England. In Upper Canada, they extended and developed their careers, writing classic interpretations of the settlement process in English Canada. Catharine's *The Backwoods of Canada* (1836) and Susanna's *Roughing It in the Bush* (1852) offer closely aligned but distinctly different ways of seeing Canada and the experience of becoming an adopted daughter of the colony. Later books such as Catharine's novel, *Canadian Crusoes* (also entitled *Lost in the Backwoods*) (1852), and Susanna's *Life in the Clearings* (1853) added to their stature as thought-provoking and engaging interpreters of life in what we now call Ontario.

Both women gave birth to large families in the backwoods. Though they lamented the kind of education available to their children in those early days, they did what they could by way of home training and maintained high hopes that at least a few of their children might make significant contributions to their country—especially after 1867, when Confederation drew the four founding provinces together. With books before us like *Fur Trade Letters of Willie Traill*, it is possible to say that neither Catharine nor Susanna would have been disappointed in the accomplishments of their children. Diligent research and archival reclamation in recent years have made it clear that several of their offspring distinguished themselves, either in the arts or by contributing in various ways to the record of the opening of the Canadian west.

Best known today are Agnes Chamberlin, Geraldine Moodie, Mary Muchall, Walter Traill, and Willie Traill. Susanna Moodie's second daughter, Agnes (1833–1913), later Agnes Fitzgibbon and later still Agnes Chamberlin, taught herself lithography after the death of her first husband in order to help her aunt Catharine produce books on Canadian flora. Agnes's initiative and executive ability led directly to the publication of *Canadian Wild Flowers* (1868), arguably the first coffee-table book produced in Canada, and to the much more ambitious *Plant Life in Canada* (1884). One of Agnes's daughters, Geraldine (1854–1945), married a young man named John Moodie from Edinburgh and followed him out west during his career as a northwest mounted policeman. She became a photographer—she was the first woman to operate a photographic studio in the Canadian prairies— and brilliantly recorded a good deal of early western experience. Her compelling photos of the mounties, native peoples, and early ranchers have been collected in Donny White's book *In Search of Geraldine Moodie* (1998).

The accomplishments of Catharine's children are even more noteworthy. Catharine's third daughter Mary (1841–1892) wrote stories and poems under her married name, Mary Muchall, and had a modest career in the 1870s and 1880s. Mary's older brother Henry (Hal) had a notable but sad fate, in that he was the first prison guard in Canadian history to be killed in the line of duty. But it was Catharine's two youngest children, William (1844–1917) and Walter (1847–1932) who left a mark on the development of the Canadian west through their letters home to Catharine and their siblings.

Walter Traill was fortunate in having a younger relative, Mae Atwood, poised to become his champion. He went west a few years after Willie did, and worked for the Hudson's Bay Company for about a decade. Walter then set out on his own, developing a large farm near the border and experimenting in the shipping of grain. His influence has been honoured in the name of Traill County near Fargo, North Dakota, and by a statue erected there. Mae Atwood diligently gathered Walter's letters and documents and put together two books, *In Rupert's Land: Memoirs of Walter Traill* (1970) and *Dawn across Canada: Oxcart to Railway in Ten Years* (1986). Walter's travels on both sides of the border, with his friendships and adventures, make good reading.

William Traill, or 'Willie' as his mother called him, went west in 1864 and devoted his entire working life to the Hudson's Bay Company. His career took him westward from the Manitoba territory to Fort Ellice and many other posts before he completed his tenure at Fort St. James in British Columbia. He married Harriet, daughter of Chief Factor William MacKay, and the two had twelve children. Echoing his mother's commitment to letter-writing and the importance of the written word, Willie, like Walter, left a rich record of observations and experiences in his letters home. I spent many interesting days several years ago in the National Archives (as it was then called), reading Willie's early letters to his mother, letters that she had taken pains to copy and arrange for possible publication. She saw in them a worthy project; age prevented her from completing that task, although she continued to write into her nineties.

It has taken further family commitment, first from Willie's grandson, T.R. (Pat) McCloy, and then from another descendant, Doug

Munro, to bring these important letters to the public. It was Pat who opened the territory in the 1950s by gathering and organizing the papers, which became the Traill Family Collection. While I was at work on Catharine Parr Traill's letters with my research colleagues, Carl Ballstadt and Elizabeth Hopkins, I received several informative letters from Pat, who was then in his late eighties. Pat was very appreciative of and encouraging about our work in collecting and editing the letters of Susanna Moodie and Catharine Parr Traill and, yet more valuable, he sent us an important letter which was still in his possession—a letter written by Catharine while she was visiting Ottawa in 1884. We were delighted to include that letter in 'I Bless You in My Heart': Selected Correspondence of Catharine Parr Traill (1996). But, in his letters to me, Pat made it clear that he wanted, above all, to see Willie's letters in print.

Together with Doug Munro, I salute Pat McCloy, Traill family historian extraordinaire. And I salute Doug Munro for his effort and vision in bringing forward the life, times, and observations of Willie Traill, HBC man to the core and, at heart, his mother's good and loyal son. Together with the photos of Geraldine Moodie, the stories of Mary Muchall, the lithography of Agnes Chamberlain, and the letters of his brother Walter, Willie's letters provide ample evidence of the significant contribution to Canada's history—both in the east and in the west—made by the descendants of Catharine Parr Traill and Susanna Moodie.

Michael Peterman, Trent University

PREFACE

DURING A 1950S VISIT TO THE ATWOOD FAMILY HOME in Lakefield, Ontario, Pat McCloy—grandson of Willie and Harriet Traill, and the first librarian at the Glenbow library in Calgary—discovered boxes of Traill family documents in the attic, in complete disarray. Annie Atwood (Anne Traill Fotheringhame Atwood)—daughter of Anne Traill Fotheringhame Traill and granddaughter of Catharine Parr Traill—gave Pat permission to remove and safeguard the material. She knew it would be in excellent hands.

The physical preservation of the Traill family documents became Pat McCloy's vocation and avocation. He sorted, deciphered, catalogued, and indeed rescued this historic treasure. He then deposited copies and/or originals with the Glenbow Archives (GBA).

Most of the original material upon which this book is based is available solely because of his outstanding efforts. Over a period of years, Pat and I discussed the letters and he strongly encouraged me to review and prepare them for publication. Willie's mother, Catharine Parr Traill, had also hoped to see these letters published.

There are more than 250 of William Traill's personal letters extant, and 177 are represented in this collection. Some letters, because of a paper shortage, were written from left to right in the normal course and then overwritten from the bottom of the page to the top. Surprisingly, because of Willie's legible hand, these letters can be deciphered with practice. Sadly, few letters survived from certain years, notably 1870, 1873, and 1875.

All of the letters contained in this book are available at the National Archives of Canada (NAC) in the Traill Family Collection, MG 29 D 81, on microfilm (Film H15) and as originals; and/or at the Glenbow Archives (GBA) in either the Traill Family Fonds, M1241, or the Pat McCloy Genealogical Collection, M8486, as photocopies, originals, or typed transcripts of originals. The Saskatchewan Archives Board (SAB) provided some letters from the S-A 104 William E. Traill fonds, as well as assorted background information. The Fort St. James National Historic Site, with assistance from the Fort St. James Chamber of Commerce, provided an assortment of Willie's personal letters.

I selected for publication the most interesting letters from each Hudson's Bay post, and supplemented those with excerpts from contemporary letters. In order to include more letters in this volume, I reluctantly cut redundant portions of many letters. For the most part, the material cut consisted of greetings such as "How are you—I am fine—hope you are the same" and repetitious notes on the weather and the children. Such cuts are indicated with this symbol: [...]. Where this symbol follows Willie's signature, a postscript has been omitted.

These letters have been reproduced from microfilm, photocopies, or transcribed copies of the originals. As accurately as possible, we present the letters in chronological order. Original place names are used throughout. Where the date and location of letter-writing is known, it is shown at the head of the letter. In some instances, the location and/or date was established from the content of the letters; in these cases, I have enclosed the uncertain item in square brackets. Because the mail service at many posts was sporadic in the extreme, mail arrived and departed as infrequently as twice a year; Willie's letters were therefore written and dispatched in clusters. He wrote many of the letters over a period of days or weeks; the date at the head of each letter likely reflects the day that Willie began writing it.

The salutations are as Willie wrote them, except where they are enclosed in square brackets. Sentence structure and wording within the letters has not been altered, although spelling has, in most instances, been corrected. Where Willie misspelled place names and proper nouns, contemporary spelling has been substituted. Other misspellings that added nothing to the meaning or clarity of the letters were corrected. Where it was necessary for clarity, punctuation has also been corrected. Words enclosed in square brackets are a best estimate of missing words or phrases. Non-italicized words enclosed in square brackets identify editorial comments. Where Willie's letters were unsigned or their final portion (and therefore the signature) is missing, I have appended "W.E. Traill." Where the signature takes a different form, it is faithful to the original.

The letters in this collection, written to family and close friends, trace Willie Traill's entire twenty-nine-year career with the Hudson's Bay Company, from his days as a raw recruit to his retirement from the Company as a seasoned veteran. These letters invite readers into Willie's life as it unfolds—giving them an intimate view of the daily challenges faced by an HBC trader and his family.

Willie's letters also reveal the substantial contributions made by the Traill and McKay families to the development of Western Canada. As Catharine Parr Traill foresaw, Willie's letters make an important contribution to the historical record of our nation. It is an honour and a privilege to offer this collection of letters to students of Canadian history.

ACKNOWLEDGMENTS

GENERATIONS OF TRAILLS AND McKAYS have demonstrated great pride and enthusiasm in order to ensure that their family's oral and written histories have been lovingly preserved. Nothing pleases them more than to gather and regale each other with tales of blizzards, buffalo hunting, feast and famine and their family's significant contribution to Canadian literature and the history of Western Canada.

The initiative, research and dedication of T.R. "Pat" McCloy, BA, BLS, one of Willie's grandsons and the first librarian at the Glenbow Foundation, was fundamentally responsible for collecting and protecting the letters that are the focus of this book.

The National Archives of Canada, the Glenbow Archives and the Saskatchewan Archives Board have been uniformly cooperative and helpful by providing me with access to all material related to, or written by, Willie Traill. The assistance afforded by their staff has been nonpareil. The Fort St. James National Historic Site, in association with the Fort St. James Chamber of Commerce, made available copies of a number of Willie's letters and information regarding him and his family.

The staff of the Hudson's Bay Company Archives (Provincial Archives of Manitoba) skillfully and enthusiastically provided vital background information regarding HBC posts, personnel and access to their photo collection.

The following splendid staff at the University of Alberta Press have guided my literary efforts with patience, humour, enthusiasm and consistently objective common sense; Linda Cameron, Cathie Crooks, Michael Luski and Amber Marechal. Brenda Belokrinicev edited the manuscript and provided a multitude of suggestions for creative changes to the text, which greatly enhanced the book's literacy and readability. The professionalism of Kevin Zak's superb design is self-evident.

Dr. Gerhard Ens and Mr. Tony Cashman were kind enough to review an early draft of this manuscript. Their thoughtful and thorough critique, and their suggestions for improvements to content and construction, immeasurably enhanced the quality and clarity of this book.

Marion Hage, *neé* McKay, a great granddaughter of Willie, spent many an hour at the Glenbow conducting research on my behalf. Diane Edgelow, my first cousin and another of Willie's great granddaughters, supplied a variety of excellent photos from the family picture gallery, a number of family contacts and continuous enthusiasm for this project.

Renie and Bob Gross of Badland's Books have provided substantial and coherent suggestions for changes to size and content and have frequently reaffirmed the value of Willie's writings.

Dr. Michael Peterman, of Trent University, has contributed a thoughtful and very professional Foreword to this volume. With his substantive knowledge of Catherine Parr Traill and her family, he willingly provided me with advice and guidance whenever I sought his aid.

And, to my wife Adele, whose patience and proofreading skills have improved this final product, my love and thanks.

INTRODUCTION

I GREW UP LISTENING TO COUNTLESS FASCINATING TALES—about my great-grandfather William Edward (Willie) Traill; his wife, my great-grandmother Harriet McKay; and her family based on their lives as Hudson's Bay Company (HBC) families in the 1800s. My great-aunts Mary and Annie, two of Willie's younger daughters, were a repository of Traill family history. These two extraordinary women were "The Aunts" to all who knew them—in name, in spirit, and in fact. Mary and Annie Traill were legends to their family, their community, and beyond. The Aunts were my direct link to their parents' generation.

For those of us raised on tales of Mary McKay's buffalo hunt, Harriet's encounter with the Sioux warriors, and William McKay's friendship with Big Bear, western history and stories of life in the HBC were family history. Imagine a member of your family hunting buffalo in the closing era of the great hunts, snowshoeing fifty miles or more a day, single-handedly nursing an entire fort through a smallpox epidemic, and you have some idea of why the Traill and McKay ancestors are an endless source of pride and admiration for all of us! Not only are the stories exciting, but the courage, resourcefulness, and decency of our relatives provides us with exemplary role models for our younger generations.

Catharine Parr Traill, Willie's mother. (Willie Traill Family Collection) Willie Traill 9

Willie's parents, Thomas Traill and Catharine Parr Strickland, married and immigrated to Canada in the summer of 1832. Thomas, a former officer in the 21st Royal Scotch Fusiliers, had been granted a parcel of land in the Township of Douro (in what is now the eastern part of the city of Peterborough), Upper Canada. Catharine and her younger sister, Susanna (Moodie), were similar in many ways: both were accomplished writers who married officers from the same Highland regiment and emigrated to Upper Canada in 1832. However, their reactions to life on a primitive homestead were polar opposites—Susanna never entirely accepted her lot, while Catharine remained consistently optimistic regardless of how bleak, miserable, and financially bereft the situation.

Thomas had neither the skill nor the initiative to operate a wilderness homestead. Saddled with high costs and an increasing debt load, and in the clutches of a major economic depression, the Traills' initial farming experience collapsed in 1839. Their perilous financial position was ameliorated somewhat when, in 1836, Catharine received 110 pounds sterling for her first major literary endeavour, *The Backwoods of Canada*. Nevertheless, financial problems remained a concern for many years.

Catharine and Susanna became Canadian literary icons. In addition to *The Backwoods of Canada*, Catharine wrote, among others, *The Canadian Settler's Guide, Canadian Crusoes, Canadian Wild Flowers, Pearls and Pebbles*, and *Cot and Cradle Stories*. Susanna's major work, *Roughing it in the Bush*, paints a bleak picture of settlers' life. Catharine's writing reflects her pragmatism, resourcefulness, and steadfast faith. Her son Willie shared many of his mother's finest qualities.

William (Willie) Edward was born July 26, 1844, on a rented farm at Ashburnham, across the Ottonabee River from present-day Peterborough, Ontario—the eighth child and second youngest son of Thomas and Catharine. His siblings who survived infancy were, in order of their birth, James, Kate, Harry, Annie, Mary, and Walter.

Little is known of Willie's formative years, although it is evident that his parents imbued him with the finest attributes of a proper Victorian gentleman. He was courteous, devout, kindly, industrious, well-mannered, honest, decent, and had a solid grounding in the English language—qualities that he epitomized until his death in 1917.

A vignette from the family's oral history underscores the ongoing poverty the family experienced. Willie, approximately age five and concerned about the family's financial plight, buried the Traill family's heirloom sterling silver spoons in their garden. When questioned about the disappearance of the spoons, he explained that he had planted them so they would reproduce. A diligent search ensued, but the spoons were never recovered.

Willie's education, while sporadic, was as comprehensive as possible considering the paucity of trained teachers and formal schools, and the lack of the financial means to provide a broad, well-balanced education. Fortunately, Willie came under the tutelage and guidance of William Tully, a schoolmaster who contributed significantly to Willie's formal education and later assisted him financially when he joined the Hudson's Bay Company (HBC).

Job opportunities in the Peterborough area were limited. However, Catharine was well connected and was determined to find suitable employment for Willie. With the assistance of James Hargrave, a former senior executive of the HBC, and George Traill, a distant relative of Thomas's, Willie was hired as an apprentice clerk with the HBC.

In 1864, Willie Traill left his family and friends in Upper Canada and journeyed to Rupert's Land. He could not have foreseen the events he would witness and participate in over the next thirty years. Willie would see Mother Nature at her worst: frosts, droughts, floods, hailstorms, famines, fires, and hordes of grasshoppers that totally destroyed crops and gardens. He would witness the dreadful smallpox, scarlet fever, and whooping cough epidemics that decimated the Plains Indians and white populations alike. He would be affected by the Red River and North West Rebellions, Confederation, the completion of the Trans Canada Railroad, and the virtual annihilation of the buffalo—which irreversibly destroyed the way of life of the Plains Indians.

Willie began his HBC career as Apprentice Clerk at Fort Ellice and concluded it, twenty-nine years later, at Fort St James as Chief Trader in charge of the New Caledonia District of British Columbia. He served the company with diligence and great dedication. His remuneration, while commensurate with HBC guidelines, was at best minimal. His duties were frequently onerous and thankless, especially in later years with the decline of fur yields and rapid escalation of costs. He resigned from the HBC in 1893.

His marriage in 1869 to Harriet McKay, the eldest daughter of Chief Factor William McKay and his wife Mary Mackay (née Cook), was a seminal event in his life. The McKays were giants in the history of the HBC and western development. William and Mary were a Hudson's

Bay Company family to the bone. They were without peer in creating a fair, rational, intelligent, workable, and mutually respectful relationship with the Plains Indian tribes. The McKays' dedication to the HBC had a fundamental and positive impact on Willie and his family. Their influence on Willie is evident in his youthful enthusiasm for the West, in his skill as an HBC trader, and in the place he ultimately held as a respected elder in his community.

Willie and Harriet's twelve children were the source of great joy and unforgettable sorrow. Tragically, three of their children died while the family was stationed at Lac la Biche: Catharine Parr (Katie), age seven; Henry, age one; and Mary (Mollie), also age one. Nine children—Walter, William (Willie), Ethel, Jessie, Mary, Maria (Yummie), Harriet, Anne, and Barbara (Catherine Barbara)—survived. All are very much present in his letters.

Willie's personal letters are the heart and raison d'être of this book. They confirm and expand on his family's rich oral history. These letters were his social lifeline and his sole link to his beloved kin. His letters were treasured, read, reread, savoured, and saved by his family. One hundred and seventy-seven of his personal letters are presented in this book, in whole or in part. They chronicle his twenty-nine years with the HBC, from his journey west to his final years at Fort St. James.

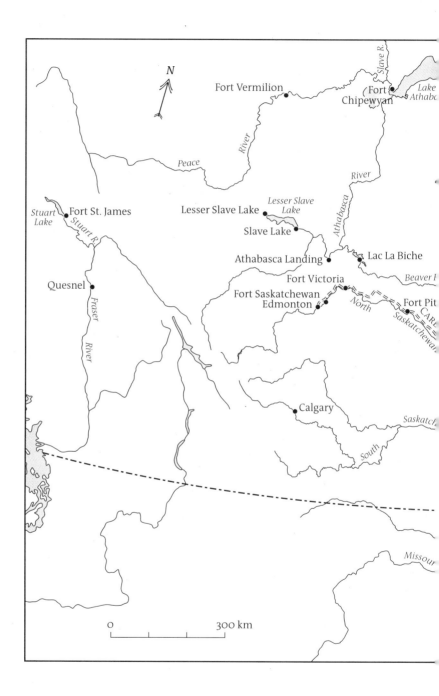

N

Fort Vermilion

Fort Chipewyan

Slave R.

Lake Athaba

Peace River

River

Athabasca

Stuart Lake

Fort St. James

Stuart R.

Lesser Slave Lake

Lesser Slave Lake

Slave Lake

Athabasca Landing

Lac La Biche

Beaver F

Quesnel

Fraser River

Fort Victoria

Fort Saskatchewan

Edmonton

North

Saskatchewan

Fort Pit

CARL

Calgary

Saskatch

South

Saskatc

Missour

0   300 km

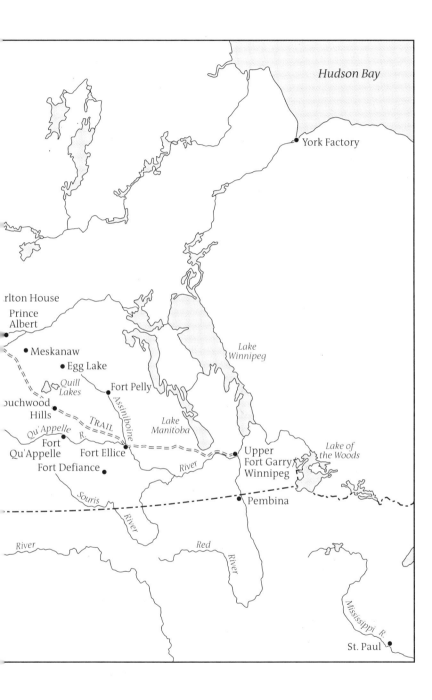

Hudson Bay

York Factory

rlton House

Prince
Albert

Meskanaw

Egg Lake

Quill
Lakes

Fort Pelly

ouchwood
Hills

Lake
Winnipeg

Assiniboine

Lake
Manitoba

TRAIL

Qu'Appelle
R.

Fort
Qu'Appelle

Fort Ellice

River

Upper
Fort Garry
Winnipeg

Lake of
the Woods

Fort Defiance

Souris

Pembina

River

River

Red

River

Mississippi R.

St. Paul

One

FORT GARRY
1864

After the merger of the North West Company and the
Hudson's Bay Company in 1821 the surviving London
concern thoroughly reorganized the transportation
system serving the Northern Department of Rupert's
Land. Thereafter, the long and costly canoe route from
Montreal—in part, the undoing of the Nor' Westers—was
largely employed in the carriage of mail and personnel.
The shorter path from York Factory to Fort Garry became
the trunk-line of the Northern Department. Without competition, the York route functioned admirably; but when
an American road arose to challenge its supremacy, it
began to break down, unable to match either the capacity
or the economy of its new rival. To preserve its position in
the fur trade, the Hudson's Bay Company was forced to
turn Southward and open up the Minnesota route.[1]

ALTHOUGH FORT ELLICE WAS TO BE HIS FIRST POST, Willie began his
HBC career with eleven days (July 16th to 27th, 1864) at Fort Garry.[2] To
get there, he traveled west to Red River by way of the Minnesota Route.
With minor variations, the first leg of the route to St. Paul, Minnesota,

Old Fort Garry (Winnipeg, Manitoba). Demolished 1881. Illustration by G. Kemp, after 1881. Original lithograph, coloured, by A. Mortimer. HBCA P–197

led from Montreal to Detroit on the Grand Trunk Pacific Railway, to Chicago on the Michigan Central Railway, to La Crosse, Wisconsin, on the North Western Railway, across Wisconsin on the upper Mississippi, and thence by steamboat to St. Paul.

The route from St. Paul to Fort Abercrombie, North Dakota, was another 280 miles—although Willie considered it to be closer to 430 miles—and closely parallels present day Interstate 94. At St. Paul, travelers boarded the St. Paul and Pacific Railroad for Big Lake, Minnesota, the western terminus of the railroad. From there, Willie continued his journey to Fort Abercrombie by Concord stage. Today this would be a comfortable four-hour drive.

In a letter to his sister Annie, Willie expresses apprehension regarding possible Indian attacks, and his concern was far from baseless. The year was 1864, and the echoes of a fierce Indian war still reverberated throughout Minnesota.

In 1862, South Central and Western Minnesota were exposed to a series of significant attacks by various Sioux bands. The Santees branch of the Sioux Nation launched the first attack in the Indian wars that ravaged the West for many years to come. Bursting from their reservation, they killed more than 400 settlers in the region before they were defeated by a hastily assembled force of raw recruits led by Colonel Henry Sibley.[3]

Major attacks were centred at and near New Ulm, a settlement on the Minnesota River some 90 miles southwest of St. Paul. Between August 17 and 24, New Ulm was attacked three times. Fort Ridgely, eighteen miles up the Minnesota River, was unsuccessfully besieged. The uprising lasted some six weeks and the punishment meted out was swift and brutal.

Although steamship service was available on the Red River, the obstacles were formidable. The Red is a narrow, usually shallow, very crooked stream—it is 250 road miles between Fort Abercrombie and Fort Garry, and close to twice that distance via the Red.

Fort Garry was the premier post in the Red River District and the most elaborate HBC establishment with the possible exception of York Factory. At that time, Fort Garry was the focal point for goods and personnel en route to more westerly forts and posts.

In 1821, the HBC built the first Fort Garry on the site of Fort Gibraltar, a former NWC post near the confluence of the Red and Assiniboine Rivers. Following the great flood of 1826 Governor George Simpson re-established the post, naming it Lower Fort Garry, nineteen miles downstream on the Red River. This new fort was completed in 1837/38. In 1835, then-governor Alexander Christie erected a large stone fort (Upper Fort Garry) near the site of the original fort, replete with high bastions on each corner and with loopholes for musketry and cannon. The new fort housed well-built and substantial stores, dwellings, offices, and barracks.[4]

Willie, like all new recruits, was processed though this fort. He spent his brief sojourn at the Upper Fort employed as a supernumerary Apprentice Clerk. His introduction to life as an employee of the HBC was indeed a halcyon one—with comfortable accommodation, tasty and diverse fare, quality potables, a gun and ammunition for hunting forays, a horse to ride, a light work schedule, and compatible colleagues with whom to sport and socialize.

In this chapter, we read Willie's first impressions of life at the HBC. He describes his journey in compelling detail, displaying a canny sense of observation, a well developed appreciation for beauty and a fine sense of humour.

SAINT PAUL [*July 3*], *1864*

[To Willie's mother]

[beginning missing] *not very often. They only stayed long enough for us to ask for some thing and the waiter hurried about in a great furor but took care not to give us any thing till the whistle was just going to blow and then we were obliged to eat up with just enough to make us wish for more though it was not so good what was of it. Ladies are always served first. They have separate cars for them. Every car we tried to enter we were told it was a lady's and we must go to the next which we would do and find it quite full. Though there were five or six cars they were all ways full. We were obliged to change cars two or three times a day and the change was always for the worse till we got so low we could get no lower. We crossed some very pretty plains which were carpeted with the most beautiful flowers but we went so fast I could not tell what they were like for said plains were composed of loose sand which rose in such clouds when we passed that it was as much as my eyes were worth to look out. On Tuesday morning we arrived at Chicago. It is the most bustling town I was ever in but so dirty and smoky that I did not feel much in love with it though for business it beats our towns hollow. We stayed till nine that night. We then for once got on a very good sleeping car. It was very comfortable indeed but not better than the one we came from Montreal to Belleville in. That night we had a good sleep which I assure you we needed.*

In the morning we found our boots blacked and were congratulating ourselves on the same when a boy came and demanded ten cents for blacking them. He did not make much out of me however for I could not boast of that sum of money. We were soon rooted out of our sleeping car and stuck in a car worse than any we were in before. That day about 2 we arrived in the city of La Crosse [Wisconsin] the most miserable place I was ever in. It appeared to be a group of houses sown broadcast over a sand pit, no attempt at streets or roads. The sand was up to our ankles in the streets. We went all over town to get something to eat but could get nothing but a box of sardines and a loaf of bread. No one could speak English but one or two and whatever we asked for they had something else but not the thing we wanted. They were all German or Norse. We expected a boat there to take us up the river, the Mississippi, but were obliged to wait till twelve at night. I shall remember La Crosse as long as I live and so will all the party. At twelve at night the vessel came for us. We went on board and procured rooms. They had two berths in each. It was very comfortable and we were asleep long before she left La Crosse and woke in the morning a long way from the above place. The time we should have taken to get to St Paul was 20 hours but we were doomed to be delayed and so about noon on the same day we stuck fast on a sand bar where we remained till daylight the next day. I said daylight but it was noon when another smaller boat came and we went on board of her and her passenger got on board of us. We then towed the Moses Maclellan, for that was the name of the old tub, off the bar and left her, but before we were out of sight she was fast again. I pitied the passengers but had as much need of pity myself for the one we got onto was very small and not particularly clean insomuch so that none of us would sleep in the berth but preferred laying on the deck. The fare was not so good as on the other and the waiters were so sassy that you could not speak to them. At dinner and other meals the passengers stood beside the table for an hour before the time to be at the table at the first ring of the bell for there was not room for more than half of us. The boat was a very slow one so that we did not make great head way. It amused me the grand names they had for the small villages we passed. One place with about a dozen houses was called Mountain City another with scarcely as many Fort [missing] City. The passengers were all kinds and all nations. There were some Southern Ladies on board. They were very handsome, a great contrast to the sunken cheeks and shallow complexion of those from the north. We got along very well for some hours after getting off the sand bar but stuck again on another for nearly a day which was very provoking. We got off again at last and arrived here this evening at 2 o'clock. The Mississippi is not a good river for navigation it being very shallow but is very pretty. The shores are very hilly and rocky almost mountainous. There is any amount of fish chiefly catfish. When we were on the bar I tried to fish but had not thrown my line into the water before I got a tremendous catfish on which took my hook off and as I had no more I could not try again. I forgot to tell you that we came across a band of Indians between Chicago and La Crosse they were the first genuine ones I ever saw. They were nearly naked and painted and ornamented in a most ridiculous manner. They were fine looking fellows however and created quite a sensation in the cars especially among the ladies who laughed and tittered at a great rate.

We are staying at the International Hotel here and paying at the rate of 3 dollars per day for our board. There is four of us Mr Hardisty who is my guardian for the time Mr Swanson, who is going to Red River and his father who has come as far as this to see him off, myself and young McTavish who we found here before us. He had passed us while stuck on the shoals. He is a very jolly kind of a fellow.

We expect to start for Red River tomorrow. There will be only four of us. We anticipate some difficulty in crossing the Prairies for there has been no rain for a long time. I have been told that there has not been a good rain for two years and the Indians are rather inclined to be hostile but I do not think that there is much fear of us being molested by them for they have a great respect for H B people. We are very well armed with guns, pistols and revolvers so that if they were obnoxious we could give them a very warm reception. I have not started my Journal yet for I could not get at my chest to get paper there from and as we were travelling night and day I could not have done so. I shall start it as soon as we leave here. If I see any strange flowers or plants as I am sure to do I shall preserve them for you. On one of the plains we crossed there was beautiful scenery. The plain itself was a dead level with here and there very high hills of solid rock towering up and ending in a spire some of them were very grand.

Young Swanson and my self amused ourselves by abusing the Americans and their customs. We had very good reason for so doing for they were the queerest people I came across. We gave those that we met in Michigan the name of Mishi Ganders and I think the name is very appropriate. My chest is all most in pieces, the men on the cars and boat handled it very roughly. The lid of it is split and it is so scratched up and chipped I can hardly swear to it except by the contents there of. I shall be obliged to leave it here for some time as we go on horse back across the plains. I have not yet learned my destiny but hope I shall be sent across to the Saskatchewan with Hardisty who I like very well.

You will hardly be able to make out this scrawl but my hand shakes so that I cannot write better. I suppose it is on account of the heat which is very oppressive and has been so since I left Canada. The air is much cooler today but the heat of the last few days has had such effect on me that I feel very nervous. I shall not be able to pay the post of this letter for I have not any money to pay it with. I shall not be able to write to any one till I get to my destination on that account. I promised to write to Lilly [Lilias Maclean, later the wife of Willie's brother Harry] but cannot do so at present. [...] I suppose you heard from Mrs Hargrave how I acted. I shall tell you however. She was going to Brockville and I volunteered to see her off in the morning. I was to get up very early and get the fires lit. She called me at six I got up and dressed myself. I heard the servants downstairs so sat down on the bed and was asleep before five minutes. I did not wake up till I was called for breakfast and was much surprised to find Miss Alcock away. I was told that she had called me but I do not think such to be the case. She might have called me to bid me good bye since I was going away so soon. I sat down at once and wrote her an apology which I hope she accepted.

When next I write I shall send a long letter to all the family.

I was much disappointed at not finding James at home. I fully expected to see him poor fellow. I hope he is in better health. Donald Maclean thinks he is in a fair way of getting better if he will only take care of himself. He was very kind to me and told me to write to him if

I was in want of money but I was in no want and if I had been I could not have asked him for any. I would have been very glad of a few cents on the road but have managed without so far. Last night I was attacked with a violent fit of toothache of the worst kind. I would not have slept all night had I not had friends whom I could ask for a glass of brandy which I held in my mouth till it stopped aching and I have not been troubled with it since and hope not to be for a long time. I am going out to see the town this evening. There is a very long Iron bridge which I must go and see. The rocks that line the River near here are full of swallows nests in holes that they have made with their beaks in the solid rock. They are the sand martins. How they can bore the rock in the way they do. There are thousands of them. A person with a net could catch thousands of them they are in such clouds. I have not got any more to say at present but will be able to give you more information per next. I shall send this by Mr Swanson. It will save postage and that is a great lookout. I fully expected to have had a letter from you on my arrival here but suppose you did not know my address. I expect to have a large packet when I get to Red River as I have not heard from Kate, Walter or Annie since I left home. I shall write to Harry [Kate, Walter, Annie, and Harry were Willie's siblings] next time but do not suppose he can be at the trouble of answering it for he does not like writing. I hope he is in better health than he was when I left. Lilly was very much frightened at his being on the River. I left my address with her. She promised to send it to you but for fear of you not getting it I shall send it you again. [...]

I hope the garden is progressing and the trees are all growing. I take as much interest in it as if I were there. I have just been about the town to see what was to be seen. Although it is Sunday all or nearly all the stores are open and the crowds that are hanging about the saloons and Lager Beer shops is enough to disgust any person. It is certainly the most impious place I was ever in. I have heard a great deal of the comforts of travelling in America but cannot say much in favour of the accommodation that I experienced while crossing through the States. I should like to give Mr Scott a description of the Americans that I have

met. He would not believe me but I assure you I do not exaggerate.
[end missing]

W.E. Traill

FORT GARRY *July* [*21ˢ*], *1864*

[Recipient unknown]

We left St Paul on the 4th of July about 8 o'clock A.M. travelling by Pacific Railroad which extends as far as Big Lake a distance of 80 miles from St Paul. There we took the Overland Express to St Cloud. The road lay over the Prairies nearly all the way to Fort Abercrombie: This place is about 430 miles from St Paul and the last military post in the State of Minnesota Dacotah territory—We passed some very pretty lakes, some like large ponds having no outlets or inlets but abounding in fish and wild fowl.

One of our leaders dropped dead from the heat. The coaches were comfortable, the horses were changed every ten or twelve miles. They never drove less than four and sometimes six horses and these at a good pace. I enjoyed the journey very much. The weather was splendid and the scenery novel to me, every object was interesting and my companions full of information on many subjects.

At 6 P.M. we arrived at the city of St Cloud. Though no city in point of size and population it is the prettiest little town I ever saw. It is built on the bank of the Elk River among a thick grove of trees. There are no enclosures, no garden fences, the houses are all scattered among the trees with green turf on every side. This gives a delightful air of coolness which is most refreshing. Of an evening the people sit under the shade smoking or otherwise amusing themselves—the women and girls sewing or knitting, the young ones playing on the green. There is an air of great quiet about this place there being no noisy rattling of wheels for there are in fact no regular streets but only bridle roads and foot-paths.

The inhabitants either walk or ride on horseback. The people are mostly Germans.

The next day we got as far as Alexandria, a distance of 90 miles. A pretty little town (perhaps I ought to have said city) consisting of one shanty and a stable. As the hotel was not first class we slept in the coach, which made a very comfortable sleeping room—not to be sneezed at by travellers.

The next day we went as far as Sioux Centre 85 miles further; a spot celebrated for the cruel massacre of the inhabitants by the Sioux Indians in 1862. The place is fortified and garrisoned by 300 cavalry. The inhabitants of the surrounding neighbourhood bring their cattle and horses into the stockade at night for fear of the Indians.

The village is built on the Otter Tail River. At the hotel here we had good rooms and good fare. Every thing was clean and comfortable.

Our next post was Fort Pomme-de-terre (a genteel name for the more homely one of Fort Potato) a military fort. 500 soldiers were stationed here.

From Sioux Centre to Fort Abercrombie the mail is guarded by six soldiers, two before and two behind and one on either side, otherwise the Indians would rob them and go off with the horses as they did a year ago. The road from Sioux Centre to Fort Abercrombie lies over the Prairies—not a tree to relieve the monotony of the wide extent of plain for 60 or 70 miles. We had excellent quarters at the hotel here and stayed till the Monday morning.

We then started at 6 A.M. and travelled for three hours before halting for breakfast. We had done with Express stages and commenced [to travel] on with our own horses. I had obtained two horses from a buffalo hunter when I was at St Paul and I got on very well till the last stage of our days journey when I found on attempting to mount my last horse that he had never had bit or bridle in his mouth or saddle on his back.

I had to get Blackfoot, the half breed boy who drove the luggage waggon to catch my unruly beast with a lasso such as they use for catching wild horses on the Prairies. This feat said boy accomplished after some trouble—He (I mean the horse) rolled over me once and made the attempt a second time. After this display of equine spirit he went as well as and as quietly as any beast could do.

After a long days travel of 80 miles we got at nightfall to Georgetown—a very extensive place consisting of one mud house and a ferry-boat on which we crossed the river.

N. B. Markets somewhat high at Georgetown [Minnesota] purchased a bushel of potatoes for the moderate sum of 4.50 cts and a pail of iced water for 50 cts. Mud hotel's accommodations somewhat limited so camped outside the town—however we fared very well on prairie chicken, ducks and fish so we did not grumble much.

We could get no good water to drink so we had to make tea when we halted with water so warm that it scarcely needed much more heating. For four days tea was our only beverage. We had it is true plenty of wine and brandy but I could take little of either. Latterly our tea ran short, a beggarly Indian having robbed us of one bag on which we were depending for a supply. In consequence of this loss we were reduced to short allowance, a great privation with the thermometer standing at 110 to 120 in the shade (i.e. if there had been any shade.)

The night before we got to Pembina [in North Dakota, about 70 miles south of Forth Garry], I had lain down as usual to sleep on a buffalo robe without a tent the weather being very fine. I slept very soundly having been on watch the night before. I am not quite sure I should have slept quite so comfortably had I been aware of the fact that part of my robe was being occupied by a large snake about six feet long—If I exaggerate lay the sin on Blackfoot our boy who told me it was the same length as myself.

He discovered it before I awoke and shot it regardless of my robe which he riddled with buck shot. When I got up I was surprised at seeing the beggar comfortably seated on his heels before a big fire eating the snake which he had roasted on a forked stick Indian fashion and I was yet more astonished when we came to pour out the tea at breakfast after a ride of thirty miles to find our tea covered with oil. I naturally concluded that we had "struck Ile" but the mystery was soon resolved for at the bottom of the kettle was found a pint bottle of castor oil which I remember our having bought at St Cloud for oiling the wheels of the carriage. Nor was it very difficult to account for its presence there as Blackfoot always stowed away all small matter in the kettle or in our provision box.

It is an old saying "It's an ill wind that blows no good to no one" so said, or if he did not say it so no doubt thought, Master Blackfoot for as soon as he found our dislike to the oily beverage he joyfully set to work and never drew breath until he had finished every drop—As we could not drink, neither could we eat the provisions prepared for our breakfast so he cleared off the eatables as well as the drinkables. He seemed much in the condition of a boa constrictor after it has gorged itself with swallowing a deer for he was incapable of catching our horses. An Indian or half-breed does eat when he can get the chance till he can eat no more.

In this instance Master Blackfoot had in addition to his usual feed consumed six feet of roasted snake, nearly all of the food cooked for four, a gallon of tea and half a pint of castor oil—He lay for nearly four hours at the bottom of the waggon in a happy state of unconsciousness but came to just at dinner time—a practical illustration of Pickwick's fat boy.

We had some good sport with our guns shooting partridge, pigeons, prairie hens and last but not least a fine buffalo calf which proved most capital eating.

Pembina is the last post office on the line between the States and the H B territory and is distant about 80 miles from Fort Garry at which place we arrived about 4 o'clock last Friday evening. We crossed the river on a ferry boat and rode up to the Fort in good style where we received a hearty welcome and I soon found myself quite at home. The Fort stands on the fork of the Red River and Assiniboine. It covers a space of four acres of ground and is surrounded by a high stone wall flanked by four towers one at either corner. On each of these towers

A view of Upper Fort Garry, built in 1835, from the south bank of the Assiniboine River. (Photo 1872.) HBCA 1987/363–F–131/25

are mounted six Armstrong guns and there are also two hundred stand of small arms for the protection of the Fort against hostile Indians. The office is a large building in the centre of the Fort. There are five clerks besides myself resident here. I am at present a supernumerary and do not know as yet what will be my destination nor if its etiquette to enquire. As I am very comfortable and happy I am quite contented to remain in such pleasant quarters.

Our living is of the best. We breakfast about eight, dine at two and drink tea at six. For fare we have fish, flesh and fowl of every variety with wine and ale and tea of the finest quality. Our office hours are from nine till two or say half past one from four to six. After tea we amuse ourselves as we like best and we have only half days work on Saturday when we take a gallop, walk, shoot hunt or sleep if we wish but that is a matter of taste. We have plenty of powder and shot free and for nothing and of this I make full use.

Yesterday I had a canter with my friend [name missing] as far as the White Horse Plains to a Fort about forty miles from here [possibly Fort la Reine]. We think nothing of a ride of 50 or 60 miles. The weather is splendid and the air exhilarating. I have been out hunting wild cattle on

The stern-wheeler S.S. Dakota docked at Upper Fort Garry, 1872. HBCA 1987/363–
F–131/26

horse back which is great fun. I have a horse kept free of expense for my use at the Fort.

The ground round the Fort is very flat as far as the eye can see and though the river lies not less than twenty five feet below yet in the great freshets of 1852 the water rose three feet within the area of the fort and the whole country was under water for miles round.

I have too much to see in this new place to waste my time on sleeping. You see that I am employing it more profitably by scribbling and giving you my notes of travel.

We Nor'westers have a great advantage over you Canadians as we get our clothing much cheaper and better than you do. We can send our measure to England and get a suit of good clothes made up in the best style for about 3 Sty. Boots however are very high and hardly to be obtained. Unfortunately I did not bring out an extra supply so if I do not get any from Canada I must wear moccasins—we get these well made and of good moose skin cheaper than the Indians charge you for the buckskin ones they make in your part of the world.

I think that it is high time for me to close this long letter which is growing to a formidable length. I hear my new friend [name missing] summoning me for a ride so goodbye. I'm off for a gallop to the White Horse Plains.

In my next I'll tell you of anything I see worth your knowing. I wish you could see the splendid horse I'm about to bestride. Don't you wish you were beside me?

Take care of yourself and don't forget
Your old friend
Magnus T-The Nor'wester

FORT GARRY *July 21, 1864*

Dear Annie

I received your kind letter dated 22 June yesterday and was very glad to hear you are all well. I had a rather rough journey over the plains for it rained 8 nights out of 13 and as we had no tent it was not very comfortable I can assure you. But it was better on the whole than coming through the States for the ground was so dry [there] that the cars raised such clouds of dust that we could not see across them. As to washing ourselves it was useless for in ten minutes we were worse than ever. The damp caused by washing caused the dirt to stick on tighter which was needless besides we were obliged to change cars very often especially at night Then coming up the Mississippi River worse and worse —the steamer made 5 days out of a 20 hour trip. The first one we got on was not a bad one but the second (for we got stuck on a sand bar and were obliged to change Boats) was a dirty small thing and also stuck on the sand banks. The berths were small and dirty, the beds so dirty that we dared not get into them so we lay on the deck. The waiter was very sassy and on the whole it was very uncomfortable. However the Scenery on the River was very grand, High hills on each side or rather small mountains on the top of which were what looked like natural forts. These hills are so steep and high that it is not possible for roads to be made down

An interior view of Upper Fort Garry from the south (river) gate. Recorder's residence, men's quarters, flour store on the right. Inland depot, fur store, pemmican store on the left. Officer's quarters and mess hall at centre back. The cannon is now at Lower Fort Garry. Photo taken c. 1860–1882. HBCA 1987/ 363–F–132/5

them. There were slides down them for supplying the Steamers with wood. It was great fun to see the wood come tumbling down the sides, several hundred feet sometimes.

At last we got to St Paul, by no means a saint like place for the shops were many of them open on Sunday and instead of going to church most of the inhabitants assembled at the saloons and taverns. We put up at the International Hotel, a very fine building with good grub though they made us pay dear for it $3 per diem but as I did not pay it I did not care.

We stayed there for a few days and then started on our trip across the Plains between 4 & 5 hundred miles and after a rather rough trip arrived at Fort Garry on the Sixteenth, where we received a hearty welcome. I would have given you a more minute description of our journey but I have just penned it for those at Westove and found to my mortification that I can not send it all which is a great grind. When you go to Douro as I suppose you will before long you will have a full account of my travels.

Some of the road over the Plains was very beautiful. We lived on the fat of the land I will give you our bill of fare. In the first place there was

Pork Ham Butter Cheese & fish Ducks pheasant Snipe and pigeons, 2 ly Biscuits Bread or Shanty cakes Crackers, 3 ly Oysters Lobsters Sardines Preserved peaches & etc with Plenty of Sugar Tea and once Milk which we got from a drover. Then there was Whiskey Brandy and Wines Port & Sherry. So you see we did not starve for the distance of 480 miles. We saw not one night house but plenty of travellers like ourselves.

Fort Garry is composed of some 15 buildings altogether enclosed by a stone wall 12 feet high with large towers or Bastions mounted with Cannon quite formidable I assure you. There is a sentry all night who walks about to guard against the Uncultivated Indians. The tribes about here are very peaceful but The Sioux are a barbarous race and committed dreadful ravages in Minnesota in Sixty two. We were on the look out for them on the plains for they are at deadly war with the Americans & scruple not to attack any one found on their territory.

You will excuse the shortness of this as I want to send a few lines to Clin.

I remain your affectionate brother
Will Traill

FORT GARRY *July 21, 1864*

Dear Clinton [Clinton Atwood, Annie's husband]

You will see by what I wrote to Annie that I had not a very pleasant trip but I am none the worse for it except losing all the skin off my face with the sun. I had also very sore lips all the time. I could hardly eat anything though we had a great variety of grub. The grasshoppers have eaten everything in the shape of grass. They were in clouds like a very heavy snow storm. They were going in the direction of Canada but I hope that they may all get drowned in the Great Lakes before they get there for they would soon leave it nothing but a waste. In the morning when a breeze sprang up they flew up and went off with the wind and at night when the wind slackened they lit in clouds. [...]

Red River Settlement is not what it is cracked up to be. The land is very good but the last two years drought has done a great deal of harm and also the grasshoppers.

The settlers' houses are of small logs thatched with reeds and clay. They are very small and do not look very inviting though they look clean enough. Few of the settlers have more than a few acres of land in cultivation though they have only to plough the land there being nothing to clear. Where they get the logs to build with I do not know. The farmers are chiefly French men or half-breeds. The women are nearly all squaws. Just about the fort there are some tolerable houses, a Good school, Catholic Church and nunnery. The English Church is 2 miles from here. There is nothing to shoot here except pigeons, there are a good many of them. I have told you all that I can think of at the present. Hoping your crops turn out well I remain yours affectionately,

W E Traill

[…]

Two

FORT ELLICE
1864 — 1867

IN EARLY AUGUST 1864, WILLIE WAS POSTED TO FORT ELLICE (near the present-day town of St. Lazare, Manitoba), where he would spend two years. To get there, he followed the Carlton Trail westward from Fort Garry to present-day Portage la Prairie, thence in a more or less straight line parallel to the Assiniboine River and what is now Highway 16—the Yellow Head Route.

Situated on a high plateau near the confluence of the Assiniboine and Qu'Appelle Rivers, Fort Ellice was the major provisioning post for the Swan River district. In 1872, the fort became the district headquarters but, during Willie Traill's era, the headquarters was located at Fort Pelly, approximately 150 km north on the Assiniboine. Goods were distributed from Fort Pelly to various posts including Fort Ellice, Touchwood Hills, Wood Mountain, and Last Mountain, as well as to wintering houses in the vicinity of the Qu'Appelle Valley. Fort Qu'Appelle also served as a collection point for furs and buffalo products acquired at these outposts.

Upon arrival, Willie reported to Chief Trader William McKay, and thus began a relationship that influenced the rest of his life. Mr. McKay was Willie's superior, his role model, and his mentor during the thirty-one months he worked with him at Fort Ellice.

Descended on both sides of his family from Hudson's Bay traders, William McKay, "Bear Skin" to the Indians, epitomized the HBC ideal. Isaac Cowie paid tribute to one of nature's gentlemen:

> Ever with devotion to his duty to the company, he was just
> and kind to the Indians, into whose affairs he brought the
> sympathy of knowledge, while his well known courage
> prevented their attempting to impose upon him. He was
> a model of what a really good Indian trader should be.[1]

Mrs. McKay (née Cook) shared her husband's sterling reputation. When she died, the *Saskatoon Star* eulogized:

> Mrs. McKay was a fitting consort for such a man. Graceful,
> dignified and courteous, she received many grateful trib-
> utes from travelers like Butler and Palliser, who enjoyed the
> courtesies of her hospitality. Like her husband, she keenly
> enjoyed hunting, and was an excellent shot.[2]

Willie was the beneficiary of Mrs. McKay's legendary kindness and generosity. With her two daughters approaching marriageable age, she clearly viewed Willie as a fine addition to Fort Ellice.

Willie refers to his outfit as being very expensive. This reflects first year start-up costs for clothing and necessities of life. He purchased these items through the HBC directly from England. He contemplated purchasing a suit of clothes for 3 pounds sterling—a substantial sum considering his first year's salary was 20 pounds sterling! His remuneration was doubtless the same as his brother Walter's:

> My contract as a Junior or Apprentice Clerk is to serve for
> five years at the usual remuneration of £20, £25, £30, £40,
> and £50 for the successive years. If I wish to remain in the

service after that I must sign a second contact for three years at a salary of £75 annually during which I become a full fledged clerk. A third contract may follow, also for three years, as a Chief Clerk with £100 a year, the maximum pay to this class of officer.[3]

It is clear from his letters that Willie felt financial pressures from time to time. Notwithstanding his modest salary, he conscientiously paid his debts and did everything he possibly could to assist his family financially.

New employees in the HBC's service were allowed an extraordinarily brief familiarization period. Willie's description of the responsibilities entrusted to him some two months after his arrival attests to the fact that Mr. McKay frequently threw greenhorns into the deep end of the Fort Ellice work pool. In Mr. McKay's absence, Willie was the acting post master. He was in charge of trading furs, buying and selling horses, and disciplining all post employees. He dispatched cart brigades as required and wrote business correspondence to his superiors.

In 1865, Willie encountered his first Sioux and Assiniboine Indians and took part in his first buffalo hunt,[4] he describes in detail. His excitement at the hunt is palpable.

Willie wrote to his mother in 1886 from a miserable one-room shack in the Moose Mountains,[5] a shack he dubbed "Fort Defiance." Fort Defiance was neither a fort nor a post, but a shack used as a trading site and staging station between Fort Ellice, the Wood Mountains, and the major buffalo hunting grounds in what is now Southern Saskatchewan, Northern Montana, and North Dakota. He had been sent there from Fort Ellice to trade with the local Indians and provide maximum competition to the area's free traders.

Willie's physical prowess was impressive and his performance on snowshoes formidable. Drivers occasionally rode, but walking or running was the norm, and Willie wrote of travelling fifty miles on snowshoes in a day, either running behind a dog team or running in front breaking trail. A major feat! Occasionally he travelled 80 miles a day, a feat beyond comprehension.

In May 1867, Willie's tenure at Fort Ellice came to an end when the Council of the HBC appointed him Apprentice Clerk in charge of Touchwood Hills. Willie left Fort Ellice with two major assets—solid training as an HBC trader under the kindly, creative, and thorough tutelage of William McKay, and the love of Harriet McKay, who was to be Willie's wife and companion for 48 years. Although the event is not clearly recorded in what survived of Willie's letters, the two were married at Fort Ellice in 1869.

FORT ELLICE *August 7, 1864*

My Dearest Mother[6]

When I last wrote I could not tell you my destination having been kept ignorant of it till the day before my departure though I had a pretty good notion for some days before. I am now as you see at Fort Ellice. I arrived here on the 4th Inst[7] after a journey of 7 1/2 days. We are the only persons who have made the trip in that time with loaded carts, 12 days is almost the fastest yet made. [...] We had very favourable weather. It did not rain once during the trip. We had good fun shooting ducks and pheasants but no larger game. We crossed a small mountain which was very hard on our beasts. It was a beautiful place. We could see it 3 days before we came to it, the surrounding plain being very level. On the eighth morning we arrived in sight of Fort Ellice which is situated on the bank of the Assiniboine which [is] very steep and high. When we first came in sight of the fort we were 4 or 5 miles off and our road took a turn away from it. At last we came to the river some two or three miles from the Fort. [We] crossed over without accident except one of the horses chose to baulk in the middle of the stream and lay down and made himself comfortable greatly to the discomfort of us [...] especially of the driver who was obliged to get into the water. [However] we got over at last and then came the tug of war. [We had] to ascend a hill about 300 feet or more and of all the walking and lifting I ever saw we had the most to [do]. When at last we all got to the top I was so [tired I] could hardly walk but did not say so. We camped [at the top] and had dinner and then Mr. McKay my future [employer arrived] from the Fort and after drinking a bottle of [wine] and some port, we bid good bye to Mr Hardisty. [He left for] Rocky Mountain House[8] and I went with [Mr. McKay to] my present home. [...]

   The Fort is a large log [house] full two stories high. The upper part is at present used for a store room the store having been blown up with gunpowder this summer with the loss of 2 lives and one or two wounded. There is a high stockade of poplar about 15 ft high on two sides of the

The house of William McKay, Chief Trader in Charge during Willie Traill's tenure, at Fort Ellice, c. 1870. GAA NA–2121–1

Fort the rest has not been completed yet. The Fort stands on one of the prettiest places I have seen. It is about 350 feet above the river which runs immediately below us. The banks of the river are all very steep and high and look very pretty. It is better than half a mile across from hill to hill the valley between being covered with small shrubbery and the river, which is small, running in the most impossible curls and crooks you can imagine. It runs in this shape as nearly as I can show you the many curls has a very pretty effect. I give you this minute description of the place for I know you would like to know all about it but I must take up no more room. Mr. McKay is the only person in charge. He is a fine stout man with a family of ten. He was born near the place at the old Fort.[9] *Mrs. McKay goes out shooting by her self and is a capital shot either flying or sitting. In hard times when prog*[10] *is scarce she goes out with 7 or 8 of her family and lives in the woods. We have little to do at present.*

I should have gone on a two days journey after Indians by myself today but was very ill last night and so weak I can scarcely stand. When the winter sets in I shall have to travel with dogs a good deal. There is about 15 young ones to break in which will be good fun. I should like to have Walter[11] *with me this Winter. We should have capital fun. When the snow falls you can imagine me muffled in as many clothes as I can*

get on running after a sled loaded with pemmican and furs with a span
of very smart dogs and travelling at the rate of from 50 to 70 miles per
[day]. The driver has to run behind all the time [except when] the snow
is deep and then he has the pleasure of running before and beating the
Track. When night comes he puts his buffalo robe in a hole scraped in
the snow wrapping himself in his blankets sleeps as best he can. He
will often make a trip of several hundred miles in this way. We live at
present on dried meat without vegetables of any description and a
very poor quality. We expect to have a very [hard winter] for very few
buffalo have been seen and on them we place our hopes of a supply of
meat. There was a large party of Sioux Indians here a few days before
I arrived. I should have liked to have seen them. They are the terror of
the Saulteaux who are meditating on trying to drive them back to their
own country which is the States. Now that I have given you a description of all that I know of I shall turn to something else. I was very glad
to hear that Robert Strickland was so kind to you. I am sure you will be
very glad of the wood. You say that Mr Hamilton will be coming from
Canada soon but that will be before this reaches you. You do not mind
sending anything unless it is very light note paper and photographs. I
find the outfit very expensive but next year I shall be able to send you
enough to pay my debts with. I wish dear Mother I could send you some
money but it is quite impossible at present and the mails are very unsafe
through the States. Tell Uncle that I do not find it half so much banish-
ment here as I should in Australia.

[…]

If you can get hold of a newspaper once in a while send it but do not
pay the post. I take much more interest in Canadian affairs since I left
home. […] I shall not close this until there is a chance of sending it off.
Always address your letters to Fort Garry for I might be sent to take
charge of an outpost any day but do not wish to change my address till
spring. There is an English Church clergyman staying here [a brother]
of Mrs. McKay's who holds service twice on Sundays but the service is
in Indian. He also has prayers every night at the Fort which I always

attend. You wished me to give a description of the interview with Gov Dallas. I did not see him at all [as he had] gone to Canada. We passed him at Port Hope. [I have been told] that he is retiring from the service. [...]

9th Tuesday As I have an unexpected chance of sending a letter to day I shall send this but am obliged to write with red ink as Mrs. McKay is writing with the black. I know of no news to tell you but this morning two miners have come from the Saskatchewan having with them 24 oz of gold which they took out in 22 days. (I have got back to black ink so I can go on) I have been out shooting this afternoon but it was very hot. I only shot one duck and came back very tired. Climbing up the big hill quite exhausted me. But the duck was very tender and paid me well for my trouble, it being almost all I have eaten since breakfast on Sunday. I find the want of vegetables very much but do not complain for I expect to have nothing else and consider myself well off to have that. [...] In your next I wish you could send me two or three Coopers pills, you can flatten them out so as to not be seen. You might also send a few parsley seeds as we have no herbs to season our soup. There is not a single set-tler here and the Company does not raise any crops which they might do; and thereby save something. Mr. McKay however has about half an acre of barley and the same of potatoes which if they come to any thing will be a blessing next year. Where ever I am I am determined to have a garden if I do the work myself if I can get seeds. And now dear Mother I must bid you good bye for the present. [...]

Willie Traill
[...]

FORT ELLICE *August 8, 1864*

Dear Snipes [identity unknown]

[...] Mr. McKay, who is in charge of the Ft is a very kind man. He is only a post master and has no education [12] for when he was young there were no schools in R. R. [Red River] Mrs Mc- is a half breed a very nice person. [...]

I use my room which is large for an office. My office work is light, keeping a journal of occurrences and making up a few small bills of Parcels is about all. Not more than ½ hours work a day whereas at Ft G-y clerks are in the Office 10 to 12 hours. There are many Indians about but I have not seen any squaw who takes my fancy. [...]

The thermometer is sometimes as low as 50 or 60 and as high as 100, 115 which I believe it must be at present, no rain since I came. I have just been trading with an older Indian and his 17 sons. He also has 12 daughters at camp, 3 wives, and any amount of defunct offspring; a middling family for one man. [...] Yesterday we all went to make a new barrier across the river. It is composed of long stakes driven in two rows from each side of the river and meeting at a point where we have an artificial waterfall [...] into a basket. The fish think it is a waterfall and go to swim over and tumble into the basket. By this we have fresh fish every day for a while. We are out of shot so I cannot shoot. The flies are very thick in my room I wish I had some fly paper.

We got a few bags of pemmican yesterday which will be a help to us but Fort Pelly which is about 200 miles from this is sure to take it from us Fort Ellice being only a provision post to supply other more important Forts. The day after I arrived we sent 50 bags of pemmican and several thousand lbs of dried meat to that place. [...] Bishop Tache from RR arrived last night but brought no letters for anyone. [...] I go out shooting now and then. It is first rate fun cantering about from lake to lake for duck. We always go on horse back and when we have shot or scared all the ducks out of one lake we canter to another. I believe there are Buffo within a day's journey of us. I expect to have a hunt one of these days.

There are plenty of elk, moose, and antelopes here in winter. The antelope are very small not so high as a calf. There are lots of wolves in the winter but none to be seen now. We also have bears black brown & grizzly.[13] I never go out without my gun for one knows not what he

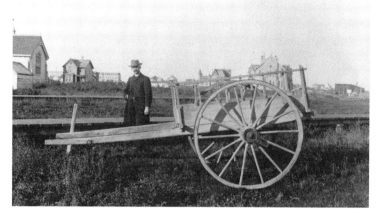

A Red River cart. Wheel ruts of Red River carts are still present in parts of the southern Prairies. HBCA 1987/363–R–7/5

may see before he gets back. There is also fear of being scalped and Tomahawked by the totally uncultivated Sioux. Bishop Tache met 500 camps of them going to RR where they are not wanted. I expect we shall have trouble with them before long.

The Barrier which I spoke of in the beginning of this letter proves a capital one. The first morning after it was finished we had a cart load of gold-eyes, pike, and pickerel. Sometimes we have two loads but are obliged to keep two men at night to keep off the Indians and empty the basket when full. [...] I went yesterday to see an Indian performance. I do not know what to call it but it was a ridiculous affair. It was a kind of religious festival. When I got to the tent which was a large one made for the occasion they were all sitting around the tent. In the centre there was a post painted red with a stone at its feet intended to represent its head. Round it were hung pieces of cloth of every description all new. These were offerings to the post which was an Idol. At its feet were two dead dogs one behind the other with their heads turned to the Idol. They smelt as if they had been killed a week before hand. By and by a couple of medicine men got up one with a drum and the other with a tremendous rattle and began dancing and drumming about. They were dressed in a most ridiculous manner. Every body was painted and dressed in a horrible way. After a while they took the dogs and threw them out of the tent when some old hags took and singed the hair off and then roasted them and the feast began consisting of the two dogs. They wanted me to have some but I very modestly declined. After the feast was over they danced & sang all evening. [Each] of the dancers carries a fire bag and as they go round they point it at each other. The one at whom it is pointed falls down as if he were dead. I did not see the end but I believe that the offerings were divided among the Indian men. Dogs flesh is considered a great delicacy by the Saulteaux. [...]

WE Traill

[...]

FORT ELLICE *August 9, 1864*

Dear Harry

[...] Pemmican is not bad stuff. It is made of buffalo meat dried and beaten up with flails and packed in bags made of the skin of the beast. The fat is then run into the bag with it. It requires an axe to cut it up. It is eaten raw. It also makes capital soup with flour and water when flour can be had and is called Bufa boo. [...] The Plains hunters arrived and brought some pemmican and dried meat for which we gave them trade out of the store. We were reckoning on some potatoes this winter but they were totally killed with frost early last month. [...] There were catfish 20 or 30 lbs. weight pike perch & gold-eyes which are very much like herrings. [...] You would be astonished at the quantities of prog that is consumed in a week here by the company's servants & their families. A man is allowed 2 1/2 lbs of pemmican or dried meat per diem, a woman 1 1/2 lbs and two children as much as a woman. Our only conveyance here is carts. They are made entirely of wood no tire and not a scrap of metal of any kind. They cost Sterling 2.0.0 and last about 2 or three years.

Mr. McKay is a jolly man, full of fun and is very kind to me and everyone else. Mrs McKay is also very kind. They gave me a feather bed the other day a luxury not known in many parts though feathers are by no means scarce.

I have not fallen in love with any of the Indian girls yet though there are some nice looking ones here. [...] I am beginning to find out how lucky I am in being stationed here. Everybody tells me it is one of the best and prettiest places in the H.B. territory. [...]

Hay grows very rank in all the damp places. In some parts that I came through you could hardly see the horses & in one place I nearly lost myself about 100 yards from camp though I was on horseback in perfectly level ground.

[...] Horses here are not worth more than from five to eight pounds except runners for which they often give £40[14]. Mr. McKay just sold one for that. He was very swift and could run down antelopes and deer which is saying a great deal. We have fifty cart horses all Indian breed not very pretty but will stand more work than three American ones. [...]

Willie Traill

FORT ELLICE *October 1, 1864*

My Dear Mother

[...] You may be sure that I feel uneasy for a letter but console myself with the hope that I shall receive several when the happy times come when the letters come from R R which I expect will be soon for Mr. Cook, Mrs. McKay's brother, is at R R at present or if not on the road home. I charged him to be sure to ask for letters for me. I wish My Dear Mother that I could take a peep into my old home and see you all but it is useless to long for such a thing with at least two thousand miles between you and I. [...]

The hard frost is beginning to make itself felt here. The leaves are all off already. We have had several flurries of snow lately. Furs are beginning to be of some value. I intend to trap a little this winter. I now have 3 rats[15] hanging in my room not a very large beginning but every little helps. The ducks will soon be leaving for the South. We see a great many geese but I have not shot any yet though we have them to eat very often but we miss onions & parsley & sage very much for stuffing them, at least I do. The others do not know what it is to have a nicely stuffed goose. I wish I did not either. Last night I went with young McKay to hunt ducks in a lake about a mile from this. I had a very spirited horse quite unfit for carrying a gun. He pranced and danced and capered. I could hardly manage him when we started to come home I tied my ducks to the saddle and got on his back. He began to prance. The ducks flapped about on the side till he got perfectly wild and in spite of all I could do set off at full gallop. I would have been all right but all of a sudden the saddle girth gave way and I fell nearly off but caught hold of his mane and managed to get on his neck where I sat till I got him stopped. All the time I held my gun, had I let it go it would have been smashed to pieces and had I fallen off I should have been smashed too. After I got him stopped I got off and fitted on the saddle. I got on again when […] off he set again at full speed when all of a sudden one of the stirrups broke and I nearly fell again however I stopped him and made a stirrup of my tethering line and got home safe in body but determined not to ride Bob Tayler[16] again with a gun in my hand. He is a splendid horse however and would fetch a very high price in Canada. We have not so much chance of starving as we had having some where about 200 bags of pemmican on hand. We also sent about 100 bags to Fort Pelly besides a lot of dried meat. We shall be obliged to send about 100 more (a bag weighs about 100). It will take 200 for our own consumption, having to winter a great many men. It makes me savage to see how slow the men work and how much they eat. It is our whole care to be as little expense to the Company as possible therefore we catch fish and rabbits and shoot ducks and pheasants to keep the table supplied. In fact, though Mr. McKay has a family of ten children we do not eat as much dried meat and pem in a year as one of the men does in a month.

Red River carts, two pulled by oxen teams and the third by a single horse. Carts were built entirely from wood and rawhide. The wooden axles made a loud squeal and could be heard for miles. HBCA 1987/363–R–7/9

A Clerk's allowance of sugar is 2 kegs of 84 lbs each of wh sugar. I wish my dear Mother you were here and you might have it all. I do not use it in my tea the only way we use it is in preserves but this year there are no berries but high bush cranberries and but few of them. We will likely get some low bush cranberries late in the fall from the Indians. [...]

7th. I was in expectation of getting at least 6 letters but Mr. Cook returned and only brought me one. It was from Annie. You may be sure it was very welcome especially as all were well when it was written. Poor Nan she talks of not being able to send me anything, but it is I that should send her help but cannot this year. I fear they will be poorly off this winter though their crops are not to be complained of. She says that Harry and Lilly were to be married in Sept. [...] I have a fine pipe to send Harry. It is a Pipe of Peace of red pipe-stone but I do not know when I shall be able to send it. [...] I received some papers from you and by them perceived that you were all well and by that token I concluded that you had not written at the time you posted them. You may address to Fort Ellice Swan River Dist now that I am settled and no likelihood of being removed for some time at least I hope not. Do not think of paying post of any letters. [...] I am in excellent health and getting fat as a seal.

I am going out duck shooting tomorrow. My washer woman is making me a deer skin shirt which is an excellent thing both for winter and summer besides being rather ornamental and very cheap.

[...] We have been busy today in packing up a supply of goods for a post[17] which we have every winter about a hundred miles from this, which is kept by one of the men who is able to read and write. It is very hard times in the settlement. The grasshoppers have eaten up every-thing. Flour is worth from 40 to 50 shillings per hundred and it is half bran. We expect Mr. Campbell[18] the Chief Trader in charge of the District here tomorrow. I have not yet seen him. Mr. McKay is going out to the plains for buffalo in a few days. He expects to be away 2 or three weeks. I will be left to take care of the Post. He will probably bring home 50 or 60 animals which we will keep frozen all winter and so have fresh meat all the time. Fresh Buff is not to be sneezed at and is better than beef or a poke in the eye with a sharp stick. [...]

12th Thursday. I was agreeably surprised yesterday by getting a letter from you and another from Mary. They came by our interpreter who left here on the 22nd ult for F Garry with some horses to fetch up some carts and part of our outfit. [...] I knew there must be some for me at F Garry and so it was proved by Mr. McTavish saying that they had not had a mail for more than a month. [...] You may be sure your letter was very welcome more especially as it left you in good health. I am very sorry to hear of the death of poor Mrs. Wolsey. It was only yesterday morning that I was thinking about her. I felt very sad when I began to think that though I have only been away from home a few weeks that one of my acquaintances should have died. How many shall I find when I return if ever that happens. I am very sorry to hear that my good Uncle was unwell. I hope that he may soon be about again. It distresses me very much my dear mother that you are in such straightened circum-stances and still more so to hear you speak of wishing to help me. I am in no want of money though I have none, for money is not of much use here at least I have no want of it. I am very sorry I cannot help you but it is not in my power but I hope to be able at some future time. I shall be able to pay my debts in Canada next year if I can manage to send money. I do not know if it can be managed without sending by some one going to Canada as we have particular money of our own in R R Settlement[19] which would not pass in Canada but I suppose there is always some means of transacting such things between two Countries. There is plenty of Gold in circulation but that cannot be sent in a letter.

Mr. Campbell has been here the last few days waiting for the carts which arrived yesterday. He left today. He is a very kind man and asked Mr. McKay to let me go to Fort Pelly about New Years or sometime convenient which Mr. McKay willingly agreed to do. [...]

So now with fondest love I remain your ever affectionate son
W.E. Traill [...]

FORT ELLICE *October 15, 1864*

My Dearest Annie

[...] It is very hard times in R R Settlement. Flour is worth 50 shillings Sterling per Cwt & further in the country is worth 1 per lb, this is on account of the grasshopper raid.

Luckily my flour is supplied to me. I get two bags of 112 lbs each for a year, [...] 14 lbs raisins or currants, 10 lbs Rice 10 lbs Hyeon Tea, 5 lbs Black tea, 6 lbs chocolate and same of coffee besides spices & as much meat and pemmican as needful so hard times have no effect except on my spirits unless it comes to starvation.[20] [...]

W.E. Traill

FORT ELLICE *October 23, 1864*

Dear Mary

[...] I have sent off two brigades, one to Fort Pelly loaded with provisions and goods and the other a small outfit to a post we are establishing[21] about 150 miles from here. Since he left here I had to write to Gov. McTavish on business and also to Mr. Campbell who is our Chief Trader. [...] He [Mr. Campbell] seemed well pleased with us. We had done better than any of the other posts in the way of prog and paid lower prices [for furs]. He says that he thought Mr. McTavish was imposing on him when he gave him me for Fort Ellice but Mr. McTavish told him he thought I would be the most useful one he knew of being used to rough it a little, and he Mr. Campbell is well pleased with me. This is very gratifying to me.

I have only 4 men who I keep at work as well as I can but they are very lazy. The Indians are very bothersome. They think that I am a Monyass as they call me or green hand that they can do as they like but they [will] find their mistake. One of their men that I sent to Fort Pelly with two carts came back the next day. He stated that he had lost one of the oxen, so I packed him off with another. This morning he came back again having lost his way and too was so tired that he could not go back & as the carts will be so far on the road having a spare ox that a man on foot driving an ox could not catch them. I let him stay but I will make him work if there is work for him. [...] I bought 2 horses on Monday for the Company. I hope Mr. McKay will approve of the bargain. [...] I find our men very lazy about getting up in the morning & am obliged to call them myself and when they work they are so slow one would think they were going to their own funeral. [...]

WE Traill

[...]

FORT ELLICE *January 27, 1865*

My dear Mother

[...] Winter set in rather later than usual for this place. I do not find it any colder than in Canada. Indeed I have felt cold much more intense there than here. I have very little to do at this end while I am at home

Dog trains. (Edgelow Family Collection) Edgelow 31

but I often go on trips after furs. We, when we hear of an Indian having furs, send off at once a man or two with a sled & train of dogs & an assortment of goods such as we think he may fancy, to try and get his furs, for when [there] are free traders here about I am sorry to say who have liquor[22] for which the Indians, who are a very degraded set (the Saulteaux I mean), will give them furs though they be starving.

    I got notice on New Year's day to hold myself in readiness to go & serve an Indian who had some furs on hand on the following morning. Next morning I started with an Indian, a son of the one we were going to see.

    We had a train of four dogs. On the sled were the following articles 2 Buffo robes & 2 blankets to sleep on, 2 pair of snow shoes, provisions for our selves & dogs besides some pemmican for trade & a small assortment of goods for the same purpose. We started at full speed, both of us running on foot and holding a line going down the hill to keep the sled from running over the dogs. We got along very well till crossing a large creek our dogs started going up the high bank on the far side. I was running before and went back to help up the sled when I discovered that one of my snowshoes had been dropped so I was obliged to go back & pick it up it being a long way back. We got up the hill after some trouble being heavily loaded and went on I still running before. About noon my man began to look at the sun and made signs for dinner but as I was anxious to get there before the traders I said Carwin which is No. We were now obliged to take to our snow shoes the road being drifted much. On we trudged till we [were] obliged to leave the road and strike out in the direction of the camp. We soon came to another large creek Bird Tail Creek (Kee-hue-whut-tan-a-see) down the banks of which we went at full speed. We then travelled about 12 miles along the valley of said creek till we struck the trail of Old Bone [an Indian hunter who periodically traded with Fort Ellice] which we followed till dark when I began to get so hungry and told my man to light a fire. He brightened up at this and quickened his trot into a gallop to the nearest clump of trees where we were agreeably surprised by finding a place where Little Bone[23] had camped the night preceding. There was a good supply of dry wood ready cut and plenty of hay to sleep in.

We got tea and went to bed each rolling himself up in his robe and blkt. Next morning we started before day light & A.M. and came up with the Old Bone at 9 o'clock. After gluttonizing at our expense we traded for his furs & started for home and camped far nearer home than where we slept the night before. Our mode of camping was thus. We picked on a spot where there was plenty of dry wood and shelter— shoveled off the snow from a piece of ground [with] our snow shoes, made a [fire of] flint and steel, got tea which [consisted] of pemmican, tea, sugar, bread & butter which Mrs. McKay had kindly supplied me with. My man I gave a cake, tea with a spoonful of sugar in it and as much pemmican as he could eat. We rolled ourselves up and went roaming the land ahead.

The weather so far was beautiful. In the morning we started long before day break and climbed the bank of the Bird Tail Creek just as the sun was rising. At about ten it began to snow and blow very hard and soon filled up the track we had made going.

We however went on till it got so rough that I could hardly stand. The wind blew my snow shoes round so that I was obliged to tell my man to light a fire in hopes of it becoming [calmer]. We had dinner and again started though it was blowing as much as ever. We stuck it out bravely & about 2 came in sight of F Ellice again. We both cheered heartily and [were] soon in the house.

Every one was surprised that I did not knock up it being my first trip with dogs & my companion being a very smart young fellow. I certainly did feel very stiff & my toes were very much galled with the snow shoe lines, but I did not tell anyone as the Interpreter had prophesied that I would knock up & would be pleased had I done so. I think that first day we travelled about 50 miles but as they often travel 60, 70 or even 80 miles I need not boast. I am now a tearer on snow shoes. There are very few if any who could leave me for a days race but I suppose they might beat me for a week as they are all used to it. I was out on a 6 days trip lately with horses & though we had no load I preferred walking on snow shoes to riding. However, one night crossing a large plain I lost the Indian trail we were following. I had been running all evening and heated my self very much. When it got dark I lay down on the sled. After going some distance my man told me he had lost the track. We wandered about in circles looking for it there being neither moon nor stars to guide us. I now began to get very cold. We could not get a place where there was any wood. I at last got so cold that I got out and ran. We at last came to a grove of small dry poplars where we camped. I worked hard cutting wood & digging away the snow which was several feet deep till I got warm. Snow always drifts into any bushes in a plain sometimes nearly covering them. In the morning I sent him to look for the road which he found a few yards from the camping ground. After this we had very rough weather but got home without accident. But you will have had enough of this. I would not have said anything of trapping but you asked me to tell you all about the Posts but you will not ask me again after this dose. [...]

I am going to start for Fort Pelly tomorrow with a train of dogs and the man I took on my first trip. The distance is 140 miles. I expect to go in 3 days and stay there some days. [...]

Love to all my brothers and sisters I remain your affectionate son. WE Traill [...]

FORT ELLICE *March 1865*

Dear Kate

My term of engagement is 5 years instead of 7 as you suppose.

I am afraid there is little probability of my being able to return at the end of my first engagement. The next term is generally 3 years. Few are allowed to return home until the expiration of the 2nd term.

No Clerk is allowed to marry during his first engagement, which is a very wise and judicious rule for the camp is almost ruined by keeping married men. We have several men who have large families. You have no idea how much prog they eat in a week. 5 bags of pemmican, each of 100 lbs, will scarcely go the round. Mr. McKay has a family of 10 but he makes it a rule that they always kill so much as they eat, that is to say the boys. The girls of which there is two are at school at present but will return with their father in April.[24]

Since I sat down to write I have been interrupted several times by Indian women who are dressing [robes] for us. They put their heads in at the door and whine out Sagarrapes (Lines) (Sama) Tobacco (Temetry) grease [or] some such want. I manage to understand well enough till they begin an overwhelming torrent of Indian [words]. [...] I enjoyed myself very much when at Fort Pelly but my visit was so short that I had hardly time to look round. Mrs. Campbell[25] is a very nice person. [...]

March 29th 1865. Dear Kate as there is a chance of Mr. McKay going to RR soon I take up my pen to finish this and other letters.

It is thawing very hard today though the wind is north.

Three geese were seen on Sunday.

Mr. Campbell was here for a day or two at the end of last week. I like him very much. He is very kind to me and gives me great lectures. I was showing him my album. He picked up his lass at the home of Strickland and was very much pleased to find that I belonged to that family. He then gave me great lectures about keeping up the family name & talent. I lent him the "Canadian Emigrants Guide"[26] [...]

Mr. C entertained us with some of his adventures in the N W. He is a really clever and good man and has seen some hard times. On one occasion he made a long journey with nothing but (Bubbice) [or] the stuff which [snow] shoes are netted of for prog. [...] We have been busy packing furs for the last few days.

I shall be left again by myself when Mr. McKay goes to RR and in the busiest time in the year. I have been very busy for some time making up the Fort Ellice accounts nor am I done yet. Mr. McKay will bring up his two daughters when he returns from RR. [end missing]

WE Traill

FORT ELLICE *July 22, 1865*

My own dear Mother

I received your kind letter of May 20 and 25th this morning on my return from the Prairies[27] where I have been for the last two weeks. I was right glad to see that it left you all in good health and I hasten to answer it as I know not how soon I may have to start for the Plains again.

[...] I heard of the death of my kind friend [Mr. Hargrave] some time since. I am very sorry and grieved to hear of it. I have lost a good friend in him. I would write to Mrs. H. but am afraid to try for I am a poor hand at offering consolation though I feel it very much.

Red River cart brigade loaded with furs. Photo by C.W. Mathers, c. 1866.
HBCA 1987/363–R–7/14

I am glad your garden is flourishing. We had a very [lingering] spring.
Our garden is not much farther on than was yours when you wrote. We
had snow and frost on the 19th of June and about 100 miles from us there
was 9 inches or more of snow. The season is much later than in Canada.
Strawberries are just ripe. There is an abundance of Sasquatoon berries
or high bush Bill berries. They use them for pemmican.

I will now tell you a little of my adventures whilst on the Plains. I
left here on the 8th Inst with 12 carts to visit our hunters and bring home
what prog they had hunted or traded. We travelled for two days at a
brisk trot to the Moose Mountain which is nothing more than a high
ridge. There I saw the last tree till we came in sight of it [again] on our
way home. We here took in a supply of wood and water as there is no
wood and a long traverse to make without water. We travelled all day
at a quick pace only stopping to eat our dinner. 2 dogs died here for
want of water. Just at night we came to the Souris or Moose River. Here
we found plenty of Sasquatoon berries of which I ate till I was none the

better of them. I am sure it was 50 miles across the plains, this the horses did without a drop of water though the weather was excessively hot. The next day we caught sight of a herd of buffalo the first I ever saw and as we had no fresh meat we were desirous of killing one. They however were of a different mind. We [dogged] them round for some time. At last I got pretty near them when they set off at a gallop down a hollow. I cut across to meet them. My horse ran straight for them till within 30 yards when just as I fired he turned short and so I missed my aim and when I tried to follow they left my horse.

You have no notion what frightful creatures they are. You can not see their eyes or their horns for hair. They are the most ugly and savage creatures I ever saw and at this time are very wicked —that is to say the bulls. So I did not get any, but that could not be called a run for my horse was not a runner and I had no one to tell me how to proceed. The next day we travelled till 11 P.M. and went to bed without supper. We saw plenty of hairy monsters but had not time to hunt them. Next morning we started early and had breakfast with our hunters. Here I saw my first hunting camp and a curious sight it was to me. Hunters always go in large parties on account of Indians. They always camp in a ring. Each hunter has an average of 4 or five carts. These are placed in a ring and they generally sleep under them except when lying in one place which is seldom as the refuse meat makes such an obnoxious smell that they move every three or four days. The ring here was about half a mile in circumference. Inside the ring the horses are kept at night, and grass cut and given them as the number of horses eat the ring bare in a few minutes. Here are stages made of [poles] brought from the Moose Mountain on which was hung tons of dry meat or rather meat drying in the sun, crowds of women, and boys cutting the meat into flakes for drying, and chopping bones for marrow fat. Then there were women dressing hides for cart covers and for dressed leather. Then there were men pounding meat for pemmican and others rendering grease others again spreading out the half dry meat on the grass to dry. For after it is half dry they spread it on the grass during the day and at night gather it into heaps and cover it with hides till morning when it is again spread out. I assure you it is a stirring scene and were it not for the stench a very pleasant one.

When I arrived Jerry McKay's brother, who is in charge of the party from home, was at the Qu'Appelle party a few miles from here. But Mr. McKay's son Thomas, a young man of 17, was here. We had breakfast on the most delicious "Buff" steaks tea and sugar and some cakes that I had left. Soon after a cry was raised that there were three herds of buff close. We got our horses and started, about 30 or 40 hunters all on fine horse[s that] pranced and capered, but none more than the one I rode a fine bay mare belonging to Mr. McKay. Tom took in hand to initiate me in the mysteries of the hunt. We rode round for some time but the ground being very hilly we could see no buffs. Sometimes when we got to the top of a big hill we all took off our saddles to cool our horses. At last we separated Thomas and I and another going by ourselves. Suddenly on reaching the top of a hill we came in sight of 3 bands immediately beneath us. We then rode backwards and forwards for a few minutes, the usual plan to warn others that the cattle were near. Others now joined us and then we set off at a trot keeping ourselves as much as possible out of sight of the cattle till we got quite close. We then went on at a canter till the animals saw us, when at the word given by one of the men we all put our horses on at full speed and I soon found myself in the midst of them and far ahead of the others except Thomas who kept close to me. I fired at a cow, so did one of the men behind me. I saw blood rush from her thigh and thought I had struck her and said so to Thomas but he said no. I then shot at another cow and struck her. She ran a few paces and fell. I was now so much excited I could not load and told Thomas so he handed me his gun. I took aim but it missed. I handed it back and loaded my own. I then picked out a large bull and fired at him and [I] think wounded him. He separated from the rest. I followed and when I got close jumped off and got good aim and I am sure struck him. He slackened his pace but I was now far from the others so I was afraid to follow so I returned and met Thomas. We then caught sight of *a bull standing and putting up his tail a sure sign that he is angry. We rode up close. When he made off we after him. I fired and struck him in the shoulder and neck which sent the blood in streams from his mouth. This would prove a mortal wound but he would run far so we chased him again. Thomas now fired but missed him. I fired again and struck him about the heart but he did not seem to mind it. Thomas fired again and struck him near the kidneys and I was coming up again close behind him when up went his tail. Thomas cried look out. I hauled my horse to one side when he made a desperate charge at me but I was too smart for him. I fired again and struck him in the neck. He stood looking defiance at us and then lay down. I was going to jump off and go to him but Thomas would not let me. It was well for when we were near to him he got up and gave us another charge but was too weak with the loss of blood to catch us. He then lay down again and in a few minutes was dead and then and only then did I realize what a monster he was —larger than 3 oxen and covered on the head and shoulders with hair that hid his eyes and horns and forelegs and a long beard under his chin whilst the hinder parts of him were as bare almost as the human skin. So it is with them in summer. I took off his scalp after a great deal of trouble. The hair was so long and thick that I could not cut through it and his skin was about 1 full inch thick or more and shall send it home sometime. It is large enough for a mat though the skin is only a strip about 1 foot long and 6 inches broad. I had intended making a powder horn of the first bull I killed but all old bulls have their horns so much worn by sharpening them on stones that those of all [old] bulls are useless for such purposes. The cow's horns are so small and crooked as to be perfectly useless. You may say I did not kill him myself but I gave him the first wound which according to the laws of the ring is the same even if you do not draw blood but mine was a mortal wound. The monster ran fully 5 miles in which he got several shots. Unless struck in the heart or backbone they cannot be knocked down at the first shot and if not killed in 8 shots cannot be killed at all, so say the Hunters.*

As the day was remarkably hot and we were thirsty we did not stop to cut them up but left that to others who followed us with carts for the purpose of carrying home the meat and hides. I was applauded by all on returning to camp for having killed 2, which was not bad considering it was my first hunt and that I was neither used to horse or gun. The gun was the same one which one of my fellow clerks announced as useless because he ran several times and killed nothing. Several of the hunters returned that day without killing. At the camp I found Jerry [McKay][28] and Mr. Hourie who is in charge of the Qu'Appelle post hunting party. We had a delightful dinner, if you can imagine dinner delightful without bread or vegetables of any description [and] water that was very salty.

After dinner we set to work to load our carts. I took 12 with me and was told by Mr. McKay to bring 16 home but had I had 50 I could have had them all loaded. I scraped up 21 in all, all loaded with pemmican and dry meat but by the time we got half of them loaded it was dark. The men then went and collected their horses and put them inside the ring for the night and cut grass for them. The next day I got the carts off at noon but did not leave myself till near sunset. Thomas McKay was to return with me to Fort Ellice. I persuaded Jerry to accompany us and sleep with us at our tent and have a cup of tea for there was none in the party. He accordingly came with us. We went talking and laughing and did not notice that we had passed the tracks of the carts for there is no road in these parts. After we rode for several miles, as we thought in the direction of the carts, we came to the conclusion that we had lost our way and separated accordingly to look for the track. We rode for some time, Thomas and I keeping together. On going up a little hill we saw Jerry in full pursuit of a buff calf. He was trying to drive it towards me but he could not and as it was very swift and would have left him he shot it. He fired twice before it fell. We skinned it and slung it on a spare horse and started as we thought for the carts. After riding some miles we fell in with some hunters who told us we were going the wrong way to find the carts. They pointed out where to find them and then we left them and arrived at camp after dark. Had we not met the hunters we should have slept out which would not have been agreeable as I had on no coat but only a cotton shirt. Jerry said it was the first time he had lost himself. He is an excellent horseman and for my pleasure raced his horse at full speed standing on its back gun in hand. He is also a capital hunter. We sat talking for a long time by the light of a small piece of buff lung in a frying pan of grease which is as good as any lamp and gives no smell more than a candle.

In the morning I raised my men early and bidding good bye to Jerry we started for home. This was Sunday so we only made half a day but had to employ the remainder of the day by taking off our wheels and soaking them in water. On Monday we ran and killed a bull and cow more to get the hides to tie our carts than anything else, for we only took the fat and hide and some choice parts. Tuesday we killed two bulls for the same purpose. At 3 P.M. of that day we saw what we thought to be an immense herd of buffalo but they proved to be a horde of Assiniboine or Stone Indians. As soon as I knew that it was them I armed all my men who were only 1 man 3 boys and Thomas McKay.

They came riding up to us and shook hands. They were armed with guns bows and tomahawk. They gave us to understand that they were camped at no great distance and had mistaken us for buffs. They gave me great uneasiness as of late they had tried to stop several horsemen and rob them of their provisions as here there were at least 100 or them all double armed we would have had no chance. I told my men to keep the carts as near together as possible. I and Thomas kept as much behind as possible so as not to give them the chance to sneak up behind our backs. We were on horseback and our guns loaded. One old man gave us to understand that we had better go as fast as we could as they had stopped some half breeds shortly before. He said he would talk to them. This made me more uneasy but after following for some time they left us but gave us to understand that they would come at night and watch our horses for us. I had no notion of this so when we camped we made a very respectable ring of our 21 carts and as soon as it was dark put our 24 horses therein counting them first to see that none were left out. I then divided our little stock of ammunition so that if they did come and offer violence we would defend the carts as long as possible but they came not. Next day they overtook us as they were [going] in the direction we were going but they did not go as far as we as Indians never go far in a day.

That night we camped at the Souris River, a singular and pretty place. Coal and iron are to be found in abundance in the sides of the bank which are very steep. There are what have been islands. Just like hay stacks in shape and crowned with cactuses and prickly pear. These same cactuses are a terrible bore. They stick into ones shoes and feet and are barbed like porcupine quills. I have some now in my feet which cause me no small amount of annoyance. That night we again kept our horses in the ring but no one came. Next morning we, Thomas and I, left them and came home with out adventure but were very tired. It took us two days of hard riding. We rode better than 70 miles per diem. My object in leaving the carts was to send a party to meet them with the new carts as theirs were breaking and would not reach home.

I am very happy to say that Mr. McKay has just received notice of his having been appointed to a Chief Tradership and richly he deserves it if ever man did. We will soon be getting our outfit from York. We need it as we are out of goods. My private order too I will be very glad of as I am rather short of some articles which I sent for.

The grasshoppers are committing great ravages in the settlement and even here they have destroyed what little wheat we sowed as an experiment to see how it could come on. We had a dish of early potatoes a few days since and are now using them continually. They are very good for the time of year. We have two tame cabries, a small kind of deer or antelope peculiar to the plains. They are beautiful creatures. We saw plenty of them on the plains but did not kill any as they are very swift. There are two other kinds, the black tail or jumping and the long tail deer both belonging to the Plains. [...] [end missing]

WE Traill

FORT ELLICE [*July 22, 1865*]

Dear Mary[29]

[beginning missing] When it is called fine pemmican choke-cherries are also pounded and mixed in with the meat. In seasons of great scarcity the dried pounded cherries are eaten by the natives but are somewhat hard of digestion and are not good for bad teeth. Fortunately for me I have as yet only heard of such diets and at present see no fear of being reduced to breaking my teeth upon pounded choke-cherries or making soup of my leather breeches, or boiling down the window or door of my shanty (or trading post) as a gentleman told me he had to do many years ago—said window or door being made of parchment or dressed skin. Such extreme cases do not often occur in this part of the country so you need not alarm yourself and picture your precious Nor'wester sitting mournfully over a ragout manufactured from a hunting shirt or a bowl of soup concocted from a pair of moose moccasins.[…] I assure you that a hunter's camp presents a stirring scene and to the uninitiated in camp life in Rupert's Land, a very novel one and were it not for the smell of the meat, I would have enjoyed the time that I spent among the wild prairie hunters listening to their wonderful tales and adventures and hairbreadth escapes. […]

Many a fine gentleman might envy your Nor'wester his life of freedom and healthy enjoyment when galloping gun in hand after game on these unenclosed wastes, with spirits as light and buoyant as the pure air he breathes—air that makes labour light, and fatigue scarcely to be felt as such. […]

I was on one occasion a few miles from Fort Union, an American trading post on the Great Missouri River—it is now occupied by troops who are in search of Sioux but the Sioux can give them a good game of hide and seek on those vast Prairies, which are impassable to those unacquainted with them on account of the scarcity of wood and water. Those Arabs of our Western deserts on their fleet Prairie horses are not to be captured on their own ground by Yankees without some trouble.

We had a visit ourselves at the Fort from a large band of Sioux. They pitched 160 tents outside our walls but formidable as was their number they showed no disposition to molest us.

"Standing Buffalo" their chief, is a splendid looking fellow. He presented Mr. McKay with a beautifully ornamented pipe of peace and invited us to a smoke in his lodge. These Sioux are a fine looking set of men though some of their braves are ferocious savages enough, but it is their interest to keep well with us and to do nothing to anger us. They were dressed some in Indian costume others in Yankee coats and trousers and some in _no_ costume at all.

The Standing Buffalo had a headdress of feathers black and white. The black he said were for the Indians he had scalped in war and the white for the Long Knives as they call the Yankees.

These Sioux Indians are far beyond our Assiniboines and other tribes—Sotos—Red Lakers and others. Our Indians are great cowards and are terribly afraid of their warlike intruders. They mean if possible to drive them off back to their own hunting grounds beyond the great River. [Sooner] said than done. The treachery of their mode of war fare is to us whites one of its most disgusting features. It is murder in cold blood. [...]

Your loving Norwester
W.E.T.

[FORT ELLICE *July 1865* [30]]

Dear Annie

[beginning missing] [...] We each took a blanket on our saddles & a little bag of pemmican about 10 lbs & a tin pot. Thus was all our travelling equipment. [...] I suppose you feasted on strawberries for some time. We have few but it was when the Sioux were here & no one could leave to pick them. However I used to be called into Mrs. McKay's room to help to demolish a pan full more than once a day. We have any *amount of berries of all kinds. Choke cherries, red cherries, Sasqatoon berries, etc. & we will have plenty of cranberries & other kinds. [...]*

We have two live cabries or antelope & a young moose tame. The former are beautiful creatures but the moose is the ugliest creature I ever saw except a lean jackass. He is very long in the legs & a neck so short that when he kneels he can hardly eat grass. He has a remarkably ugly head. He is too young to have horns. If ever I return I shall try & take 2 young buffalo home with me. [...] [end missing]

   W.E. Traill

FORT ELLICE [*August 17, 1865*]

Dear Kate

[...] I hear that the government of R River Settlement has been given over by the HB Company to the Canadian Government but do not know whether it to be true. [...] Our carts came back from the Plains this week with nearly 50,000 lbs of pemmican & dry meat which will keep us in provisions for a while, were we not to send it to Fort Pelly. [...] I had a letter from my friend Mr. Wm Tully a few days since which I must not fail to answer at once. I must also send him a Bill[31] for what I owe him so soon as Mr. Campbell comes from York though he never once hinted on the subject but his letter was very kind & full of good advice. [...] The Misses McKay are very nice girls. The youngest Kate is the best looking. She is dark with splendid black eyes. They are both rather shy but not afraid of a fellow. Mr Watt who is beginning to look for a partner for life was very anxious for an introduction to them but as there was such a press of company they did not present themselves all the time he was with us. They bring me a drink of milk every evening and often strawberries & cream so long as they lasted. [...] I am still at Fort Ellice. I should be sorry to leave it now that there are such attractions at it. [...] I have had my own troubles this summer. First I had a sore finger. Next came a whitlow[32] which caused me many sleepless nights & days of pain.

Next came [a] toothache unbearable. Next a bad gumboil. Then I had a sore foot which I hurt going into a lake for ducks. I had also many little aches & pains but my health is nevertheless very good, I am thankful to say. [...] [end missing]

W.E. Traill

FORTS ELLICE & PELLY *September 29, 1865*

My dear Mother

[...] soon after, I was sent to take charge of Qu'Appelle Post[33]—about the same distance from FE as Ft Pelly but in another direction. Here I made the acquaintance of a Mr. McDonald a very fine fellow indeed a Highlander. I mentioned Walter[34] to him. He took up the subject very warmly & said that he would write to Mr. Ellice who is a relative of his. He said that there was every prospect of success & that if Walter was of my own turn that it would be a good thing for the Co.

I have since spoken to Mr. Campbell for I am now at Ft Pelly in the room of Mr. Finlayson who was obliged to go to RR on business. Mr. C thinks that there is no doubt but what they will accept of Walter. My own name is the most wide spread of any Apce Clerk in this district. This you will think is conceit, but it is really the fact though why I do not know unless it is because I am steady & take a great interest in all that concerns the Co & that I have been brought up to a rough life which is a great recommendation of itself. I wrote to Walter telling him all about the work & pay etc. The Co Service is not as paying as in old times but still there is independence for all who make up their minds to go through. [...] It would be very agreeable for both of us, for it is for this district that Clerks are most wanted & to this District he would most likely be sent.

The papers passed me in the winter packet & were taken up to Saskatchewan. From thence they were taken down to Norway House & round by Swan River to F. Pelly so that I got them in September. [...]

Ft. Pelly is rather dull owing to the absence of Mr. & Mrs. Finlayson but there is a very lively person Mrs. Des Chambeault. She is a ventriloquist in a small way & very lively. She is a half-breed French woman. Her husband is a Clerk & her father a Chief Trader in the service. The living here is very good duck, geese, beaver, moose etc. They have a tolerable garden but not so good as at Ft. E. Our carts from F E, which started from there the same day as I, arrived here yesterday. The river was high so we had to float the pemmican across on a boat made of skins. There was 100 Bags pem & 60 bales Dd meat so it took us some time. [...]

Will E Traill

FORT ELLICE *October 22, 1865*

My dear Kate

[...] I have been to Fort Pelly for a month & only returned 2 days ago. I passed a very pleasant time at F P. I was left alone there for a week. That is to say Mr. C came here & left me in charge during his absence. [...]

When I returned to F.E. I found Mr. McKay waiting my arrival anxiously as he was ready to go to the plains for fresh meat. He left yesterday with 23 carts & will be absent more than a month in all probability. I am therefore "Monarch of all I Survey" but have my hands full which will keep me from getting too despotic in my government. [...]

I got a present of a very pretty little pointer dog from Mr. McKay. His (the dog's) name is Frank. I call him Frank Traill. By the by if you see Frank be sure & remember me to him. [...]

I was away today setting traps. Last year I only caught 1 wolf but there is nothing like perseverance. On my way home I shot ten rabbits & could have killed more but ran short of She-sheep-an-win which being interpreted means shot.

At present we are living on rabbits & beaver. The later are as good as suckling pigs & very much like them in flavour. Moose nose is a very dainty morsel. I think it is the nicest thing I have eaten in this country. As we have plenty of vegetables, we are better off than last year & we shall soon be reveling in Buffo tongue & Boss. It is very cold nowadays & winter will soon be setting in & then dogs & snow shoes will be the order of the day. I intend to have more pleasure in the way of cariole driving than last. The Miss McKays will be very good company on such occasions.

I am afraid I shall be too busy to make any long trips to the Indians this winter. As it is so late in the season Mr. Campbell thinks it advisable that I should wait till the first of June before I draw money which is the usual time for such transactions. I will therefore send a Bill through Montreal 1st of June for £15—which will I hope pay of all my old scores. At least keep my creditors from giving you much bother until the following year when I shall be able to send home a like sum if all goes well. [...]

I must soon try my hand at making a double cariole also to rig my skates. I shall try & induce the girls to learn to skate. [...]

I suppose Walter has ere this got my last. I hope he will come out here. Mr. C thinks there is no doubt about his getting an appointment. He is at the right age. [...] I think also that this kind of life will agree with him. I wish Harry had had such a chance before he ruined his strength. There is a remote chance of my going to York in Co with some other gentleman in charge of the boats but I am not anxious as it is a very disagreeable trip. Be sure & send me the recipe to make vinegar from maple sap. Mrs. McKay & I tried it last spring but it failed. I think it was owing to the sap being boiled down too much. [...]

The river froze over last night but a more lovely day could not be. We have not had a drop of rain since the later end of August but we are so much the better off on that account.

We have no Service today as our parson is away with Mr. McKay hunting. It is very dull on Sunday when there is no Service. Mrs. McKay, the girls & I & Mrs. Cook the parson's wife generally go for a walk. Mrs. Cook is a very nervous person. There are constant reports that Sioux are in the neighbourhood which puts her in constant alarm. I always tease her & try to make her believe that they are really about. I have no patience with people who are so nervous. Mrs. McKay is a model in that respect, so are the girls. I have got both Mrs. & Mr. McKay's likenesses which I shall enclose in this if I have room but expect you to send me a couple in their place.

You must not criticize Mrs. McKay though she is plain. Her likeness does not do her justice & makes her look fully 10 years older than she really looks.

I wish I had a photograph of Fort Ellice or Ft Garry to send you but may in the course of time. [...] [end missing]

W.E. Traill

FORT ELLICE *October 30, 1865*

Dear Annie.

[...] I received it just on my arrival from Qu'Appelle Post about 15th Sept & would have written before but was ordered off to F Pelly & was there a full month. I went to fill the place of the Clerk of the trade store as Mr. C does nothing in that line but has his hands full of other matters. I had only 1 days warning. [...] I spent a very pleasant time of it at FP. Mrs. C is an excellent hand at making a person comfortable. I took only 2 shirts & 1 coat with me & felt very shabby. I did not expect to stay so long. I went on horse back in two days & came back in almost a day & a half though Mr. C who is a most indefatigable rider told me it would take me better than three. The distance is better than 120 miles. [...]

I do not think you need be alarmed at present about my choosing a native for a partner for life but as far as that goes though I am not in favour of the ladies of this country in general. There is a couple of them [the McKay sisters] at F E who I am very fond of. No one [would] know that they were half-breeds nor are they for their grandfather is only a quarter breed & he is the nearest half-breed relative they have.[35] [...]

Cariole driving will soon be the order of the day. I can hardly say that I had a single ride last year but now there is some one to drive & it will give me no small amount of pleasure. Dog travelling in winter is quite a different thing from pleasure riding in a cariole. When on a trip you can run behind all day, but pleasure riding you sit into your cariole with plenty of robes & lie back & smack your whip & make a dreadful noise to keep the dogs in constant terror. A cariole is made more like a shoe or slipper than anything else & is a very comfortable conveyance.[36]
[...]

WE Traill

FORT ELLICE *October 31, 1865*

Dear Clinton

[...] Mr. McKay bought 2 Yoke of American oxen lately which were sent to Fort P. No one could drive them but myself, so I was looked upon as a great Medicine Man by the Indians & as a very smart fellow by the people in general. They could not conceive how I could make the oxen do as I wished them to. I made a hay rack & drew several large loads of hay with Mr. C's help.

Mr. C is a very fine person. He used to entertain us with his adventures in the N and what he says may be relied on as strictly true. On one occasion he had to eat his windows but it must be remembered that they were made of parchment. He says that the nicest thing to ever eat was an otter which was killed in the fall & lay in the river till the ice went off the Spring following. [...]

I went shooting rabbits this evening with Mrs. McKay & her daughter Katie. I killed 5 & Mrs. McKay only one which is something for me to brag of as she generally kills more than anyone else.[37] I often bring home ten & some partridges. [...]

WE Traill

Dear Mother

[...] I had the day before started on my way out to this place. I had
taken in tow an old squaw who was coming out to her brother in law.
She had an old mare on which I was obliged to bestow sundry tastes of
buckskin to make her keep up with my horses of which I had two. The
old brute was quite knocked up when we stopped at night & lay down
in her trams & never got out of them for there she died in half an hour.
Now I was in a fix you may be sure. A day's journey from the Fort & an
old woman & her little girl to take nearly 100 miles in very cold weather
& both my sleds loaded. To crown all, the old witch took sick & kept us
awake all night with her lamentable howlings. I thought she would die,
so in the morning I told Pierre my man to put in one of our horses into
the old woman's jumper & take her & the child back to the Fort.

I was met that evening with a whole budget of letters. [...] You may
be sure that I resumed my journey with a light heart for all along I had
been wondering at your long silence.

My light heart however did not prevent my nose from freezing. It
froze 3 times that day. I was in fear afterwards that I would lose part of
it but I am happy to say I have still the enormous proboscis that I used
to have. Later that day we came on the fresh track of a bear but had no
gun & besides it was Sunday. I arrived here my 4th day & immediately
bought the house I am now living in for 15%.[38] It is not a castle but not
dear. It is about 15 x 15 x 5 feet 10 inches high, so I frequently hit my head
on the rafters when I forget & raise it. I call the place Ft Defiance for I
bid the [swarm] of free traders defiance.

I have now 4 men & 5 trains of dogs. It is little more than 1 month
since I came here first & I have already more than 200 robes besides
plenty of furs which is more than any of the traders have though they
have been here since fall. I am just preparing for a trip out to the Woody
Mountains on a [trade] with the Assiniboines. I am sorry I cannot go
myself but I have my hands full here. I made a trip to the Souris River

*about 80 miles from this place. I went in 1 1/2 days and came back in the
same. It is a place without interest being a small stream along which a
few Indians winter in mud houses. [...]*

*We took our wood with us and a sufficient stock to rely on coming
back which we hid about half way for people are sometimes frozen by
others finding their wood & burning it.*

*Coming home it blew up a storm towards night & as there was
no shelter we travelled on till near midnight & reached Moose Mountain Creek about 15 miles from here, having travelled 65 miles with
heavy loads.*

*I have since sent out 2 of my men to the same place but the weather
is rough so that they cannot return at present, though from the hill in
front of us you can almost see the place.*

*I forgot to mention that we saw plenty of buffaloes but did not at-
tempt to kill any but we were often obliged to hold on to the tail ropes
of our sleds to keep the dogs from running after the brutes. Many a good
run they gave me in this way. [...]*

*The old Gov's letter was very kind & communicative & contained
a great deal of valuable advice & also gave me great credit for my
steadiness & the interest I take in HB Cos affairs & recommended
my continuing to study which advice I shall profit by when an opportunity presents itself but I wish the old Chief was here & he would not
think much of studying anything but how best to out do our enemies—
the traders. I will now put up this for the night. I am writing on the lid
of a box which I hold on my knee & not the most brilliant of lights.*

*Here I am again with my box lid on my knee. I did not get any paper
till yesterday. I sent one of my men to the Fort a few days back for
fresh supplies. He returned yesterday & brought me some letters but
none from Canada. [...] Amongst the letters I got yesterday was an
invitation from Mr. & Mrs. Campbell to go & spend my new years at
Fort Pelly. Of course I could not go as New Year's Day is past & gone,
but I heartily thank the kind friends who sent me such a cordial invitation. [...] Mrs. McKay kindly sent me a lot of nice cakes & a cold plum*

pudding & some flour. You may be sure I am very glad of them for I have not tasted bread of any kind for a dog's age.

You may be sure I was overjoyed when I came to that part of Kate's interesting letter which said that you had at last got your money & that it was fully as much as you expected. You will now be out of extreme want which has not been the case for many a day. Mr. McKay seems very well pleased with my trade so far. He says he is going to give [a] grand dinner to me & my men when we go to the Fort, which will be the 1st of Feb if possible as he is going to Fort Pelly then & wishes me to be there during his absence. He will send out 2 men to take care of this place so that I & my men may all op'in.

Joe Hargrave's letter was kind & interesting. I shall answer it as soon as possible. The old Govr said nothing about Walter to me. Perhaps he had only just arrived from Canada. [...]

17th. I have just started my men to the Woody Mountains. It was quite an imposing sight to see them start with their 5 trains of dogs. All the howling you ever heard put together could not be compared with what was done this morning. At starting, all my dogs, 25 in number, set up a most doleful consent & all the countless dogs in the neighbour-hood joined in full chorus. I have now only one man with me, the man with whom I first travelled last year. He is a nice cheerful willing fellow especially at eating the plum pud which Mrs. McKay sent me. You would stare if you were to see him pitching into it. He evidently thinks that he is in duty bound to finish all that I warm up. He is at this moment mak-ing an [axe handle]. I am lying at full length on a robe on the floor with a foul light which upset just now & very nearly gave me the trouble of re-writing this page, which under the existing state of affairs would be no joke. I spent my new years as last year by making a trip with dogs, but this time I was able to ride & enjoyed myself very much. I could not help thinking of the many pleasant rides I have had at home on that day.

My man is just now making a second descent on the pudding having finished his [axe handle] & finding I suppose that he had still a little

Pressing fur. (Edgelow Family Collection) Edgelow 15

room to spare though not 15 minutes ago he put his hands on his stomach & said it would <u>Break</u>. You ask do I wear beard & moustache. I did boast a slight development of each but as <u>Jack Frost</u> chose to sit on them I was obliged to cut them off as the moustache was the means of freezing my nose. I wish you could see my house as it is at the present but this morning it presented a still more chaotic appearance. One side was filled up with 120 robes & the small stock of goods I have. The other side is with a promiscuous collection of furs, guns, snowshoes, pemmican etc etc. so that I really have no place to put my leather breeches. I had a bed stead but was obliged to pull it down today to make room. The wall is covered with furs nailed against them to dry. I have a space about 6 feet wide from the door which is made of parchment & serves as a window, to the fireplace & this serves for bed room kitchen & office for myself & 6 men when they are all at home which only happens occasionally. When they return we shall be in a queer fix for house room if they bring anything like what I expect.

19th. I am all alone today having sent off my man George on a trip in quest of furs. It is very dull here with no books & no one to speak to but savages. They are a great nuisance. They come in just to bother me & ask me the prices of every article of trade at least once a day when they do not want to buy. I am sure they must know the price of everything by this time. It has been extremely cold for the last two days but is some what warmer today. We have not 3 inches of snow yet & on one side of the mountain there is scarcely an inch, it having blown off to the other side with a heavy storm about 10 days since. In the middle of which storm I started for Fort Ellice with my man, about 3 o'clock in the morning. We got to a place on the other side of the mountain where there is a few houses & there I heard news of furs that changed my plans so I sent my man on to the Fort light & I returned with the furs we were taking home. I got back about 11 A.M. having travelled full 40 miles since I started. Not a bad half day. […]

This morning just after I got up an Indian came to tell me that I was wanted to go over to Ne can e qua ape an Indian living about 1/4 mile from home.

I went thinking he was asking me to a feast as is their custom but no. I sat some time & then he told me to bring my man to interpret for me. I came back & had my breakfast & then went with my man but he only wanted to ask me a trifling question. This was very provoking but nothing more than common. […]

Since August I have seldom had a day to myself excepting when Mr. McKay was out hunting. I wrote to you then I think. I intended to write to all hands from this place but as I am going to the Fort in 10 days at the latest I shall postpone till then. I expect to stay 10 days or a fortnight whilst Mr. McKay is off to Ft. Pelly. […]

I have just been analyzing a bag of fine pemmican & find its constituent parts to be as follows 1 per cent squaws hair 2 per cent blankets 5 per cent buff do 20 per cent blue berries 5 per cent stone berries 5 per cent miscellaneous trash 62 pct pounded meat & fine grease. So you may judge what a nice dish it is. How blankets get into it is thus. The Indian women when picking the berries break of the bushes & shake them into their blankets & of course a great deal of wool goes along with the berries into the pemmican. I have been teaching my man George to understand the price of goods. In writing I find him very quick and attentive. He has been taking lessons from Mr. Cook our parson.

22nd. This morning I started for the tail of the mountain to see Mr. McKay's brother in law whose sons went out hunting nearly a month ago. I had four good dogs & was able to ride some times so that I went [fast]. I got to a place about 20 miles from here & about 15 from the tail. Here I heard that the hunters had not returned so I turned back after eating my dinner having only traded 1 robe & 1 kitt fox & a bag pemmican. I found a dog which we lost, which pleased me more than if I had made a good trade. It was near sundown when I started home. Whilst still in the mountain I saw some traders with 2 trains [of] dogs about half way from this place (one can see far from the mountain). They were about ten miles a head of me but I determined to over take them and play them a trick. I put my dogs on to the gallop & ran as hard as I could, jumping on once in a while. I over took them before they had got 3 miles from where I saw them first. I kept beside them for a little while but passed them before long. Now for a race I drove up my dogs. They had about 250 lbs on their sled. The trader's dogs had a 5 gallon jug rum on one sled & literally nothing on the other.

As soon as they saw I intended to leave them they urged up their dogs but as they could not run far with out jumping on their sleds I soon left them far behind. I would not ride so long as they were in sight which was not long for it was getting dark. It was quite dark when I reached the foot of the mountain & I was very tired & the road very bad & I found great difficulty in keeping pace with my dogs. The inequalities of the ground made but little difference to my dogs, but to me toiling up the steep ascents was no joke. The traders did not arrive for more than two hours after me. I feel sore & unwell after my race. My object was to get my man ready to start in the morning to be before the traders. If I did not they would get every thing as they go along having rum, for which the poor deluded savages will part with everything. These traders played me a trick the other day & I think now I can pay them back with their own coin. [...]

24th. I sent off my man early this morning. I find that the traders have not gone yet.

My man returned today having fleeced the traders out of everything the Indians have.

Jan 31st [...] We had a great deal of trouble coming home. The ground is as bare as in summer almost. I was obliged to leave 80 robes & 150 wolves about half way. We sent for them yesterday with horses. [...]

The day I left we had a great fuss. I will try & describe the scene.

All the Indians had been drinking for a day or two. That morning about 3 A.M. we were all wakened by an Indian rushing in to our house calling out in Indian I will kill you all now we all jumped up but there was no fire & we could not get a light.

The Indian got amongst the kettles & began pitching them about & spilling meat, liquor, etc all about the house & striking right & left. I groped about to find him but got a terrible blow with a [kettle]. I caught him by the waist and felt if he had a knife. I found he had none so I told my men to haul him out. I caught hold of him & dragged him to the door & told my men to out with him telling him at the same time in Indian to go.

The men opened the door when in rushed another Indian & caught hold of the other & they began to fight. They got amongst my furs which were laying loose ready for packing & there they fought scratching & pulling hair etc. I told my men to light a candle but it could not be found. I then told them to make a fire which they did. We could then see what was going on. My men tried to part them but it was no go so we let them fight till they began to get tired. [end missing]

W.E. Traill

[To one of Willie's brothers]

[beginning missing] [...] *The ducks and geese will soon come and then we shall not be so badly off—but then again we have little or no shot, [so] we will have to cut balls & roll them in a frying pan which is the general plan of making shot. We owe the want of prog to the great depth of snow which has kept the horses very poor. Many have died. We have lost 14. The traders (freemen) have lost great numbers. One man who came to Moose Mountain [last fall] with 6 horses has none now—all dead. Some again have eaten their horses to save their own lives & the lives of their families.*

At Edmonton House in Saskatchewan they have lost 70 horses & 40 oxen. [...]

The Blackfoot have been making terrible demonstrations in Saskatchewan but have done no damage as yet. [...]

The RR Settlers are anxiously looking out for a change of government but I doubt much if they will relish taxes, school rates & strict authority. They do not deserve a government at all. [...]

Be of good heart my dear brother. Perhaps there is yet better days in store for you, but should such be the case set no store thereon but strive to be found ready let the hour come when it may. [end missing]

W.E. Traill

FORT ELLICE *April 3, 1866*

My own dear Mother

[...] I heard from Mr. Campbell a few days ago. He tells me that Walter is appointed for the Swan River district & will probably be out in May or June if not when Mr. Mactavish returns from England where he has gone on business.

I do not know what Walter's notion is for keeping things so close from his relations especially from you. He accepted the apptmt at once but desired me not to tell anyone so do not question him about it. Perhaps he might back out if he knew that I had made his [motives] & intentions known. [...]

I am glad that you have at last got your money. I intended sending you the sum I promised but since it will be fully as acceptable next year when I shall much better be able to spare it I shall send only half this year or even less for I must also send £5.0.0 to my good friend Mr. Tully who has been such a good friend to me & as he has no legal hold I think it my duty to see that he does not lose by me. [...]

You might send some more by Walter, also a book if you have a nice one of your own writing. The Back Woods would be a nice one but I suppose you cannot get one in Canada. [...] Walter might [bring] it also. I have the 1st Vol. The money you expended in improvements is well laid out. It is a pity you could not purchase the lot in front of you. It troubles me much my dear mother that I have given you no assistance as yet but that I have continued so long an expense to you. My wages have been small as you are aware & my expenses large but after next year I shall have a yearly increase of £10 for three years & from that I shall jump to £75 which will be good wages. I have been obliged to buy a gun which a person cannot dispense with in this country but I shall not have the same expense for years I hope. If you can manage to get the lot I should be able next year to send you enough to pay [something] on it & besides what I owe you or will owe after what I send you in June. It would I am sure be a capital investment of money for I am confident that the land will be worth a great deal in the village before many years.

[...]

Mr. McKay started this morning for Qu'Appelle, about 120 miles from here. It was not then so rough. I am sure he did not get 10 miles before he would have to camp & such a day to camp without a tent or cover of any kind more than a robe & blanket. I made a trip to my old winter quarters not long since. I was only 4 days absent as I travelled fast. It often takes 8 days to go & come. I went with two men but returned alone. I came home in a day & a half. I ran almost the whole of the way as I had about my own weight in the sled & only 3 dogs. The last day I got quite snow blind towards night & was quite blind for several days. My eyes are hardly strong yet. It is a very painful thing. [...]

Every one seems to be in a great hurry to be married in Canada. The new Bishop passed here during my absence at the Plains. He is I believe a very fine person. [...]

Will E Traill

FORT ELLICE *April 18, 1866*

My dearest Kate

[...] I expect to go to FP next Monday to see the folks there & superintend the bringing down of some bateaux & timber. I have had many invitations from all hands to come up. I expect we shall have more company this summer than last. Mrs. Finlayson from F.P. will be with us a couple of months. Mrs Campbell & another will be passing & stay a few days with us. One of the girls is going up to F.P. to stay part of the summer with Mrs. C- whilst Mr. C is down [at] Norway House.

It is quite probable that I shall miss all the Company as in all probability I shall be on the plains for some time but this is not certain. I should not like to miss the company even at the expense of missing my hunt. [...]

The snow is going pretty fast the past two or three days & geese & ducks are making their appearance. We had a roast goose & apple pie for dinner today & tomorrow we dine on beaver which to my taste is preferable to goose. We lived two days on a wild cat that I killed. It was excellent eating very much like mutton. Mrs. McKay is just commencing sugar making. [...] I have since been at Fort Pelly but only stayed 1 $\frac{1}{2}$ days. All were well & very kind but every one was in a desperate hurry like myself. [...]

We had good times of it whilst I was there. Cakes & wine & singing. They pressed me to sing so I gave them "Widow Mahoney" which made them hold their ears. Some sang Gallic & French. Smith the Clerk there is a really capital fellow. I went on horse back with ten men to fetch down 4 Bateaux loaded with robes but they were off before I arrived. In them went Mrs. Finlayson & Mrs. Des Chambeault. They are here, the former for some time & Mrs. D for a few days till Mr. McKay goes to the settlement which will be on Thursday next. [...] I suffer agonies from toothache at times. Mr. C gave me leave to go to RR during the summer to have my teeth extracted.

I shall go in all probability with Mrs. Campbell & Mrs. McKay who are both going in August. [...]

I expect Walter out next month. He will probably come with Mr. McKay from RR. If so I shall take him on to Qu'Appelle after a few days. I leave him there but it is not far so we are sure of seeing each other now & then. Mr. McDonald, his future boss & his wife were at Fort Pelly when I was there, both very nice folks. I am sure they will make him very comfortable. [...]

Will E Traill

FORT GARRY *August 29, 1866*

My dear Mother

I arrived here on Monday last and found Walter [Willie's brother] here. He is looking very well and has grown so much and otherwise changed so that I should hardly have recognized him had I not expected to meet him here.

He is very much improved in every respect and is in good favour with all the Clerks & Master here. He will, I am persuaded, make the smartest man of the family. By the Minute of Council he was appointed for Fort Pelly but it seems uncertain whether he shall be sent there or kept here. He would prefer being kept here chiefly on account of being

Walter J.S. Traill, Willie's brother, 1870. GAA NA–1010–2

more in the way of learning business. It would have been much better for [me] had I been kept at one of the Factories for a year or so before I was sent to inland. I came down with Mrs. McKay & Mrs. Campbell. My excuse for coming was to get some of my teeth filled but I really think that I was sent to take care of the ladies. Mrs. C is now staying at Lower Fort Garry. I am going to pay them a visit this evening and will probably stay a day or two. […]

4th. I have just returned from a stay of two or three days at Lower Fort Garry. Mrs. Campbell is staying there. I enjoyed my visit there exceedingly.

I drove her out to make some calls and was quite surprised at the number of nice people I met there. I fell in love with half a dozen girls but not dangerously.

Mr. Campbell arrived yesterday evening. We will be leaving the settlement about Friday. It is not settled whether Walter goes inland or
stays here for a year. We will know before I close this.

I hear by Walter that you are very much alarmed for our safety
among the Indians. You need have no apprehensions [end missing]

W.E. Traill

FORT GARRY *September 4, 1866*

My Dearest Kate

[…] I am really very much distressed to hear of the close of James
[Willie's brother] & Tom's [Willie's brother-in-law Thomas Muchall[39]]
partnership. I feared it would be a smash long ago. It must be a great
blow to poor James ill as he is. I am afraid it will be the ruin of him in
health as well as in business.

It seems to me that Tom did not act right toward James. I should
write to Mary but hardly know how. It seems as if ill fortune attends
James.

My salary after this year will be more than sufficient for me so that
I may reasonably expect to be able to give assistance to those at home.

5th Last night I went down and got one of my grinders filled for which
I paid 12 [shillings]. This morning I had another pulled and was able to
eat with my side teeth for the [first time in] the last two years. […]

WE Traill

FORT ELLICE *September 16, 1866*

My Dearest Mother

As I said before I passed a very pleasant time of it whilst in the Settlement, I have formed quite a different opinion to that which I formerly
held of R.R.S. […] I am sorry for my own sake that one of the girls is

going to winter at Qu'Appelle but the eldest stays at home which is great consolation. I am very fond of both of them though Miss McKay is my favourite. I suppose however that I shall be obliged to winter from home or be from home the greater part of the time.

You spoke of trying to write something in the way of H B life. I have not the slightest objection so long as places or individuals are not mentioned. I should be only too happy to give you any information respecting the habits of Indians & animals etc.

Not long since, 4 of our Indians left here with the intention of stealing horses from the Sioux. It appears that when they got a short distance from here they met a Sioux and shot him dead. They then ran for it and [are] now hanging about the Fort not daring to go out of sight for fear of the Sioux. I hope the Sioux will come and give them an awful thrashing & scalp about 60 of them and then the cowards will behave. [...]

W E Traill

FORT ELLICE *November 4, 1866*

. My dear Mother

[...] I wrote you since I met Walter in RR and so did he. I have not seen him since he left this place but hear from him every week (almost). He is at the Qu'Appelle Lakes with Archd McDonald where he [is] in good quarters and is contented and comfortable.

He was then on the eve of departure for the plain hunt. Of all the Clerks I know, I know none so well calculated to do well as he. I have just received my order from Orkney and am well pleased with every-thing. Amongst other things I got two nice neat suits of clothes (scotch tweed), a nice writing desk, four flannel shirts, 2 under shirts & drawers, 6 cotton shirts and many other things which were very necessary and useful.

I wish you would all set your minds easy about the Sioux and Black-foot question. We are as safe here as at home. The company have few enemies amongst the Indians and it is seldom or never that we hear of anything befalling company officers or men.

Mr. McKay is off to the plains for the annual fall hunt. He has been off two weeks and will be off as many more. He is having very rough weather I am sorry to say. Snow fell the day after his departure and still lies on the ground and the weather has been very blustery & cold for the time of year. Mr. Campbell was here when he (Mr. McKay) left and stayed two weeks from the time of his arrival waiting for his sister in law Miss Sterling who has come out to join Mrs. Campbell. She however did not come till Mr. C had returned to Fort Pelly having given her up. She, Miss S- arrived here on Tuesday last and only stayed one night and then I sent her on to F.P. Miss McKay accompanied her I am sorry to say for we (Mrs. McKay & I) are very dull without her. Miss S is a very good looking lady but cut out for an old maid. She is very tall and better looking than her sister.

Miss Catherine McKay is staying at Qu'Appelle with Mrs. McDonald and consequently Walter will have the pleasure of her society all winter. [...]

W E Traill

FORT ELLICE *December 16, 1866*

My own dear Mother.

[...] I have been doing something in the way of trapping having killed twelve red foxes, one kit fox, two badgers and twenty musquash which nearly clears off my inland account of leather etc. I hope to clear it all off before Xmas. I made or rather got a pair of mittens made of badger skins. They are pretty and very warm and come up to my elbow. [...]

One of the suits I got out was far too small in the sleeves so I traded it off last week for a silver watch and 2 chains. The watch has cost me just £3—I hope to sell it soon.

I do not think that I shall have so much traveling this winter. The buffalo are scarce. Mr. McKay returned sometime since with sixty buffaloes in his carts. Were it not for that we should run a good risk of starving this winter. [...]

I had to transact a great deal of business during Mr. McKay's absence and got a kind letter from Mr. Campbell expressing his [approval] of the able manner in which I got through it all.

The greater part of our trade this winter will be with the Sioux but as I said before I will not bear a great deal of traveling. [...]

There has been a great deal of sickness here lately. Mr. McKay is (and has been for the last month) ill with a skin disease. Miss McKay has also been ill: so also many of the Fort people. [...]

W E Traill

FORT ELLICE *[Early 1867]*

To Annie[40]

[beginning missing] [...] *Some who come to the country do nothing but openly abuse, and despise the half-breeds who I despise as a nation [but] I do not believe to be half as bad as they are thought. In fact I know that what some affirm of them is untrue. I to be sure, am with the head man amongst them, and tho he and his wife have no education beyond what they gave themselves are everywhere respected as they deserve to be. The girls are also a credit to their parents. They have what we in Canada would call a good sound education. They are amiable and kind & the youngest is real pretty. [...] I was kindly treated at Fort Pelly. Mr. & Mrs. C excel in kindness and I flatter myself that I am a great favourite with them. Walter is also a favourite. I only stayed there three or four days at F. Pelly and then returned.*

I have trapped quite a little this winter, 17 foxes, 1 wolf, 1 kit and two badgers, which pay my advances at this place in moose skins &c. &c.

I got goods from home (Orkney) last fall and I am now sending home another order. I get things cheaper and better than at Factory. Walter also sends with me. I will be able to send mother a Bill for £10 or 12 this summer, which will I have no doubt be acceptable. [...] [end missing]

W.E. Traill

FORT ELLICE [*January 1867*[41]]

Dear Annie

[beginning missing] [...] At New Year we gave a great feast to our men and all the women and children, also the Indians men, women and children. It was a fearful sight to see all the stuff they crammed down. One little boy about 14 drank 12 half pints of tea, and ate enough to keep three men alive for a week. The only disagreeable [thing] was that complained of by Ballendyne in his life in H B, that of being kissed by all the old hags.

I took the hint given by that author and use to jerk up my head and so let them kiss my chin—Some of their mouths were certainly open sepulchres. Such yawning toothless chasms I never saw.

The weather so far has been good but we had two weeks of very tempestuous weather during Mr. McKay's absence at the plains last month. They were caught in the big Plain by weather that drove them back to Moose Mountain. A party of traders who were further out in the plain lost 6 of their horses.

The Sioux are wintering out there and are in a state of destitution & starvation.

We are all in a fair way of having little enough to eat next spring as there are no buffalo near nor have we much meat in our store and less pemmican, and the Indians are all starving so also our enemies the [free] traders. It will do the latter good to live for a few weeks on rabbits. [...]

W Edward Traill

[...]

Three

TOUCHWOOD HILLS
1867 – 1869

TOUCHWOOD HILLS WAS WILLIE'S NEXT POST.[1] He would be based
there for three years (1867 to 1869). Clerk Joseph Finlayson was Post
Master at Touchwood Hills, and Willie, as Apprentice Clerk, was his
second-in-command. Willie was also Post Master of Touchwood Hills'
satellite post at Egg Lake, and he periodically commuted the approximately 140 km between the two sites.

The post serving this area had been moved from site to site before
it was finally located at the intersection of the Fort Qu'Appelle/Fort
Pelly and Carlton Trails.[2] Touchwood Hills was fifty kilometers due
south of Little Quill Lake, on the southern branch of the Carlton Traill
—the most travelled route between Red River, Carlton House, and
Fort Edmonton. Egg Lake's exact location is obscured by the mists of
time, but the post seems to have been a few kilometers north of present day Kelvington, Saskatchewan, on the eastern shore of Nut Lake.[3]

Captain William Butler,[4] who would later become a casual friend
of Willie's, painted an appealing portrait of the countryside around
Willie's new post:

> About midway between Fort Ellice and Carlton a sudden
> and well defined change occurs in the character of the

country; the light soil disappears and its place is succeeded by a rich dark loam covered deep in grass and vetches. Beautiful hills swell in slopes more or less abrupt on all sides, while lakes fringed with thickets and clumps of good-sized poplar balsam lie lapped in their fertile hollows.[5]

The winter of 1868 was severe, and Willie's time here was spent in hardship. Still, he was reunited for a time with his brother Walter, and this must have compensated for the shortages. Willie tends to make light of the perils of winter travel on the northern prairie, probably discounting the dangers to allay his family's concerns. Occasionally, Willie wrote home about the violence of life in the region. When he did, though, he was careful not to mention his own close involvement.

Except for the 1885 rebellion, fatal confrontations between Indians and whites were rare, and deadly conflicts between HBC employees and Indians almost non-existent. However there were periodic clashes, usually brimming with suspense and potential danger. Cowie describes a potentially deadly confrontation:

> Jerry McKay, having joined a party from Touchwood Hills under William Edward Traill, apprentice clerk, reached the big camp a few days after I left it…. Upon leaving after completing the trade, a heavy tribute was demanded of them. This Mr. Traill absolutely refused, and as the cart-train was starting, with Henry Jordan leading the foremost ox, shots were fired "across the bows" of the leading cart and its harness was cut by Assiniboines with the chief, Red Eagle, at their head. While Jerry was parleying with Red Eagle, Traill had the latter covered with his breech-loading Henry rifle (the first ever seen in that country), behind Traill was an Assiniboine with a gun leveled at the formers head, and behind the Assiniboine was a Cree with flintlock aimed at

the Assiniboine. Had Traill pulled the trigger, and he was within an ace of doing so, the train would have been lit to an explosion of intertribal war in that tumultuous camp. Fortunately for the future peace of the plains, Jerry, foreseeing the inevitable consequences of refusing, took the responsibility of conceding the demand, and, in spite of Traill's protests, paid to the Warriors' Lodges goods to the value of fifty pounds ($250), and so averted much greater loss.[6]

We can well imagine that, for Willie, navigating with a broken compass over terrain nearly devoid of identifiable landmarks (except for bodies of water and the occasional knoll) required a great deal of skill and a measure of good fortune. In the best of circumstances, long-distance travel by snowshoe demands considerable know-how and endurance. Traveling on snowshoes with bloody, damaged feet must have been pure agony. Willie faced bitter cold, severe frostbite, gale-force winds, white-outs, and snow blindness—travel was hazardous in the extreme.

TOUCHWOOD HILLS *May, 23, 1867*

My dear Mother

I left F. Ellice on the 13th Inst having stayed after my companions were off, to accompany my love across the river and having her safe and sound across a piece of very rough road. She was going to RR where she will stay nearly as long as I shall be at Touchwood Hills so that neither of us lose much by the other being from home. We (Mr. Finlayson & I) encountered very rough weather en route but arrived safe & sound at this place on Saturday. We found Jerry McKay in charge. Mr. McDonald was at F. Pelly. He arrived on Sunday and with him Walter, who did not go to York as we expected but is to summer here. You may be sure we were both very well pleased to meet and be so long together. He is looking well and quite happy. He feels rather poor today. He and I have been out spearing whitefish for the last few nights & it is to that that his indisposition is owing.

I have been detained here on account of the miserable conditions of the horses. They are in an almost starving condition. There is not a mouthful of prog in our stores here but we have a daily supply from the barrier & nets which, with what Walter & I kill at night keeps us going. There is but poor prospect for me at Touchwood Hills. They have been starving there for a long time and have killed several cattle. They are not half as well off as this place for they have no fish.

I am to start tomorrow for that place of renown. I am not the least afraid of starvation for I know that I can always feed myself and my house keeper Mrs. Finlayson. She is a nice body. I have mentioned her before in former letters. Her husband is to relieve when he returns from Y. F. or I should say I am just stepping in to keep things together till he returns.

This is a really beautiful place. I hope it may be my lot someday to settle in such place as this. I am sure I should be happy with my Hatty.[7]

The Cree & Blackfeet have lately had a great fight in which 46 of the latter were killed, women & children included. The Cree treated some of

*their prisoners with great cruelty. One Blackfoot woman was compelled
to dance on the body of her murdered husband & sons.*

*Some of them were put to death & that not in the most merciful
way. I do not believe however that they ever practice the same amount
of cruelty as one would suppose judging from the novels of Cooper[8]
& others. They have danced the Scalp Dance several times of late and
keep up a continual drum from dark to day light. The Indians are now
dancing the Scalp Dance before the door & making the most diaboli-
cal din imaginable. They have five or six scalps on poles which they are
flaunting about in great triumph. You can hardly imagine what a savage
aspect they have. They are dancing for tobacco. They tell us that it was
our balls that killed the scalps and that we are in duty bound to help
them. We of course would sooner that they had killed one buffalo than
100 Blackfeet.*

*Mr. McDonald [Post Master at Fort Qu'Appelle] is going to R. R.
soon and will I hope bring up lots of letters. He is a fine fellow. Walter
is lucky to be under one who is so apt at business and so well qualified
to teach it to others. Walter is a universal favourite. I am quite put in
the shade.*

*We both have been unusually lucky in getting a good name &
patronage at once.*

W.E. Traill

FORT QU'APPELLE *June 6, 1867*

Dear Kate

*Walter and I rode down (from Touchwood Hills) on Monday and I have
been here ever since. [...] We had a fine pageant yesterday. The Crees
came in in a large band and danced & drummed all day. They made
long speeches & behaved themselves very well.*

*I enclose a lock of hair which I cut from a Blackfoot scalp. I suppose
you will be horrified with it.*

We live chiefly on fish just now. Buffalo are far and few between.[...]

Walter is going to act as Captain in a bateaux which is to start for F.E. in a day or two. His Indian name should now be "Ohiman Okemah" which is Captain or else it should be Okemah Maskanow or Captain Trail (track or road). [...]

W Edward Traill

P.S. The next Blackfoot I kill I shall send you the scalp entire. A young one would cure best I suppose.

TOUCHWOOD HILLS *August 4, 1867*

My dear Mother

[...] Tho I dearly loved my poor brother James,[9] the intelligence of his death did not give me the grief that it would had it been under different circumstances. I could even thank our heavenly Father for having relieved him from this world of misery to his own arms whither I trust he has now gone.

Poor James! his life has been indeed a short but by no means a happy one. It would be very selfish of us to wish him back to this world which has nothing but cares and toils to recommend it to us. It is wonderful how we still cling to it as if we were never to leave. It would be well if we always had in mind that beautiful paraphrase

'Tho trouble spring not from the dust

Nor sorrow from the ground

Yet ills on ills by Gods decree

In mans estate are found'.[10]

I often call this verse to mind. If man was put in this world to prepare himself for a better and more beautiful one, that end gained what does it matter how soon we leave this?

I wrote one or two letters after the one that reached him in his last sickness. I should much have liked to have had one letter more from him ere he was taken away. I often read his last two or three. Amelia

[James's wife[11]] will feel his loss very much, not from any affection she had for him but for his protection. I feel she will have great cause to regret the little care she took of him. I hope her brother will do something for her, Henry I mean. He certainly aught, but I think that they are an extremely selfish family.

I am appointed now to the charge of Egg Lake,[12] a wood post about 100 miles from this. Of course I am not very much elated by the promotion not that I let any one know that I do not like it. I only dislike it on account of being separated from Harriet. There is another Clerk coming from F.E., a green hand or Moneass as the natives say. It is very likely I shall never be at FE again unless in after years as Master. It is seldom that anyone is put [subservient to another] after once being in charge of a Post or Fort.

I have only heard once from Harriet since she went to R.R. She got her carte taken and sent me one. She promised to send you one from R.R so I will not send you the one I have here, which is but a poor one.

When I last wrote we were very hard up for tucker. We were on short commons from the time I took charge till the 20th Ultimo [the previous month] when ten carts from the plains brought about 5000 lbs provisions. This set us on our legs, but we sent the most of it to FP and were getting low again when the rest of the carts returned with good loads so now we are quite independent.

I see Walter every week or two. I returned from Q- yesterday where I spent four or five days. The distance is not great. I left yesterday morning after sunrise and was here by dinner. I was on horseback—Walter rode about 12 or 15 miles with me and then returned promising to come up on Saturday next if possible. He is quite alone [...] It is very agreeable for us both to be so near each other. I shall be much further off next winter but still we may be able to see each other often. [...]

The whole of June and the greater part of July was very wet. June was almost incessant rain. Our garden was looking magnificent when the grasshoppers, those scourges of this country, came in clouds and in one single day left the ground as bare as if it had been ploughed. I never saw anything like it. The trees and shrubs were bending under the weight of them, so you may form some idea of the myriads of them [there] were and still are—tho the most of them took wing after doing their worst. I fear in R R they have completely annihilated the hopes of all the farmers. They come in clouds and almost obscure the light of the sun. Riding against the wind yesterday was very disagreeable. They are unable to [steer] themselves and come against one with great force like heavy hail stones. They are [so] hard that when they strike one in the face they cause considerable pain. They even come into the house and are on the window panes like flies.

I fully believe that they eat the mosquitoes which were in great numbers but which decreased immediately after the arrival of the grass-hoppers. 'It is indeed an ill wind that blows luck to nobody.'

The summer has been so cool that the bull dogs[13] have only just appeared. They generally commence in June. The last three or four day's heat must have brought them. I fear they are too big for the grasshop-pers and to the cattle they will [prove] much worse.

When I first saw the grasshoppers coming, I said to one of my men (an Orkney man) "Look at the snow Nicolson". He looked up and after staring a while said "Is that snow it is too hot for snow". He soon found out what kind of snow it was when they began to come down. Even now they look like snow to look towards the sun. [...]

I had some trouble lately with an Indian who I had bought a [horse] from this spring soon after assuming charge of this place. He stole a horse from FP. I was advised of it by the person in charge, so when the Indian Sha-wen-a-kapon came I recognized the horse by the descrip-tion given. I asked him for the horse but he would not give him to me so after reasoning [with] him 6 hours I got out of patience and went to his tent & took him [the horse]. I then dared him to take the horse before my eyes but he was afraid. I then made him promise to leave our horses alone in future or else it would be worse for him or any one else who tried to play over me. They are a great set of cowards and when they see the white man resolute they'll seldom go beyond words. Next day 5 of our best horses were missing. I thought they had been stolen by the party that had pitched off of which Sha-wen-a-kapon was one. I got 4 men and armed them & gave chase on the tracks of the horses. We overtook the horses but not the Indians. The horses had been stampeded by the flies and had taken to the plain where the mosquitoes are not so bad as in the woods. They were about 15 or 20 miles from the [horse] guard. I like a little excitement like this it drives dull care away and arouse[s] one's energies which might otherwise stagnate. [end missing]

W.E. Traill

My dear Kate

I have to thank you for your kind and very welcome letter of August 16th. I got it on the first of this month and from the hands of no less a personage than the Earl of March who is traveling in this country for sport. [...]

I had sent off LaPierre with a Brigade of Carts as a kind of safe guard against the men getting drunk in passing a lot of Freemen who were reported to be en route to Saskatchewan. I heard that there were [two] gentlemen going up to Saskn for sport but had no idea who they were. I had just done dinner when I heard some of the people of the Fort calling out O Remowuck which is gentlemen.

I had just sat down to write and the table was in dire confusion. I tried to put past the papers etc. but before I could do so a young gentleman rode up to the door. I received him in a very free and easy manner thinking he was no great beer but what was my consternation when I heard Alex McKay [Chief Trader William McKay's brother] [...] call him Lord March. You may be sure I was in a fine fix. The house was quite dismantled, as Mrs. F had put by everything to give room to the carpenters who were to work at the house. I had eaten up some rice and Apple jam that she left so had nothing to set before his Lordship but Currie

Red River carts going through Portage La Prairie. In a brigade, each driver controlled half a dozen carts, tied together with line astern. On long journeys, parts—particularly axles—were often replaced numerous times. Photo by Leonard Callendar, 1880. HBCA 1987/363–R–7/12

meat and bread. I luckily had the keys to F's canteen, so I got there from a flagon of pale brandy to give a kind of aristocratic appearance to the table.

I could have got him a better meal but with him came a whole swarm of free traders who soon set the Indians drunk as pipers. They filled the house in swarms, so also the Traders. The latter were for bargains. I assure you I had my hands full so that I had scarcely time for a smoke with his Lordship. He was very free in conversation. When the Indians came forward to shake hands with him with the usual salutation Bon jour and a few words in their own language he would take their hand and say "how do you do" and "my dear fellow but I don't understand you". They bothered him a great deal sending messages to the Queen telling her of all their wrongs etc. from the hands of HBC. I was fortunate in being able to furnish him with everything he wanted for his journey. He asked me where he had better go. I told him to the Cypress Mountain where game of all kinds abound. He said "Ah they tell me so but there is some danger of losing ones scalp by the Blackfeet". I admitted that such was the case but at the same time if I were out for sport as he was that is the place I would go to. He seemed to think his scalp was better where it was than fastened to a pole and paraded about a Blackfoot encampment.

Novr 3rd. Dear Kate I have just returned from Egg Lake where I have been equipping the Indians. I intend to give you a short account of my trip. […] When I began this Mr. F- was absent at F.P. He returned on the 9th Ult. and with him came my good Burgoise Mr. Campbell. He stayed a day or two and was very kind. He gave me marching orders for Egg Lake but only for a trip. I am to winter here but am virtually in charge of E. Lake. I left here on the 12th for the latter place with a couple of men and four carts and oxen. I myself rode on horse back.

We jogged along without any accident till our 6th day, when we came to the Fishing Lake where we found a camp of EL Indians. I had no one for an interpreter but a young fellow who stuttered awfully. The Indians who were a rascally set were very saucy but I told them I did not care for them. They threatened to drive me back but I told them plainly that if they wanted me to go back they would first require to shoot me and then perhaps my men [would] go home. They cooled down at last and I proceeded on my journey and the following day I reached the Fort. About 5 miles before I reached it I overtook my interpreter who had been sent from F P to meet me there with the outfit of goods.

When we got to the house, we found it in an awful mess. A whole host of Indians were camped inside the house & you may be sure had it in a horrid state. Daniel & I turned out les savages and went to work and with a shovel & hoe. Got a room or two cleaned of the rough dirt before the carts came. I put all the goods in the room which I had appropriated for myself.

We had forgotten the hinges for the doors, and as the house had been dismantled last spring we were in a fine fix. I hung the house doors with leather hinges and for the door of the store was obliged to manufacture hinges out of copper hoop which answered as well as any thing could.

The house is small and not pretty but that does not matter for it would be very much out of character were it pretty for it is situated on a large [marsh]. The Egg Lake itself is not much more than a [marsh] and the water in summer is not fit to drink and smells horribly. I do not see why in the name of reason the Ft, if such it can be called, was ever put here.

I got through equipping the Indians in fine style. I arrived there on Thursday and the following Wednesday I was all through and started home via Fort Pelly.

I did not expect to go that way but found it necessary on account of business. Before I bid fare well to E. Lake for the present, I will tell you that there are about 100 [graves] close to the Fort. The Indians died there in great numbers the summer before last and were buried close to the surface and not 200 yards from the Fort. The foxes and wolves & other beasts of prey have disinterred them and feast nightly on the carcasses. The ground there about is fairly beaten smooth with their feet. Daniel & I set 4 traps the night before I left and had four foxes in the morning.

The skulls & bones are lying round in every corner and you won't see a dog but that has a thigh bone or an arm in his mouth. If I was there I would make a small fortune picking up tobacco, knives, [steels] etc. & selling again. As it is I picked up a splendid fire [steel] & scalper. [...]

I have no fear of the poor fellow I robbed of the steel being without fire in the next world if he is in any way like his relations who still inhabit this. I consider them worse than either Sioux or Blackfeet only they are such arrant cowards they dare not do anything. The one with whom I quarreled last summer is now the best friend I have amongst them.

My third day from E.L. I reached Fort Pelly where I was received with open arms by all hands especially by Mrs. C- & her sister. I only stayed a day and a half and was then obliged to come home for Mr. F- was wanting me and I knew he could not dispense with my valuable services especially as he was to leave for the plains as soon as I returned. My fourth day from F.P. I reached home I met Mr. Finlayson several miles from the Fort looking for me. I found all well and glad to see me. The following morning Mr. Finlayson started for the plains for fresh meat. I hope he will get good loads else we will starve this winter. It is hard times all over the country and especially in this Dist. I must now tell you of a horrible murder that was committed about 10 miles from this place. Two men Francis Matooney and Joseph Cadatte went out hunting foxes. They were absent several days and when last seen were drinking liquor which they had bought from the trader who last saw them. On Wednesday the 17th Ult as one of our men was going to Fort Pelly he found Joe Cadatte lying on his face on the road. He thought he was asleep and tried to wake him but when he uncovered him for he had a blanket spread over him he found he was dead shot through the breast with a ball. About ten yards from this place was an encampment and the ground all about beaten down as if by persons quarrelling. The dead man had his gun in his hand with the muzzle from him. It was not loaded but had the gun coat on.

Another gun coat lay beside him which was recognized as belonging to Matooney. He went to the Ft and told Mr. Finlayson who sent for the body being too busy to go himself. The man Matooney has not made his appearance so there is little doubt of his having shot him tho whether in self defence or otherwise it is hard to say.

He has since been seen by a party of men en route to R R from Saskatchewan. He told them he was going to Saskn and that he had been nearly killed but did not mention having killed any one. [...]

W. Edward Traill
[...]

EGG LAKE *November 4, 1867*

Dear Annie

[beginning missing] [...] One of the rooms was an inch deep with dead grasshoppers which had got in through the cracks but could not get out again. The Fort or house as it might much more appropriately be called is "an ugly [blot] on a swampy spot". [...]

The buffaloes have been very scarce all summer and the grasshoppers destroyed most of the crops so that we expect a famine. The rabbits which are the staple food of the Wood Indians have entirely disappeared and all kinds of game are very scarce.

I have been trapping a little and killed 8 red foxes and two minks. I intend going heavier into that line of business when I have more time. [...]

There is a few settlers here both half breeds & Indians—They do not do much & this year are quite destitute. They were obliged to eat up all their [feed] last winter and now are almost entirely destitute. At best they are of too exotic habits to do much in an agricultural way.

The person who last had charge of this place was a regular gonk. He starved all winter while others farther from the buffalo had enough & to spare. Besides this he let everything go to rack & ruin so that all my endeavours will be of but small avail to make a good trade. Had I horses I might do something but I have only 4 cart horses—the rest are at R R whither they have been sent to bring up carts & goods.

I made a bargain with an Indian this morning for a fine American horse. I gave him two horse carts & harness & an old plough. The bargain is good for both parties. The Indian is certainly a gainer in his way & the Company also. Mr. McKay paid forty pounds for such a beast last winter. I was told I might give 3 horses & carts for this one. [...]

Walter has just arrived from Qu'Appelle. He came on horseback. He left that place about 8 AM and was here by 3 or 4 PM. He is looking very well and hearty & is in good spirits. He says he is going to write you from his home so I will not burden you with any of his news—merely his love. I think it more than probable that I shall return with him to Qu' on Monday.

He and I have been walking about ever since his arrival looking at the place & talking of old times. He is now fast asleep being pretty tired from his long ride.

We have a Mission here. The parson, if he may be so called, is Mr. Pratt, an Assiniboine Indian by birth who received a slight education at RR. He is a truly good man but unfortunately he is cursed with a most reprobate family. His wife & children & their children are the bane of the poor mans life.

His horses & animals died last winter and he was obliged to eat all his seed potatoes etc. etc. He has no other way of making a living but by his gun. He is on the tramp from morning till night often walking 40 & even 50 miles in a day looking for game. He had little or no ammunition for a long time & could not afford to shoot anything smaller than a goose. He often goes 2 days without eating. He has about 15 mouths to feed solely by his gun. Poor man. I pity him from the bottom of my heart. I help him in every way possible. I take great pleasure in the old mans society. He has lots of stories to tell of his adventures etc.

His sermons though in pure Cree are to me more impressive than those of many of the English preachers. [...] [end missing]

W.E. Traill

TOUCHWOOD HILLS *December 25, 1867*

Dear Mother

[...] This day which used to be a very happy one when the family circle was yet unbroken is now anything but that to me and so I am sure to all the members of the family. It only seems a few months since we were all together at the old house at Oaklands. I can hardly believe that such a length of time has elapsed since then. [...]

I fully expected to spend this day at Fort Pelly as usual where I expected to meet Walter as Mr. & Mrs. Campbell with their usual kindness had invited us both but owing to circumstances which I will now relate I was unable to go. In the early part of the month I made a trip to Egg Lake of which place I have the charge. I took a horse and cart and one train of dogs. There was then scarcely two inches of snow. We went in five days and found all well but the Indians doing little in the fur line.

I found it necessary to send my man in by Fort Pelly returning myself to this place with the horse and cart. I brought one of the men with me, a regular green Orkney man who was more bother than good. Not liking the route by which I went I struck a course of my own. The weather became very rough and had it not been that my man had a compass we would undoubtedly have lost ourselves. As it was I got entangled in a heavy woods and was obliged to cut the road for the horse with my axe which I carried in one hand and the compass in the other. The compass gave me a great deal of bother as well as help for it was a broken affair, the needle coming off continually so that every time I wished to consult it I was obliged to take it to pieces to put on the needle. Of course this delayed me a good deal and was rather cold work on the fingers. We managed to get through the woods and struck a large plain which I had crossed going so was all right when once on it. We reached this place in 4 1/2 days which was half a day shorter than the time taken to go. The last half of the way we were up to the knees in snow without snow shoes but as the snow was light it was not very heavy traveling. As I had appointed to meet the man I sent to F.P. at E.L. on the 15th Inst I only stayed a few days and then started back, intending to go from thence to F.P. and return direct after Xmas. I accordingly started again on the 13th Inst with the same man that I returned with and a train [of] dogs. The very first day turned out rough in the afternoon snowing and drift-ing. My man left his compass so that I could not keep a straight course and as I was going by guess there being no road I soon lost myself but of that I was not aware till morning when I got a glimpse of the sun just as it rose. I knew at once I was wrong so [steered] my course accord-ingly. We soon struck the proper track and kept it all the time but with much difficulty it being drifted over. The snow fell heavily our second day and night so that walking in snow shoes became very labourious. I was obliged to beat the track all the time for our former track showed so slightly that my man could not follow it. Indeed it gave me much trouble to do so myself. My feet began to cut with the lines of the snowshoes to such a degree that the blood oozed through two pairs of moccasins and a pair of thick duffle socks. There was no help for it so on we went.

Our fourth day I came to a good track, at least a road that showed so that my man could follow it. I was now quite unable to walk so made him take the snow shoes while I took his place in the sled where I continued till we reached E.L. about ten miles on this side of the fort. It was then sunset so I knew if we kept on at the pace we were then going we would be obliged to sleep out again. In spite of great pain I put on the snowshoes and started ahead of the dogs. I never stopped running till I got to the Fort which we reached soon after dark. You may be sure I was not sorry to get there. We had taken so much time going that with the bad roads I knew I would not be able to reach F.P. by Xmas so I determined on returning to T Hills. I was sorry to disappoint the good folks after having accepted their invitation especially as I expected to meet Walter there. I think however that he will not be able to go.

I stayed one day and then started home with two men and trains [of] dogs. I was determined not to walk a step going home for I could hardly put my foot to the ground. We went along fine for the first two days but the weather getting rough and more snow falling the dogs could hardly drag the light cariole so that I was obliged to walk up to my knees in snow for I could not put on snow shoes. We reached home our third day late at night, at least one of my men and I. The other man did not reach till noon next day.

The last day we made a distance that on two former occasions it had taken us two days & a half to travel. This month has been exceedingly rough. We have not yet had a fine day in it tho it is well nigh out. We just got home in time, for rough as the weather was during our travel the two days following my return were infinitely worse, so much so that no one could possibly travel. The cold yesterday and today has been intense with very high wind and drift. I fear our hunters who are out on the plains are having a hard time of it. [They] will be well enough however for they have a tent, but the poor horses exposed as they must be to the wind and at least 45 or 50 degrees of frost on the barren plain will I fear feel it severely if they do not [perish] with the cold.

I am very glad I did not go to FP. I would still be on the road. […]

W Edward Traill

TOUCHWOOD HILLS *August 16, 1868*

My dear Mother

Your welcome letter of June reached me the other day along with one from Kate of a rather later date. Also the view of Westove[14] of which I am proud. It is a very nice one. The place must be very much improved since I saw it. […] Since last I wrote I have seen a little more of savage life on the plains which is a great advantage to me as a trader. Things did not turn out to my satisfaction on the plains, so I determined to see what I could do in person so I started off on the 2nd Ult with five men and 9 horses and carts. I had heard shortly before of a camp of Crees across the south branch of the Sask. […] said to be rich in provisions so made up my mind to go there, but after two days travel in that direction I changed my mind and struck out for our own Indians and well it was that I did not go across as the sequel will show.

I cannot bear to ride on horse back traveling slow so I shouldered my rifle and walked in advance of my carts. We took little grub as we trusted to our guns. I fed the whole party for ten days myself. I killed all we could eat and more which is saying much.

You could hardly believe me when I tell you that five men and a boy ate 5 large and four small antelopes, 1 bull and part of another, a badger, two eagles, 84 lbs dry meat a keg of cakes, about 10 lbs flour and all this in 13 days. I forgot at least 20 or 30 ducks.[15] Not a small ration you will think but we were short enough the last two days. Well our 8th day we came to a hill called "Where the Stonie was killed". We had dinner about five miles on this side of it and while the horses were feeding I walked ahead and went up to the top to have a look as we expected to see the camp soon. As I was going up the hill I saw two cabrie (antelopes) lying in a valley. After a great deal of maneuvering I succeeded in attracting their attention without letting them see what I was. They came running to me and I killed both of them. I now took out their entrails and hauled them all the way to the top of the hill for I thought the carts would pass on the opposite side of the hill. I assure you that I had a job for it was a roaring hot day and the bull dogs would give me no peace. I was quite done out when I got to the top. When I got there at last I saw the carts passing on the side I got the Antelopes so I had the extreme pleasure of hauling them all the way down a distance of a mile. Of course it was easier than hauling them up but it was provoking to think I had been at so much trouble for nothing.

Our 10th day we came to buffo—the first we had seen. They stood in thousands and the noise they made was like the roar of waves on the sea shore. We killed one (I do not say I did) but I would not let the men kill more as [end missing]

W.E. Traill

TOUCHWOOD HILLS *September 11, 1868*

My dear Kate

[…] Mr. Cowie from Q was here so we had a jolly day. This morning he left [for home]. Tomorrow I start for Egg Lake where I will remain till April I suppose but I will visit this place frequently. I will have an Interpreter and two men and a boy besides the family & the former.

You may be sure I will be very lonely this winter but I hope it will be the last I will pass alone.

Mr. Campbell told me he had hard work to keep me in the District. I wish he has not been so helpful in keeping me for I am tired of the trade here and so are most of the officers in the District. The Indians are getting very troublesome to deal with and the whole trade is more difficult than in the rest of the country.

HBC post at Touchwood Hills where Willie was Apprentice Clerk in Charge during 1867 and 1868. Photo taken 1905. HBCA 1987/363–T–16/2

My darling girl too was far from well and Mrs. F- who saw her says she was looking very thin and pale. I have not heard from her for some time—before I wrote mother. There has been no chance from F.E, for a long while. I fully expected to find letters waiting me from her but was disappointed.

I wonder where I shall be this time next year. Perhaps in Saskatchewan but most likely in this District but here or there I hope not to be alone. There is a probability of this post being abandoned or moved further out. I should prefer to be at Egg Lake for the summer there to build and make myself comfortable for the future. As the place is, it would not be comfortable for my Hatty not that the house is bad but the site is an abominable one. [...]

I wrote the Governor a day or two ago at the same time sending him a fossil which I picked up which resembles a heart. He is a great lover of natural curiosities and has large collections of the curious so I think he will be pleased with it. This is to pave the way for another letter in which

I intend asking for leave to marry when my contract expires. I think I am not a bad diplomat. We will see how the [ploy succeeds]. […]

> W Edward Traill
>
> […]

GUARD POST *February 25, 1869*

My dearest Mary

[…] I am not going to pick your letter to pieces but lest you fall into a similar error in future I beg you will remember that McKay tho spelt so does not rhyme with way but is pronounced McKie. […]

Your advice comes rather late in the day but to Walter I have no doubt it will not be so tho […] to tell the truth I think he is too discreet a young man to require such advice as he undertook to lecture me in your own strain but seriously it is not right of you now when I have 'axed' the Governor. Not that I would have you to suppose that all the good advice you could volunteer could have made me forsake my love tho I am not sure but if you had pitched in sooner you might have made me to wait a year or so. And yet if you had to spend the prime of your life at a hole like this and having a dear little woman (I mean you to imagine yourself a man and in my shoes) breaking her heart to be with you and yourself longing to have her by you. […]

I dare not let Harriet see your letter, a privilege which I often allow her. She got hold of one of your old ones and found in it some advice about making my wife cut her toe nails. […] She likes Kate best of you all except mother because you and Annie give me such prudent advice but Kate resigns me to my fate and writes little notes to her. […]

But I am only going on at a great rate about this little woman and forgetting all other subjects.

I really think [were] it not for the safety of the Co's property I would fall out with some of the Indians just to have something to write about.

Unless I give you nothing but small talk I know of nothing else. Gossip there can be none where there are [no] women to run down their neighbour and no neighbours to chase.

There were two tents of Sioux pitched close to the White Horse Plain fort [between present-day Winnipeg, Manitoba, and Portage la Prairie]. The men were off begging or hunting. Two Chipewyan came and asked the squaws leave to pass the night in their tents. They got leave and after getting something to eat went to bed if you can say that lying curled up in a blanket is going to bed. Well during the night when all were asleep the two got up and killed them, all but two children who in the darkness got out under the eaves of the tent. The wretches scalped them all not leaving not so much as a hair on their heads, and then cut sticks. No one knew till the husbands came home and found their wives and children all killed. They raised a party and immediately started in pursuit. I hope they may have caught them and I could hardly regret if they burned them alive.

Few have any sympathy for the Sioux. My Hatty is very much in dread of them, in fact it is her greatest failing. Even Mrs. McKay is rather nervous when they are about not on her own account but on that of her numerous children. She used always to wish to go and hide with her family when they were reported as intending a visit.

I am sure you will believe me when I say it was a somewhat fidgety feeling writing old Mactavish. The worst of it is I have a dread that I enclosed another document in the envelope to his address. Would it not be a lark; [but] then my case would be next thing to hopeless as he would justly say that one so careless was not fit to have the responsibility of a wife and a Co's Post at the same time. [...]

When at F.P. I enjoyed myself as well as possible under the then existing state of affairs; but I had much to do. To pack goods and make a [packing] account of the same. Read my letters and try and answer some amongst others one from the Govr. Mr. McKay was fat and jolly as ever, but I had little time to spend in his company nor he in mine for except after supper when we all gathered in the sitting room for cakes & toddy we had no time for anything but business and not enough for that. [...]

And now my dear old Mary I hope you will always write in verse. It is so clever and amusing.

[...]

As I suppose you hear from Walter frequently, I will not say more than that I hear from him frequently and that he is quite well, and happy when at home and from home also but he says he never comes home without feeling sad to have to leave it even tho for a few days or weeks at most. Is it not nice that he is so well contented and happy and so attached to the good folks? You know he is not one who takes sudden fancies at least not now.

[...]

I hope Tom will like the shanty well. Please remember me kindly to him and tell him about the squaw that his uncle Will will bring home some day and the buffaloes, grizzleys, scalps, etc.

How would you like me to send him a stuffed Blackfoot [baby] to play with?

Now old girl I must take leave for a while. [...]

Your loving old playfellow and Brother Snipes

[ORIGIN AND DATE UNKNOWN]

[Addressee unknown]

[beginning missing] [...] We were now at our wits end [...] not knowing where to find the camp. I suggested keeping on the inside of the buffalo till we came to them but our guide thought he knew better so he led us in a different direction. Near the Cypress Hills[16] which is close to the South branch and more than half way to the Rocky Mountains we came on the trail of the big camp. I assure you I was glad to see the track and thought to catch them at once but we travelled hard three days before we came up with them and then they were just in the place where we first came on the buffalo. Had we taken the course I proposed or even had we stayed there we would have fallen in with them several days sooner and had not have knocked up our animals.

The camp was a very large one about 300 tents—more than 1000 souls—a mixture of Cree Saulteaux & Stonies—There are several different tribes of each, so there was no small amount of jealousy amongst themselves as is always the case when many Indian tribes meet. We had not a very pleasant time of it in camp but got our loads and were ready to start home when Jerry McKay in charge of Qu'Appelle carts arrived in camp. He had been hunting and had loaded some of his carts which displeased the Indians. I saw that he might be delayed a long time so I determined to stop and help him till he could get off and go altogether. This we could not effect for several days for there was not meat enough dry to load his carts—I had one run after buffo while in camp. I am sure there were full 300 riders. You can hardly imagine what a picturesque scene it was to see so many Indians all dressed off and armed with guns and arrows. I [killed] three [buffalo] and then jumped down to take out the tongue of one when my horse broke his line and ran off so I had a run of about 2 miles before I came up with him. An Indian had caught him for me—I ran two some what narrow escapes of being tossed for the bulls are very wicked just now.

After Jerry got his loads we all started home but not without great opposition from the Indians. One party was for letting us go the other for detaining us. I thought they would come to bloodshed amongst themselves. However we got away all right but had to be careful of our horses for several days lest they be stolen.

Once while we were in the camp there was a report of enemy a few miles beyond.

One would have thought all the Indians had gone crazy—Every one of them jumped on the first horse he could catch whether his own or that *of another person—Out of 25 horses they only left me four and those were only kept by force. One of my men threw an Indian off our best runner. Well they rode at full gallop to the place where the enemy were supposed to be but no enemy was to be found so they* [end missing][17]

W.E. Traill

Four

SASKATCHEWAN RIVER POSTS
1869–1874

FROM 1869 TO 1874, WILLIE SERVED AT THREE POSTS on the Saskatchewan River: Fort Pitt, Prince Albert Farm, and Carlton House. He was
posted as Clerk at Fort Pitt in the early fall of 1869, under the command of Chief Trader William H. Watt. Fort Pitt was located on the
north bank of the North Saskatchewan River, near the present day
hamlet of Onion Lake, about 5 miles east of the Alberta border.[1]

In late 1870, Willie was transferred from Fort Pitt to temporary
charge of Carlton House, also called Fort Carlton,[2] where he was appointed temporary Clerk-in-Charge. Effective June 1871, Willie was
assigned to manage and operate the HBC farm near Prince Albert,
which was also called Carlton Farm. It began operation in 1867/68,
and Willie was one of its first managers. The primary function of the
farm was to provide vegetables and cereal grains for Carlton House
and the Prince Albert posts.[3]

Willie's time at the Saskatchewan River Posts was very difficult.
During his five years in this area, he was faced with smallpox, starvation, and rebellion. In his letters, he speculated that, without major
changes within the HBC, a bleak future was in store for the Company and its employees. He mentioned rumors of such much-needed
change, including increased remuneration for staff.

Willie was nearly killed in 1870. His mother's June letter to her great friend Frances Stewart paints a vivid picture of the attack, as well as of conditions within the HBC at the time:

My dear Willie was very near meeting with as sad and even sadder fate at the hands of an enfuriated half-breed at Fort Pitt. Who gave him a blow on the back of the head with an axe knocking him senseless and inflicting a wound. The wretch who attacked him was about to finish his dreadful work when an old Orkney man came to his rescue and struck back the uplifted axe and tried to unclasp the grip that he had on Willie. Ten others stood by and never lifted a finger in his defence. On this crisis Harriette the young wife flew to her husbands help—The men called out that he was *killed!* hoping that he was so—but, the brave girl—Willie writes, 'did more to save me than even the old man.' The rebellious state of the men in the forts back have been very great for as W- says they have now lost all respect for the Co—since the outbreak at F Gary and know that they will be upheld by the rebels in power....

Deeply disgusted my two sons seem to be with those men who should have staid to defend the property of the Co- and who have deserted their charge. Willie was left utterly at the mercy of the lawless half-breeds and Indian mercenaries—My brave honest boys would not desert *their* posts of duty—When the officers who had the higher command did so. I must not write more on this subject for I feel my blood rise when I think of it all.[4]

In late 1870, while Willie was Acting Post Master at Carlton, a savage smallpox epidemic tore through Carlton House and much of the Western Plains. Willie was credited with saving many lives through his tireless attention to the sick. Captain William Francis Butler[5] commented most favourably regarding Willie's conduct during the smallpox epidemic.

> The circumstances attending the progress of the epidemic at Carlton House are worthy of notice, both on account of the extreme virulence which characterized the disease at that post, and also as no official record of this visitation of smallpox would be complete which failed to bring to the notice of your Excellency the undaunted heroism displayed by a young officer of the Hudson Bay Company who was in temporary charge of the station. At the breaking out of the disease, early in the month of August, the population of Carlton numbered about seventy souls. Of these thirty-two persons caught the infection, and twenty-eight persons died. Throughout the entire period of the epidemic the officer already alluded to, Mr. Wm Traill, laboured with untiring perseverance in ministering to the necessities of the sick, at whose bedsides he was to be found both day and night, undeterred by the fear of infection, and undismayed by the unusually loathsome nature of the disease.[6]

After all this hardship, Willie's fortunes at last began to improve, although the West was facing new challenges. The vast buffalo herds were rapidly disappearing, adversely impacting the Indians, the hunters, and the HBC. In 1874, a second epidemic—this time, whooping cough—swept the Plains.

That same year, Willie was appointed Clerk-in-charge of his first important post: Lac la Biche. The post had suffered a series of lean years and desperately required a competent manager, presenting Willie with an excellent opportunity to showcase his abilities.

FORT ELLICE *July 29, 1869*

My dear Mary

I have only time for a few lines so you must not complain. I send this and a small parcel by a Mr. Graham, a gentleman who is passing and who kindly offered to take any parcel or anything I might wish to send. As I know you will all be glad to see anyone who has seen us, I have given him a letter of introduction to Mother. I think you will find him a very nice person and I am sure he will be welcomed by you all.

I am sending a small parcel containing a pair of slippers each for yourself, Kate & Annie. You must take them as a small token of friendship from Harriet whose work they are, at least some of them. I also send a pair each to Tom & Clinton. I am very sorry they are such common and ill made things but we were not looking out for a chance so were not prepared.

Harriet [now Mrs. Willie Traill[7]] and I are very happy and expect to be so. I do not yet know for certain where I am to be stationed so I will not be able to tell you. I will write Kate before I leave here for I am in daily expectations of being removed. As Mr. C is expected up from Council I would write to Kate now but have not time for more than a few lines and I promised her a long one and will not disappoint her.

I forgot to say that Harriet has been very unwell for some time, but it is nothing serious and I hope she will soon be quite well again.

Walter too has been very unwell. He suffers dreadfully from headache. He is all right now.

Of course we are all very anxious about our appointments. I hope mine will be to the place I hear it is but we cannot rely on reports so must wait till we hear something more definite.[...]

W Edward Traill

[...]

FORT PITT *January 2, 1870*

Dear Mother[8]

A happy Christmas and merry new year to you my dear old mother and to all at home with you at Westove; if you be there I doubt not that Mary and Annie are with you and their little ones. How much I should enjoy being one of the party!

[Harriet] & I spent Xmas with Mr. Watt. We gave a dinner to the men & women of the Fort so we had not much time to ourselves. After Xmas Mr. Watt started for Edmonton so we were left to spend New Years day alone. As soon as we got up we were pestered by every man, woman & child, both white & Indian coming to kiss us. I assure you I would as soon be excused as to kiss some of the old Indian women. [Harriet] had a greater share of the kissing than I for she had both men women & children whilst I only kissed the "ladies". The worst of it is that we commenced giving them a cake each to get rid of them not calculating on the crowd who came. We soon ran short of every cake, bun etc. so that bread had to be made for tea. [...]

It is a day that calls up old recollections and one misses faces which have been [want?] to surround us. This is the first New Years Hal has spent from home since her school days. On the whole tho not jolly we were quite happy tho both thought much of home and would [fair] have peeped into the "future" which a merciful providence wisely hides from us. Where we may be when the day comes round who knows. So long as it finds us as happy and as well contented with our lot together it will be sufficient.

We have not been at this place 4 months and have become more reconciled to the place & people.

I have been from home twice since I last wrote. The first trip was for fresh meat. I was absent 14 days. The last time I was away 15 returning on Xmas eve, the day I promised. Both trips were successful.

5th What a contrast between your summer in Canada & ours! You seem to have had a very wet one and ours on the contrary has been excessively dry. Our winter began early in November. We have had deep snow since the latter part of that month but little cold to speak of.

I find myself getting lazy at letter writing. I suppose it is because there are so few chances and I get so few letters now. Perhaps it is that I find my spare time more occupied than when I was single. There are many little things to be made for the house such as tables, sofas etc. which I never thought of before. When we first came here, Mr. Watt had a great bulk of a Horse Marine in the kitchen as cook. Harriet thought she could manage a great deal better without her but as she was paid by the year and we are entitled to a cook Mr. Watt preferred she should stay. Since he has gone to Edmonton, Harriet has done the cooking etc. herself and gets on much better besides effecting a great savings in every thing. The expenses of the house are hardly equal now to what they were when Mr. Watt was alone and we live doubly as well—in fact we live like princes.

I have bought Harriet a stove which is not provided by the Co. They think we should use the fire place but that is very awkward to cook by for one used to a stove.

I hope you don't think I try my wee wife too much. I do not think I can—how can I when her every thought & act is to try & please her Will.

Jan. 20th The Packet has arrived and goes on tomorrow so I must close.

The Packet is 13 days late. We have looked out for it for a long time and at last concluded that something was wrong with Watt but he is all right. He says the packet was delayed by two of the Company's servants leaving a young gentleman along the road and they had to wait for him two days.

They were traveling from Slave Lake to Edmonton with two trains [of] dogs. When about half way between the two places, and just past a road that led in to a post to one side of the route, they left this young gentleman in the camp. They drove off and left him without dogs, snowshoes, blanket or a mouthful to eat. They arrived at Edmonton on Saturday evening, danced at night and lounged about all Sunday without even mentioning that they had a companion. On Monday they mentioned having left "a mooneas" Green Horn on the road and wondered that he had not arrived. A couple of trains were immediately dispatched to look for him. They found him at Fort Assiniboine. The day before they deserted him, he saw a track forking off and on inquiry found it led to F Assiniboine. No sooner did he find himself abandoned than he retraced his steps to the forks of the road and followed that track to F Assiniboine. It was well that he did for the weather was extremely cold and he must have perished. Of course the fellows cannot be brought to justice but the young fellow is a son of the Hon- Young of Canada. I sincerely hope they may be made to suffer for such a heartless piece of brutality.

Mr. Watt I am happy to say goes no further. I hope I may remain with him as I would not like to be with any other officer in this District that I know.

There is a probability of my going to Edmonton to be in the sale shop there. I would be pretty well off but would rather stay here. [...]

Ever your loving son
W Edward Traill

CARLTON HOUSE [*Fall or Winter, 1870*]

Dear Mother

[beginning missing] Dear girl how I should miss her should I fall ill, but for her own sake and the dear little boy I would rather they should be from me if there is anyone else to nurse me—one who has recovered.[...]

Poor Harry [Harriet], what a blow it would be were anything to happen [to] me. I know not what she would do for she loves me as few wives love their husbands. I know that I should indeed be bereaved were any thing to happen to her. I fear were she at home I might forget my duty to my neighbours in my solicitude for her and my little son—indeed I hardly know which would be [duty]—I believe the Indians have suffered fearfully. Some who arrived lately say that they found the bodies of 20 Indians lying along the road in one single pitching (days march) which with Indians traveling with their families is seldom more than 12 or 15 miles. I expect that fully half of the Cree will die, but in their case I look at it in the light of a merciful dispensation of providence for I expect they would all have died of starvation soon if not this, next winter. We anticipate a hard winter. No provisions have been made this summer. The buffalo seem to have disappeared for the time. We have not got a bag of pemmican in the Fort and but little dry meat, whereas last year at this date we had several hundred bags pemmican and some hundreds of thousands of pounds of dry meat. [...]

It is now past midnight. I am sitting by McDonald who is very uneasy. I had to leave Ballendine who has a wife to look after him to come and watch here. We are daily expecting Mr. Christie. I hope he may soon come and relieve me of the charge. It is hard for me to be man of business, doctor and nurse. Yesterday I did not get time to wash my face. [...]

W Edward Traill

CARLTON HOUSE *November 13, 1870*

My dear Mother

I am sure you are wearing to hear from me again and as there will soon be an opportunity I will now reply to your kind though sad letter informing me of the sad end of my dear brother [Harry].[9] What a shock I got when I happened to fall on a paragraph in the Globe some time since. I could not realize it, but since I found it was but too true. Poor fellow. When I left home I hardly expected to see him again as he had then been in bad health for a long time, but little did I think that he would be taken off by the hand of a fellow mortal. It is a dreadful thing to die,

A view of Fort Carlton (Carlton House), where Willie Traill was Clerk-in-Charge during much of 1870. Photo by C. Horetzky, 1871. GAA NA–675–1

but to be hurried into eternity in an instant of time by the hands of a murderer is something too dreadful to think of.

I have had a very narrow escape as I wrote you before, and since that time have run a great risk from the smallpox which has carried off young and old, rich and poor, in hundreds in this District yet my unprofitable life has been spared. Truly God is good to us erring creatures. I suppose you have received the letters that I have from time to time written you since the disease broke loose. I am thankful to say we are now clear of it at last. I have had my own trials, but through the mercy of God both myself and family have been spared. We are all in excellent health now. [...]

You will be sorry to hear that in spite of my having been apptd to Swan River again, I have been kept here and am now in charge of this place. Mr. Clarke[10] who was previously in charge left in the early part of the fall intending to go to Canada & Ireland but what was my surprise a day or two ago to see him back accompanied by an officer Captain Butler of the 69th Regt. They are both on Government business. Mr. Clarke will proceed on to Edmonton and will pass down again soon. This time will be a genuine start for Canada. No doubt Walter sends you the new newspaper, "The Manitoban". If so you will be better up in all matters connected with the Government and the Co than I can be so I will not venture any R R news.

I understand that the Co. is to be thoroughly reorganized and the whole thing turned upside down. Commissions are to be discontinued but all officers are to be rewarded according to merits & ability etc. I take for granted that wages will be increased. I sincerely hope that things will take a turn one way or another very soon, as the standing is very unsatisfactory for a year or two past. All has been well enough for the present but a very doubtful look out for the future. [...]

Now I must give you a peep at our fireside. There behold my darling wife attending to the household [affairs], which are manifold just now as the house is full of strangers and she is quite alone having no one to help her but a young girl who is only good at washing dishes & potatoes and nursing at times.

Angus (who is my big brother in law and who came up with Harriet) and baby[11] are playing all sorts of capers. The dear little fellow is just able to get up on his feet without laying hold of anything and to stand quite alone. I hope to see my darling walking in a week or so at any rate by the 26th when he will be 9 months old. He is very fat, fair and good natured, but the little scamp has not a tooth in his head. Mr. Clarke seems very fond of him and the Captain who is a sensible man takes a deal of notice of him. He (Walter) is only able to say mama and na na and a few uncouth sounds which he delights in repeating. I am sure the dear old grandmother's heart would warm at sight of her little Nor'wester.

On the whole we are more comfortable here now than we have been since we married. I have just made an agreement with a woman to act as servant, so that will take a deal off Harriet's hands.

I see Harriet is enclosing a cutting from the "Manitoban" which will give you an insight into the amount of disease, though no numbers of deaths are mentioned. I suppose you know that all the places therein mentioned are in the vicinity of Co's posts in this district. I might mention that when I last heard from Edmonton there had already been 215 deaths amongst the half breed population at that and neighbouring places, and still the disease was raging. All that number in two or three weeks out of a population of say 1000 souls. Indians of all tribes have died ad infinitum. [...]

Winter has again set in and I fear it will be one of scarcity. No Buffalo here or in Swan River [Manitoba] and little or no provisions on hand. In Swan River they can easily procure grub from the settlement, but here it is not possible in winter. So far we have lived well and I expect to do so throughout the winter. We have a farm about 50 miles distant. Tho it don't pay it supplies a few commodities which we could not procure elsewhere. We have plenty of potatoes. A few turnips, barley etc. The only thing we are short of is butter. [...]

W Edward Traill

CARLTON HOUSE *April 6, 1871*

My dear Mother

[...] Enclosed you will find a Bill for Twenty Dollars which if you do not need please give to dear Mary with my love. It is but a small sum but I hope some day to be in a position to make more acceptable gifts.

We have had a long and tedious winter. Starvation has been general. Many of the poor Indians have starved to death, tho none in our imme-diate neighbourhood, tho they would by scores had we not fed them out of our scanty supply. Our own people have been on half rations the greater part of the winter. I have on two occasions saved whole families from starvation by sending provisions a distance of 90 or 100 miles to the poor creatures. What would they do without the Co?

Smallpox has at length died out amongst the whites & half-breeds but reports say that the Crees have it yet. [...]

Mr. D.A. Smith[12] wrote me a very kind letter in which he expressed his appreciation of my conduct last summer etc. etc.

Mr. McKay was in Red River and there met Mr. Smith, Mr. Hamilton & others, all of whom he says spoke most highly of both Walter & I. Captain Butler who I mentioned in winter he also saw and he spoke of me in the same terms and that to Gov. Archibald. You see tho a stranger in a strange land I have many friends.

It is the universal opinion that there is to be a favourable change for the HBC Officers and I assure you reform is much needed. There are many in the service who do not a hands turn and are as well paid and as much thought of as those who work hard, but I hope a new regime will be inaugurated in which every man shall be paid according to his deserts.

My little wife is not well today nor has she been for some time but I don't think it is anything more than a little biliousness. Little Walter is now weaned and is quite a man. He has only four teeth yet and those make him a little cross at times but on the whole he is a very good boy and I trust is not much spoiled—at least we don't allow him to have his own way. He cannot speak yet. I wish he would begin to as it is then that children begin to be interesting. However he has very funny little ways. [...] He chooses to feed himself now and a fine mess he makes.

Angus has gone home. I sent him down by our packet men as Mr. McKay wants to put him back to school again. On his way to Ft. Pelly they ran out of grub and were a whole day without eating which Angus stood like a man. He is only 12 years old. One of Mr. McKay's boys is studying for the Church. [...]

Your Loving Son
W Edward Traill

CARLTON HOUSE *April 23, 1871*

Dear Kate

[...] I have only 3 bags pemmican in store and no prospect of getting other provisions soon but as the warm weather is coming we shall not starve. [...]

Since I wrote you we have had a supply of fresh meat from the plains 3600 lbs but we have so many depending on us that it is all done and we are again living from hand to mouth. Last night we finished all our grub but this morning we got 5 sturgeon from the nets, so that will hold us one day longer. I always find that something turns up to keep the Pot boiling.

Mr. Christie did not come. He has changed his plans and will not be here for ten days at least.

He wrote me that Mr. Hardisty is to take charge here. I am to have the charge of the farm, which is 50 miles from this. I shall like it very well. We will be able to live better on the farm than at any one of the Forts. [...]

I am looking for my hunters daily. I sent them out as soon as they arrived. They should be back again now. Yesterday I started a party to the Plains to hunt & trade dry provisions. [...]

Mr. Nesbitt the Presb'y Parson from that quarter was here on Sunday. I could not go down with him which I should have liked to do. By living at the Farm we shall have the advantage of a local preacher as well as the society of himself & family. [...]

W.E. Traill

[...]

CARLTON HOUSE *June 3, 1871*

Dear Mother

[...] I do not know where I shall be stationed this winter. I am here for the summer to attend the equipments. Christie told me that in all probability I would be in charge of Prince Albert, a post near this place to which a farm is attached but he said he could not promise me anything as it would be [decided] at Council. I feel very unsettled, and so does every one. I wish we could hear any thing definite. I am afraid the Co. will have to wind up its affairs in this Country, in which case we will be set adrift. For my part if the country was a little settled I would not care much, but as matters are, any one out of the Co's pay has a poor chance to get on. I am quite confident that I could succeed on a farm as those who live on a farm can eke out an existence without working and an industrious man could not fail to do something better. But I suppose we will have to hold on. I am sure that the Co cannot get along without military force. You have no idea what a wild set we have to deal with in this district. I do not mean the Indians but the servants & freemen who are worse than Blackfeet.

Watt has gone down in the boats to Norway House. I do not think he will be coming back. He and Christie do not get on well.

I have not heard from Walter since March. He took the Fort Ellice furs to Georgetown in April and has not yet returned & had not when Mr. McKay's man came. I hope to hear from him by the first arrival that takes place.

There is an abundance of wild fruit but Harriet being away I am afraid I cannot preserve much. I wish she was home for I miss the dear girl and our sweet child very much. I am almost idle here and have no company that I relish. There is a French priest staying here who gives me daily lessons in French. He does not speak sufficient English to make a good teacher, but still I get along pretty well. I have very little Black-foot news to give you. The day that the boats arrived at F Pitt there was a party of Blackfeet came & stole 19 horses from the Indians. The horses were within a quarter of a mile of the Fort but the rascals were so sly that they were not seen tho it was a little after dinner. [end missing]

W.E. Traill

PRINCE ALBERT *October 22, 1871*

My own dear Mary

I am very busy getting some alterations made in the house which it is quite necessary should be completed ere winter sets in, and I am as busy as a nailer but make slow headway as I have so much to look after and

the cooking occupies a great deal of my time. But I forgot, I have not
yet told you that my darling Harry & Walter are away on a visit to Fort
Ellice. Mr. McKay promised that Kate should pass the winter with us and
H- has gone for her. She left on the 28th Ultimo, but I hope my term of
house keeping has well nigh expired as I am going to Carlton tomorrow
with the expectation of meeting her there. If not I shall go to the crossing of the South branch the next day when I shall be almost sure to meet
them if all be well. I heard from her once when she was close to her old
home. She was only to stay two or three days as the season is getting on
and it would not do for her to linger on the trip. Fancy going between 3
& 400 miles to see one's parents and then staying two or three days.[13]

I was going to buy a sewing machine for Harriet and was on the eve
of closing the bargain when I received a letter from Mr. McKay saying
he had bought one for her—also a gold watch which he promised her
as a wedding present. I gave her a very pretty gold chain during our
engagement. He is a generous old boy. [...]

Dec. 10th [...] I went to meet Harriet at C but met her about half
way. She had Kate with her. You may be sure I was glad to see them.
Harriet made the trip in 23 days only staying one day with her parents
at F.E. It was well she staid no longer for the day after she returned
was wintry and from that time till now the weather has been unprecedented for severity. All the month of November the thermometer staid
very low—seldom above 10 below zero and several times at 30, 33 &
35. There were plenty of frozen ears & noses. But now I must tell you a
piece of news which will interest you more then cold or frozen noses. I
mean the birth of a little daughter on the 29th Ultimo.[14]

We are both very proud of the daughter. She is fair of course dark
blue eyes, of her hair you can judge as I will enclose a little for the grandmother. She is very good as Walter was—sleeps all day & cries but little
at night. Her Aunt Kate dotes upon her.

Harriet is going about again but is not very strong, but I am very
thankful that she is so well. Poor little Walter is quite cut out in his aunts
favour but we both seem to love him more. He is very fond of "Babby"

and wants to nurse her. You should see him singing to her & trying to keep her quiet. Poor wee man he is not in the least jealous. He is beginning to say every word he hears but seldom contrives to put two or three together. He is very fond of his Aunt who he calls "Aunty" [or] "Cake". When she reproves him he comes to me with a long face & says "Aunty mad" (bad). He is a wonderful boy for climbing and is always falling from beds, tables, boxes etc but does not learn wisdom from experience.

We think to call the baby Kate. She will have many namesakes in her grandmother and aunts. Harriet wants to call her Mary Catherine but I detest double names.

I have suffered considerable from toothache the last month or so. There is a Doctor at Carlton who I shall get to haul one of my grinders. He drew one last spring—a regular whopper.

We find it a great treat having [Harriet's sister] Kate with us. She is such a chatter box that we are never lonely. [...]

WE Traill

CARLTON FARM *July 14, 1872*

My dear Annie

I now sit down to reply to your kind and very welcome letter of 28 Jan'y, which I received nearly a month ago on my return from Fort a la Corne whither I have gone on a pleasure trip by the passing Boat Brigade.

You ask how I like farming. Well enough tho I have my own troubles. There is however one consolation: that is that a failure does not affect my pay. The crops look well again, but yesterday we very nearly had a repetition of last year's loss. A hailstorm passed over us but tho the hail was large it was not accompanied with much wind so it only broke a few potato stalks. After we were in bed there was another hailstorm but tho more fell it was not so large. I was afraid that everything would be cut to the ground: some of the hail was as large as partridge eggs. [...]

Tho farming we have little farm work to do more than the [overseeing]. Last year it was different as Harriet had the cares of 12 cows and all the dairy work they entail, but as I was in no way bound I would not allow her to do it this summer.

I don't know how we shall get along when Kate leaves us. Tho fond of my little pets I am [no great nurse] and Walter is still too young to look after his sister. He is very fond of her and calls her "Michel" (Miss [Traill]). [...]

Walter is a great chatterbox now tho he can't speak plain. He knows all his uncles & Aunts by name. He wears trousers & a coat and "puts berries in Pack" (Pocket). He is fond of horses and claims all the colts he sees. He says "Plenty colteys Alter have". [...]

I am very uncertain as to whether I shall get leave to go home this year. I fear not, but I shall probably find out when Mr. Christie comes in Aug or Sept.

I expect Mr. McKay will come up to Sask on this summer probably to winter at F. Pitt but I am not sure. I shall be very glad to see him again as I have not seen him since I married. [...]

I wish I could go home next winter but tho I intend to apply for leave I am by no means sanguine. I long much to see you all again. How short the time seems since I saw you last and yet how many changes have taken place. How many dear ones have departed and what numbers have sprung up. I am sure I should be almost bewildered with the number of cousins & nephews & nieces the most of whom I never saw and then my own little family. [...]

29th [...] I went to Carlton expecting to stay a week but found that my services were not required so I only stayed one night. [...]

Since I began this we received a parcel from mother containing some beautiful dresses for the children and some nice books and other things. Harriet is very much delighted with them especially the little dresses. They all fall to Katie's lot as they are small for Walter, he being in coat & trousers for some time. [...]

We expect to have steam communication with R.R. some time next month but whether the steamer can come this far is a question that will not be settled till it is proved by actual experiment.

I ran the Coal [Falls][15] (the only impediment to navigation) and am of opinion that a comparatively small outlay would render it quite navigable but that point will soon be settled.

There is a great deal said about the settlement of the Saskatchewan but the influx has not yet [begun] unless the few R.R. settlers who have lately come this way are taken into account. [...]

Harriet starts for Carlton tomorrow if it is fine. She goes to take supplies for the year. She will leave Walter with Kate & I and will take the wee Katie & a girl as company. She does not expect to be long only staying one night.

I hardly think you would undertake a journey of 50 miles & back with no other escort than a girl of 13 years. [...]

WE Traill

CARLTON HOUSE *April 14, 1872*

My dear Mother

[...] The general opinion seems to be that our prospects have not improved. I myself in a conference with Mr. Christie asked him in confidence what was his candid opinion on that score and he said he thought that tho the trade would be on a better footing that the prospects of Officers for the future look blue enough—worse than before. [...]

The Indian Commissioner will be here in July and if an amicable settlement is made with the Indians there are many who will turn their steps hither ward.

As you say in R.R. things look troubled. I think however that any dissatisfaction there may exist is on the part of a few political malcontents who have ever been troublesome and whose aim seems to be entirely selfish. [...]

You should get Hargrave's book[16] on R.R. It is well worth reading. I have not read it but have sent for it. I would send you a copy were I not so much out of the way. I hear everyone speak highly of it. [...]

I am glad you saw Mr. McMurray and that you liked him—indeed everyone likes him. I have seen very little of him but that little was enough to make me like his kind manner. He is as perhaps you are aware married to a second cousin of Harriet's. [...]

I do not know how long I shall retain charge of this place. I have refused to continue in charge unless I have proper men under me and have a woman for the dairy work. There is no other officer in the service who allows his wife to do such work as Harriet is obliged to do. Mr. Christie promised to see that other servants were engaged. [...]

WE Traill

CARLTON HOUSE *July 7, 1872*

My dear Mother

[...] As regards changes in HB economy I have heard nothing more than what I already wrote you. [...]

I am sorry to say that Mr. McMurray when last heard of was dangerously ill in London. His complaint was dysentery of which C.F. Clare died under distressing circumstances in '67. I sincerely hope Mr. McMurray has recovered and that you may be able to forward the parcel you speak of. [...]

Little Walter is now of an age to take interest in pictures. I was greatly pleased with a wolf sent him by "Coz Kate". [...]

He has a cart in which we put a dog and then he & Katie drive to church—a full mile & a half. They both enjoy the ride.

The spring has been rather wet but the crops look well. There has been no frost in June. I hope we shall have a favourable season throughout. [...]

Very few of the Junior Officers are contented with the turn HBC affairs have taken. None seem to doubt that the trade will revive but all are discontented with the way they have been left out in the cold and with their prospects for the future.

I hope to be able to enclose a draft for $50 which you will accept my dear Mother as a new years gift from your affectionate son & daughter in the wilderness. I would send it or part to the girls but think best to send to you knowing that if they require help you will know best where the help is needed. [...]

Harriet and I paid a visit to Carlton last week. We went with horses & carioles and slept going. The night was rough but we were comfortable. We came home in one day. I ran nearly the whole way, only riding down hills. The road was bad so you may think that I felt tired after a run of 50 miles, not having been on a trip for a long time. [...]

W E Traill

CARLTON HOUSE *August 11, 1872*

My dear Kate:

[...] We are daily looking out for the Indian Commissioner who with Messrs Christie, Fleming and others are to treat [...] with the Indians of these parts. I expect Mr. McKay to accompany the party. [...]

I hear that my old friend Captain Butler is coming out with a lot of immigrants (Irish I suppose) and intends settling in this neighbourhood. Whether he himself will settle I do not know but I hope he may.

We expect to see the steam boat during the course of the present month—that is if the Coal Falls does not prove a temporary barrier to navigation but I hardly think that such will be the case.

Saskatchewan is destined to be something yet, tho I doubt if it will ever be a great wheat growing country. Our crops look magnificent at present but owing to almost daily rains they are not yet ripening, and unless the weather changes I fear we shall again lose the whole by frost. [...]

Harriet had been up at Carlton in the covered wagon & I went to meet her about half way as she returned. Shortly after I met her the storm came on. She would have been frightened had I not met her before the storm.

I have taken up a [claim] here and intend getting a house of some kind erected so that I can hold the land. It is quite probable that Mr. McKay will settle here in the course of a year or so in which case it is possible that I would turn farmer if the HB service does not hold out more satisfactory inducements than it does at the present. [...]

WE Traill

PRINCE ALBERT *January 15, 1873*

My dear Annie

[...] Life here is more monotonous than ever. True we have more society and more reading as people begin to come from R.R. & elsewhere and settle, but we appear to be more than ever shut out from the world as the more fortunate Manitobans are brought in closer contact with it.

However the day is fast approaching when we will be no further behind than our neighbours. There is little doubt but that the P.R.R. will pass not far from this and then if we are a little farther from Canada we will be a little nearer the Pacific. When the R.R. is in operation it will be but a weeks trip to go home. I hope however that I will be able to go home long before the completion of the Pacific Rail road. [...]

There has been a great rush from Canada to Manitoba. Do you know any farmers who have left for these parts. I think they are mostly from the extreme west of Canada.

I can hardly understand why so many leave comfortable homes to come out here & yet judging from the majority of young men I should say they had 'left their Country for their Country's good.' They are said to be an awfully wild set.

Our Parson is a Canadian from near Bowmanville. His wife is from the West of Canada.

We like them very much tho they are very much Yankified. It seems to me that all Canadians I meet (not very many by the way) are very much like Yankees in speech and manners. [...]

Harriet heard lately from Walter. He seems to have recovered his health quite which at one time rather alarmed me. He spoke of going to St Paul to buy goods for the store. I have no doubt that you hear from him more frequently than you do from me or I from him. He is much nearer you than he is to me—not [in] real distance but in facilities for communication.

Our winter so far has been rough and cold. We have had 70 degrees of frost twice and the general average has been very low. I hope we may have an early spring to make up for the cold.

Captain Butler of whom you have no doubt heard is wintering at the Forks which is about 35 miles distant. His companion and brother officer (Capt Mansfield) came up on a visit lately. He had a hard trip as some of his boys left him and he had no bedding as he started with the intention of reaching here in one day. He had to sleep out without bedding with the thermometer at 40 below zero. He reached here with his nose pretty well frozen but otherwise quite well. He stayed two nights with us.

It is wonderful what hardships these fellows go through for the love of martyrdom as it were. It is well said that an 'Englishman is only happy when most miserable'.

The Captains have offered me the management of a large stock farm which he proposes to establish at the Forks. The offer is a good one but I hardly think the Company would let me go.

I do not think I shall stay longer than my present term in the service unless they treat their officers more liberally. The first step of a promotion for a Clerk is to the position of Junior Trader. Now it is the general opinion that the berth of Trader is even less remunerative than that of Clerk or in plain terms—less than £100 [per year]. [...]

My farm here yielded well this year. In R.R. the crops were good but many lost all they had by grasshoppers. They are a great scourge and for that reason were I farming I would prefer farming here to R.R. Here we never have grasshoppers in numbers. [...]

W E Traill

HB FARM, PRINCE ALBERT *August 12, 1873*

My dear Mother:

[...] I am glad to hear that you got The Great Lone Land[17] and liked it.[...]

We are in daily expectation of the steamer. I hope we may not be disappointed. We are to have a Mounted Constabulary force here and four Stipendiary Magistrates.[18] The force is much required as we are living in turbulent times. Not that there has been any out break but there is a strong spirit of discontent throughout the country both among the half castes (French) and the Indian tribes who have been promised a treaty for some time past and have as often been disappointed. [...]

23rd We have just heard that the steamer has come to grief. After stemming the worst rapid on the River it sunk on a [rock] 10 miles from where it was built. All the stuff 4800 pieces was in the hold and was 3 nights under water so you may be sure the whole stock will have received great damage. We depend on those goods for our winter supplies so will suffer in consequence.

We have Kate with us again. Mrs. McKay will be down from Pitt in September about which time you may expect another grandchild if all is well.[19] [...]

The whooping cough which has been very fatal in R.R. has found its way out here and causes us [no] little uneasiness, tho as yet none of our little ones have it. [...]

WET

Still no word of leave to go home. I fear my chance is small as Mr. Christie has retired and I have heard no word of permission.

CARLTON HOUSE *January 27, 1874*

Dear Kate

[...] I left Harriet and my two pets Katie & Mary all well. You know that Walter is at Fort Pitt with his grand parents. I had a letter from Mr. McKay lately. He says Walter is quite well and happy. He is very fond of his grand parents. His Uncle Joe has no chance of getting near his mother for Walter appropriates her all to himself. He tried to fight his grandfather when he pretended to fight his grandmother.

Wee Katie's a sweet child tho not pretty. She is fond of the baby but fonder still of a dirty leather doll that her grandmother made for her. She says of her sister you's baby mama and this is my's baby. She is very fond of her uncles and aunt but Angus is her favourite. He stays with us and attends school.

He is a very fine boy and ahead of all the boys at school and even the Master.

Since I left home Harriet has hurt one of her breasts but she thinks it is getting better. She has Kate with her as well as Gilbert and Angus.[20][...]

I fear there is no prospect of getting away next summer. My only chance of doing so is to leave the service and I really hate to leave it after spending ten years of my life in it to no mention. I mean to say that by remaining I have good hopes of promotion in the course of two or three years, but if I leave it now it would be throwing away the ten years that I have already served. At any rate I cannot get away this year as I have a year to serve after the first of June next. If I see no prospect of getting a furlough by that time I will leave. I have been promised by the officer in charge of the Dist that he will exert himself in my behalf both as to furlough & promotion. [...]

I am president of a literary association. Of course we are not a very literary set but you have no idea what an improvement has been wrought in society in a few weeks.

Our minister Mr. Vincent gives lectures now & then. We have weekly debates which are conducted very methodically & orderly. We have rare old fun. You may guess what fun there would be where a question such as the last was discussed. The debate was as to which leads [...] the happiest life, the married man or the bachelor. The married members advocated matrimony and the bachelors the reverse side. The married men were defeated. I was not there but I believe there was grand fun. Had I been there I hope I would have turned the scales in favour of the married men.

We have had several political meetings at which I had the honour to preside as secretary & sometimes as chairman. I felt cheap enough when first called on to act in the latter capacity. [...]

We have started a subscription for a library and have already got some 100 dollars.

I am really sorry to leave but such is life in HB Service. When a man begins to get comfortable he is removed.

This is a rather hard year for provisions. The buffalo are far so the Plain tribes are starving. The Wood Indians are better off as this is a year for rabbits. [end missing]

W.E. Traill

CARLTON HOUSE *January 4, 1874*

Dear Mother

[...] I am thankful to say the little ones are well. The whooping cough is still in the settlement, tho confined to one or two families. It has made the round of all however except our own family and one other. I cannot be sufficiently thankful for this mercy.

Our little baby is a remarkably good child. She has never put us to the necessity of even lighting a candle or getting out of bed since she was a week old. She is growing well. Harriet is quite strong again. [...]

I heard from Mr. McKay lately. He was suffering from lumbago. Little Walter was quite well and happy.

He will be four years old the latter part of this month. We miss our dear boy very much.

I left home on the 9th of Jan and have been here ever since. I worked hard for 10 days but since then I have done nothing to speak of, indeed I have been very unwell. I have suffered from a somewhat heavy attack of dysentery which has stuck to me for some time. I am now getting round all right. [...]

Starvation again reigns on the Plains. There are no buffalo within 3 or 4 hundred miles.

I do not think the Crees will suffer so much as last year for the bulk of them have followed the buffalo.

I have just been appointed to take charge of a Post which for some-time has been greatly mismanaged. I have been promised a tradership in three years if I am successful in suppressing opposition in that quarter. To do this my presence next summer & the following winter is indispensable, but when once things get in trim it will not be hard for them to let me go. [...]

Mr. McKay very kindly offered me 100 lbs if I wished to go home & take my family with me. Now that sum would pay all my traveling expenses and perhaps more but I must wait.

W.E. Traill

CARLTON HOUSE *February 2, 1874*

My dear Annie

[...] I expect to be removed from Prince Albert in spring. Our farming operations have been discontinued. Probably I will go to Lac La Biche which is above Fort Pitt. [...]

The McKay family are our close neighbours. The old couple of course are at Fort Pitt but there is Tom & his family, William, Henry, Angus & Gilbert & Kate. On the whole it is very pleasant. We have horses and can drive about when so inclined. Unfortunately the whooping cough has been very prevalent so that Harriet could not go where she liked. It is now dying out and I am thankful to say so far our little ones have not had it. [...]

WE Traill

CARLTON HOUSE *February, 15, 1874*

Dear Mary

[...] My Walter is at F. Pitt with the grand parents. Katie says "Che che off O pit" I am longing to see my dear little Katie & the innocent baby. Dear little baby she don't know me yet so she will evince no pleasure at seeing me—not so Katie who will not leave my arms for a long while. God bless my darling children & give us both grace to train them up in His faith fear & love. [...]

I should like to get some of your publications. I came across one in The Favourite, & liked it very much. I see that the two Crawfords write for that paper. I have not read any of their stories. [...]

I left my family at the farm more than a month ago and came here to work but except the first two weeks and the last two days I have done nothing. [...] The day following I expect to start home but to stay only a short time. [...]

The McKays being near us is very pleasant. And there is scarcely a day but what some of them come & see us or we go & see them. [...]

Old Mr. & Mrs. McKay are at Fort Pitt. He is now a Factor. [...]

La Biche is a very dull, out of the way hole. There is however, a Roman Catholic French Mission close to the Post. Some of the priests are very intelligent men & the nuns are very nice creatures. One of the priests is a good painter and a very cultivated man.

The post is very comfortable in some respects. There is a small farm. A mill. Cows etc. so if the person in charge does not live comfortably it is his own fault. Fish is the staple article of diet but with all the conveniences I have mentioned any one of any recourse can greatly add to the cuisine.

This winter is a hard one for the Indians. There are no buffalo on the Saskatchewan plains except in that quarter occupied by the Blackfeet and of course it is death to the Crees to go and hunt on Blackfeet grounds. [...] [end missing]

CARLTON HOUSE *July 6, 1874*

My dear Mother

[...] I am glad I am going to Lac La Biche. If I get on well, I will not remain a clerk more than three years. If not I may as well bid good bye to the service. One thing in my favour is that I cannot do worse than my predecessor has done. [...]

I might have sent a little more but was anxious to make up a sound sum to invest in Canada. I have made up my mind to be far more economical and hope to be able to add yearly to my nest egg. [...]

Hence forth at this season of the year you may expect from me ten pounds annually. I could not expect a blessing on anything I do if you my dear mother were in want—Little Walter wanted to sell a colt & send the money to his Aunt Mary when he was told that she was poor. Instead of selling his colt I send this $35.00 which was owed me and which has just been paid. [...]

Harriet has had better health this summer than any time since we married. [...]

Clarke will go to Canada this fall. I don't think Kate [Clarke's wife and Harriet's younger sister] will go with him. [...]

WE Traill

Five

LAC LA BICHE
1874 – 1881

IN 1874, THE COMPANY MOVED WILLIE to its post at Lac La Biche, where he would be stationed for the next seven years. A few miles away, the Athabasca River flowed north to Lake Athabasca, up the Slave to Great Slave Lake and through the Mackenzie system to the Arctic Ocean. Until the advent of passable roads and railroads, these waterways were the highways of the West.

The 1870s were worst and the best of times in what was becoming Western Canada. Sales of furs were falling off in Europe, and this was hard on the HBC. Manitoba joined Confederation in 1870 and British Columbia joined in 1871. The Canadian Pacific Railway Company, on its way to the Pacific, reached Manitoba October 9, 1877, with the arrival in Winnipeg of The Countess of Dufferin. This railway marked paid to HBC's Minnesota Route and slashed many days from the transportation of freight, personnel, and mail. Telegraph service reached the west, but was too costly for the average person.

The slaughter of buffalo continued unabated, rabbits (a dietary staple for the Indians) were scarce, and at Lac la Biche even the supply of fish—once considered inexhaustible—was low. Scarlet fever raged across the plains and famine was an ever present spectre. The

Company did all it could to provide for the starving Indians; even placing its personnel on half rations to meet the need.

Natural disasters darkened the Traills' landscape. The impact of periodic flooding of HBC forts and posts was undoubtedly exacerbated by their location—always near, and often on, the shore of rivers and lakes.

Living under such hard conditions, Willie and his family were beset by tragedy.

My dear Mother

It is with a sad heart that I now take pen in hand to address you.

God has seen fit to take from us the flower of our little flock. My
darling little Mary (Molly we always called her) was taken from us the
day after we arrived at this place. On the 27th of July we left Carlton on
our journey to Lac La Biche. Our dear ones were then all in good health.
Little did we think that we would so soon be bereft of our little lamb.
Three days out from Carlton, our children caught a bad cold which
turned out to be whooping cough. Last winter all the children at Prince
Albert had it but ours, and when we got to Carlton they were constantly
in contact with children recovering from it. Long ere we left Carlton, the
complaint had disappeared and we hoped that our children had quite
escaped, but they caught it when no one was near that had it.

For nearly a week, the weather was very cold & raw which of course
was unfavourable for the little sufferers. Still they bore up well. The darling Molly was good and playful never giving the least trouble. She had
a smile for every one. She was beginning to stand by catching hold of
anything and was crawling about. At Fort Pitt they all got worse, especially Walter who rather alarmed us, but when we left that place he &
Katie got livelier, but the dear little Mollie began to get worse, our third
or fourth day she began to give us some alarm. At last we left the cart
brigade hoping to reach this place our second day and thought it probable that some one here could give our little one relief if it was the will
of God that she should be spared to us. Our horses were not good and
the road execrable, the worst I ever was on, so instead of taking 2 days
we only arrived here our fourth day at noon. For the last two days our
darling took no notice of anything. Her dear eyes wandered unceasingly
from side to side and she moaned slightly but unceasingly but never
once from the time she left Fort Pitt did she utter the slightest cry, dear
little soul it was very distressing to see her. When we arrived here all
was done for her that could be done but it was only too evident that our

darling was to be taken from us. We arrived here on Saturday at noon. We sat up with our darling that night. We had intended taking her to the Roman Catholic Mission[1] on the Sunday but when the Sunday came I saw that it would be a risk, but as one of the people from here was going to church I sat down to write a note to the pere with whom I was acquainted asking for assistance, but whilst writing I was startled by a cry from the poor mother who was holding the dear child in her arms, I started up to find my child in the throes of death. A fit of coughing had carried her off. Dear mother, you who have experienced the same alone can know the agony of the moment. We were prepared for our child being taken from us but not so suddenly. Oh how hard it is to part with a loved child in a strange place & among total strangers with out one kind friend who could comfort us under our sore trial.

We had our darling buried in the garden from whence we will have her removed in winter to Prince Albert where we expect our future home to be. The poor mother had to dress it with her own hands. Dear dear little Molly, now that she is gone we can say, 'Our father thy will be done.' We could not wish her back knowing that what is our loss is her eternal gain, but yet it is hard to bear. We will console ourselves by the hope of joining her in that realm of bliss where parting sin and sorrow shall be known no more.

I had promised to write to the girls and give them a full account of my trip up, but how can I dwell on anything but our sad troubles on the journey.

This is a pretty place. The Post is built on the south shore of the lake—a fine sheet of water. The lake is 25 miles in extreme length and varying from two or three to eight miles in width. There are islands in it, but so large as not to be distinguishable from the main shore. The lake abounds with whitefish, pike, perch & suckers. There are also dog fish but they are not eaten except in very hard times. We have our nets set just in front of the house from whence we get our living—not that we live entirely on fish for we have potatoes, turnips & some other vegetables. We can also get ducks and other waterfowl so you see we are not likely to starve as at a Plain post.

Now my dear mother, short as my letter is I must close as I have a great press of business on hand which cannot be put off.

Harriet sends her love and a lock of our lost darling's hair. Poor girl, she feels our loss very much. She is left much to herself as I am always busy and there is only one woman in the establishment and she is blind.

The other little ones are far from well but we trust they will be spared to us.

Good bye my dear mother. I will write again as soon as an opportunity occurs meantime.

Believe me to remain your loving son
WE Traill
My love to the girls. I will write if I had time.

LAC LA BICHE *October 15, 1874*

My dear Kate

[...] Our trip from Carlton to this place apart from the sickness of the children was somewhat tiresome. The road from Pitt to this place is execrable and one of our two horses chose to lie down at every creek and mud hole. Some times we had to unharness the brute and haul out our wagon ourselves. We only had a little Indian girl with us so you may be sure we were relieved when we came to the chief obstacle—Beaver River which is a considerable stream & rapid to find it was low. The water just came into the wagon box. One of our two animals gave out entirely before we got here. [...]

This is a pretty situation tho I cannot say much for the dwellings and other buildings. The establishment consists of the officers house which is a long low bark roofed log house resembling a byre.[2] [Then] there is a smaller one but just like it with two rooms for the men. The trade shop &

fish store are much the same only smaller. There is a pig sty, stable & tumble down byre, and that constitutes the establishment of Lac La Biche.

The situation is on the south end of the lake, which is not a stone cast from the house. The lake is a fine sheet of water 25 miles long by 18 broad but it is shut nearly in two in the middle by narrows.

There are several islands but at some distance from the Post and so large as not to be distinguishable from the main shore at a distance.

In summer we set our nets just in front of the house for you must [know] that living at LLB consists of fish three times a day or as often as you like. I do not want better living than we have had since we came here—fish cooked in half a dozen different ways. Boiled, fried, fresh, split & smoked, salted fish etc etc. Then we have had ducks, prairie chickens, partridges, rabbits, with a taste of beaver & moose nose etc. with vegetable. We will soon have beef & pork to add to our bill of fare so you see we are in no danger of starving, more particularly as the fish stock is inexhaustible.

Harriet is very proud of her accomplishments as a sportsman. She has been practicing with the gun lately, to the sorrow of the prairie chickens. She is now off on a visit to some rabbit snares she made yesterday. I will let you know the result of her labours. She says she wants to learn how to put down a net but I fear it will be some time ere she conquers her fear of water. She does not feel at home in a canoe. She has just come in with six rabbits, the result of 13 snares set last night. You see I need not starve with such a wife. But hunting is not her only accomplishment. She can cook & make my clothes as well as any wife I could have found in a civilized country, and above all she is a loving & true wife. Am I not a fortunate man?

We have been very busy getting one room made decent. It is an addition to the house and was neither floored nor plastered when we came. I have had it lathed and plastered and floored. It is now not only comfortable but quite nice. We do not intend to let the natives have the run of the whole house as they have been want at this place.

I am getting along pretty well so far with the trade and hope in time
to get things in good order.

In a day or two I will be starting out my fishermen to the fall fishing.
The spawning grounds are about 10 or 12 miles from here. We will haul
the fish by [dogs] in winter. I hope to get from 10 to 15,000 white fish. If
I get even 10 thousand I shall have abundance for the whole winter.

I have one of the best fishermen in the country.

We have just got our two cases goods from Orkney, about £30
worth to which Mrs. & Mr. McKay have added several nice presents.
Mr. McKay's present to Harriet is a very neat tweed walking dress. Mrs.
McKay sent her several things for the children with several pounds of
sweets for the little ones from their Aunt Kate. [...]

19th [...] We had a visit from a missionary yesterday and enjoyed
the service exceedingly. His name is Steinhaur, a full blooded Indian
from Lake Simcoe. He was brought up & educated at Alnwick by old
Father Chase. He knows Rice Lake and was at the Indian village there.
He came out here in '55 just after the Rice Lake bridge was built. He is
stationed about 50 miles from this and will visit us once a month. [...]

WE Traill

LAC LA BICHE *November 22, 1874*

My dear Mother

[...] I was sorry to hear my dear mother that you had been so unwell but
glad to hear that you are better.

When one is taken away at the age of Aunt Agnes we cannot grieve
the same as for the young, for at the age of 80 they have passed the al-
lotted span and when their lives have been good & useful we trust that
it is well with them.

I hope you will not be defrauded out of your share in her bequest. It
seems very selfish & hard of Aunt Eliza to contest the Will at her age &

single as she is. How does she found her claim? Did she help her sister in the authorship I cannot understand how she can dispute the Will.

Harriet has been unwell for the last month past. Poor girl she frets too much. She finds this place so lonely, only one English speaking family in the vicinity [and] they live two miles from us. I thought she was resigned to the sad loss of our darling but when she is feeling ill she frets very much. [...]

Winter set fairly in on the 1st of this month. The lake did [not] freeze over till the 15th.

Yesterday & today have been very rough & stormy. We have had the thermometer at 25 already.

Last winter we had the severest weather before Christmas.

I am surprised that Walter had not visited you by the date of your letter. Mr. Smith, I understood to say had given him liberty to go home for a few weeks. Perhaps he found [too] great a press of business at that time & would defer his visit till the close of navigation.

It will be long before this finds its way to Canada. It will be taken from here to Victoria by Bishop Grandin. [...]

I have heard no word from Mr. McKay since last I wrote, but Kate wrote to Harriet. Clarke (Kate's husband) was off to Canada. He should be back to Carlton by this time. When he returns Mr. McKay will return to his charge at Fort Pitt. I hope we shall see the old gentleman this winter.

I hope we shall have a pretty comfortable winter.

We have about 10,000 white fish, 20 bags pemmican. I have killed 2 oxen & will kill several pigs.

I rather fear we will not have an extra good winter for furs however it is hard to judge by the country round here as several of our hunters go for some on the Athabasca & some towards Lesser Slave Lake where furs are more abundant than here. [...]

Every one kills fish for their winter. Most families have from 2 to 3 thousand according to the number of persons & dogs, for all keep at least one train of dogs and as each dog must have a fish per day they require a good stock.

While my fishermen were off to the fisheries I had to fish for the establishment & cut & haul wood etc etc. I liked fishing when the weather is not too cold but it is no fun to overhaul a net when the ice is floating in the water, though these men do it in mid winter at any possible degree of frost and that bare handed. If possible I intend to try a drag net next fall. We get enough as it is but take rather too long for my liking. I am fortunate in having the best fisherman and net maker in the north but I nearly lost him. He was overhauling his nets in a storm and upset & was about drowned. When rescued by others he could not stand when put on shore. He was a couple of hours in ice water. He was nearly drowned a second time trying to cross the ice before it was strong enough. [...]

There is a probability of the Company making a road through this part of the country from some point on the Saskatchewan above Fort Pitt to the forks of the Athabasca, in which case this place would be one of some importance. I hope such may be the case as we are altogether shut out from the civilized world.

If the Peace River route for the N P R R is adopted it would pass through this neighbourhood.

[...]

W E Traill

LAC LA BICHE *January 3, 1875*

Dear Annie

[...] We were altogether alone on Christmas, and on new years day we had far more visitors than was either agreeable or convenient. We had to feast every one of our neighbours as well as the people of the establishment. They came in early and we only got rid of the last about bed time. [...]

We have no friends. There is one very respectable family who live about two miles off and then the Mission people. They are all French but speak tolerable English. The nuns are very kind. One of them is an old friend of Mrs. McKay's and very kind to Harriet & the children. [...]

The trade however is poor, there being a wonderful scarcity of fur bearing animals.

The people with whom I have to deal are a tiresome set.

I sometimes wish I was at some other occupation than trading furs, which is by no means congenial to my taste. It is the meanest occupation out, for one is constantly being abused by every old Indian that comes along. If I could afford it I would leave the service.

However two & a half years will be all I will serve [with out] I get better encouragement than I have at present. [...]

I do not know when my turn will come but one thing is certain and that is that when I will get a furlough I will not lose any time in availing myself of it. Had my trade this year been successful I might have stood a chance but such not being the case tho it is no fault of mine my chance of getting away is very small.

It was a down right swindle leading me to suppose at the first that I should have a chance of going home after seven years. Such is never the case—no nor at the end of ten years. Very seldom anyone gets leave except on a plea of ill health. Of course commissioned officers are different. In HBCos service the higher you rise the less you have to do and the higher wages you get. I wish I had my foot on the first rung of the ladder. [...]

W.E. Traill

FORT PITT *June 1, 1875*

My dear Mother

[...] Mrs. McKay goes with me tomorrow to Fort Pitt to be with Harriet till her after confinement, after which she will go down to Red River to see her boys who are at school. [...]

I left Harriet and the children well. I trust they may be still so on my return. I shall be about 6 days on my journey.

The winter here seems to correspond very well with yours. We have had an extremely long winter and remarkably deep snow and consequently the rivers are all, or have been, remarkably high. The spring has been almost unprecedented for floods on all the rivers rising in the Rocky Mountains. This north branch broke up before the ice had in any way melted. This fort […] tho built on a high ground was nearly flooded, and at Carlton built on still higher ground the ice blocked against the bastions of the Fort. Still lower down at Prince Albert the people had to take to the hills for their lives and five Indians and some cattle were drowned. On the south branch matters were much the same but no lives lost.

But the most remarkable flood occurred on the Athabasca at Fort McMurray on the forks of the Athabasca & Clear Water River. The river rose in the course of half an hour to the remarkable height of 63 feet carrying off several of the buildings of the Fort and drowning all the transport oxen. Mr. Moberly the officer in charge came on foot to Lac la Biche to try and get animals to replace those drowned. I supplied him with the number required and am left without any animals & had myself to make my way here partly on foot.

My trade has not been a good one but Mr. Clarke writes me that he is well satisfied considering that it was a hard year for furs. […]

I have just received a letter from Walter. He seems down on his luck. Poor fellow he takes things too much to heart. I have just written him a long letter trying to cheer him up and [at] the same time giving him some advice which I trust he will take. He would be better had he done as I did and married young. He was I think sweet on Kate but too prudent to marry. I think he is sorry for it now that it is too late […]

I have saved about half my wages for this year and trust while in the service to be able to put by an equal sum say $250.00 which I will always invest. Of course trouble may come and prevent my realizing such a saving but I think I can do so. I have need to put by a little because I shall soon need to put Walter to school.

I lay no store on money for moneys sake but for the sake of those who are dependent upon me. Education for my children shall be my great aim if it please God to spare them to me.

[...]
WE Traill

My dear Kate

[...] Before going any further however, I must tell you a bit of news that I know will interest you. The day before yesterday, Harriet presented me with a fine little son. I say little but he is quite a giant, bigger than Walter was. He has very large hands & feet and a nose that will do credit to both Traills & McKays. Both mother & baby are doing well I am thankful to say.[3]

I dare say you know that Mrs. McKay came up with me from Fort Pitt. We arrived here on the 5th. She goes home in a day or two but has to go to RR at once to see her boys who are at school there.

We shall miss her much, so will the children. She had only just re-turned from Carlton when I went for her. Before she gets back from Manitoba she will have travelled over 2000 miles.

I had a rather rough trip to Fort Pitt. Owing to an accident in the north I had to give all my animals to make up an otherwise irreparable loss, and was only left with one horse with which I had to make my way to Fort Pitt. Chiefly on foot, as the horse was carrying. I had to send my packs by the R C Mission carts. I travelled in company with the R C Mission people one day & then forked off to Whitefish Lake where I had business. The people at that place were next thing to starving so they ate up all my provisions after which I had to make my way through the woods back to the Fort Pitt road, depending on my gun for provisions. Every creek was a river and every river a flood. We nearly drowned our horse in the Beaver River & at another creek we assayed to cross on a temporary bridge that had been in use but which at that time was afloat. The horse broke through the bridge & would have been drowned but we managed to haul him over the bridge on his side. We were nearly to our knees in water on the bridge. Of course the saddle bags got wet & my papers were not improved by the soaking they got.

We would have had some difficulty finding our way but happened to fall in with an old half breed who knew the country and who I hired to guide me through. We came out on the road far in advance of the [R C Mission people]. [...]

W.E. Traill

LAC LA BICHE *December 30, 1875*

My dear Mother

A happy Christmas & new year to you my dear mother, and tho you can scarcely expect to see very many returns of the day yet I trust I may yet see you & the dear ones at home. [...]

They should in justice let me go next summer. Mr. Clarke promised when I consented to come to this place that if I was successful in trade he would use his influence to procure me leave this coming summer.

I have been so far successful that the returns of this outfit far exceed the returns of any year for some time past so that I have good grounds for claiming the promised reward. [...]

New Years is the busiest time in the year for me but this year is more so than usual. [...]

The winter has so far been a pleasant one altho we have had some severe cold as high as 66 degrees below zero. We had a very heavy gale of wind one night about the beginning of the month which I thought would have carried off the roofs of the houses. It damaged the roof of the stores & some of the settler's houses. It was by far the heaviest gale of wind I ever experienced in winter. However we have had very little wind besides & very little snow. [...]

We heard lately from Mr. McKay who is well. The old couple is quite alone as all their children are at school in Red River. I intend if all is well taking Harriet and the children out to Pitt with me in spring and if we go no further I will return leaving them there for some time. Should I get leave to go home[4] it is probable I may leave one or more of the children with the grand parents. My means are limited & it would be a great expense and not a little trouble to take them all with me although Mr. McKay kindly offered in case of my going to defray part of my expenses. Of course I should not like to take anything from him but I know his kind heart & if I refuse to accept it he will give it to Harriet.

I have not heard from Walter since I received your last but received some canned fruits & sweets for the children from him. [...]

One day Harriet heard Katie saying to herself in Cree I will tell grand papa. I will tell grand papa that when he send sweeties mama only gives Walter & I two or three & she & papa eat all the rest. I will tell her all about it. [...]

W E Traill

PENNSYLVANIA *July 18, 1876*

Office of The National Surgical Institute (Eastern Division)
N.E. Cor. Broad and Arch Streets, Philadelphia
My dear Mother

You will doubtless be getting anxious to hear from me as I promised to let you know from time to time how I get along.

I stayed at the Pages the night I left Rice Lake. I was sorry Mr. Page was away. Mrs. P. was very kind & pressed me to stay longer but I could not spare the time.

Next day Saturday I got only as far as New York as the cars did not run on Sunday. I cannot understand why unless indeed the R.R. people be the only religious people in the States, for the shops are open all Sunday.

Willie Traill during a visit to Philadelphia. Photo by A. Newman, 1886.
GAA NA–3455–1

I arrived here yesterday & am now quartered at the establishment. It will cost me a queer sum but I have not a doubt of their ability to cure me. They do not deem a surgical operation necessary. They have given me no pain so far. […]

Please draw for me $100.00 and forward by Post Office order as I shall be short of money. They charge me $150.00 irrespective of board so you may guess that I shall be short. […]

I will probably be back about a month from the time I left you as my ticket was only good for 30 days. […]

W.E. Traill

MONTREAL *August 17, 1876*

My dear Mother

I write you a few lines to let you know that I took it into my head to return this way so don't be anxious if I don't turn up as soon as I intended.

I may not be able to leave here before tomorrow and will probably stay a day & night with Mrs. Hargrave and perhaps a day or so between Belleville, Cobourg & Port Hope or Rice Lake.

When I leave you I will go direct to Winnipeg unless I stay a day or so at Toronto, however I cannot delay long anywhere.

I have received considerable benefit from my treatment & trust that with the means at my disposal I may cure myself fully.

I am writing at the Company's office where I am waiting for Mr. Smith who is out. I cannot leave till I see him. […]

W.E. Traill

TORONTO [*August 1876*]

Dear Mother

I should have written you yesterday to let you know of my arrival here, but was hurried all day trying to see as many of my friends as I could intending to leave tomorrow night, but now I find that tomorrow is a bank holiday so I shall have to stay over until Tuesday to get money for my trip. I got in on Friday night about 10 and found the Vickers all well and very kind and glad to see me. […] Yesterday I called at R. Moodie's[5] office over & over again and at last succeeded in finding him home. He is looking well & wanted me to go out to his place but I fear I cannot do so as he lives so far from here. […] After a long chat I went to the Tully's and passed a very pleasant evening with Mr. Tully […] & Aggie.

Robert Moodie asked me if I thought you would be able to come down here this summer. He seems anxious you should go and stay with him for a while. Of course I did not know. I suppose dear Katie will be going home tomorrow to look after the garden. […]

Altho you might not think so from my manner I found the parting from you all a most trying one. I was obliged to appear unconcerned and I may have appeared heartless, but it was only by a great effort that I controlled myself.

If as I trust a railroad is built into the Peace River within a few years I may yet see you once more in the flesh my dear Mother, but if it is not the will of God I have a sure & certain hope of a happier meeting where there will be no more partings. [...]

I cannot write the others until I get to Pembina. I fear I shall have to go straight through not staying at Chicago on account of the delay here. [...]

Your loving son
Wandering Spirit

FORT GARRY *September 7, 1876*

My dear Mother

I arrived here on the 6th at 2 AM but of course slept out the night on the Str-. I am sorry to say I passed Walter on the road, that is I met the steamer on which he was. He has been down here and was on his way up with Hamilton and the CC & some others so we only saw each other without being able to speak. [...]

It appears to be no new commissions given which seems strange as Mr. Smith gave me to understand that there were several. [...]

WE Traill

CARLTON HOUSE *Autumn, 1877*

Dear Annie

[beginning missing] Altho the Governor had promised me that I should be at no expense in returning home from Garry, I had to buy a horse & conveyance which cost me above $200.00 which I could ill spare as my expenses have been very high.

I certainly shall not be able to afford a like holiday for sometime to be sure of the $1700.00 I have spent this summer. I have bought 480 acres of land in the States which in the course of a few years should pay me high interest. [...]

I heard from mother lately. She is pretty well but bothered by the Longman affair[6] of which you have doubtless heard. I trust every thing will turn out well.

I suppose you will wish to know something of my trip from Fort Garry to this place.

I left Winnipeg on the 8th September in company with R. Hardisty (invalid) a clerk & two young ladies, one the niece of a brother officer going to see her uncle. The other was a Canadian girl going to marry a doctor at Edmonton who she never saw.

We had seventeen horses & 5 four wheeled vehicles & a cart. I was proprietor of a buckboard[7] and a mare. I had also two horse (so called) supplied by the Company for my use but one I had to leave en route quite done up tho never used.

The ladies were green & Hardisty being rheumatic was helpless and our only man was lazy so I had to stir my stumps especially as our horses were very wild at least those that had life enough to be so—some on the other hand were so tame they could hardly be induced to move. The roads were bad and it took long to hitch up and get underway. Things were dull enough were it not for the ladies who used to vary the monotony of the thing by driving into each other now and again at the expense of the wagon wheels which generally were two or three spokes the worse for each encounter—You may be sure that in the long run they did not improve in appearance. I mean the wagons nor yet the ladies. For that matter for the wind and weather did not improve their appearance much.

As spokes began to be at a premium with us and the game of breaking them got somewhat monotonous, our ladies varied their amusement by breaking an axle now and again. Considering that they generally came out head foremost at each encounter I was surprised they did not try some other way of amusing themselves.

We broke axles not less than five times—When we reached Fort Ellice we had two mended but before we got forty miles they broke another. I wanted to put in a wooden axle but H insisted in waiting while we sent Breerton back to Ellice to get the axle mended.

We waited till next afternoon when Hardisty & Miss Bun & the man left me & Miss Coulson to wait for Breerton & follow on.

Sundown came & no Breerton. We had nothing to eat & no tent however I had an oil cloth with which I set to work and made a shelter for Miss C—when just as I had finished & it was dark Breerton turned up.

We went to work and got the axle on and started off but did not go a mile when the axle heated & stuck fast.

We could do nothing but camp so camp we did without wood (it being a Plain) but as luck would have it Mrs. McDonald had sent some bread by Breerton so we ate some bread and then made a shelter for Miss C and left her to pass the night—no doubt in fear and trembling— next morning some of the horses were astray so we were absent from camp quite a while looking for them. When we returned we found Miss C crying. She thought we had deserted her. We overtook the rest of the party at noon after which we had no adventure more than a few breaks downs of axles etc. I was head carpenter and wheelwright. I made wooden axles with no tools but an axe & butcher knife.

But I find my dear sister that I have only got to Carlton and already my letter is up to weight and I have not had half my say. I must there-fore wind up by telling you that I found H-[8] at Carlton with Walter & Willie, Kate being with her grandmother at Pitt.[...]

WE Traill

LAC LA BICHE *December 24, 1876*

Dear Annie

A happy Christmas to you my dear Annie and Clinton and many of them. Christmas is always a busy day with us fur traders so I take time by the forelock in writing you.

It was a great disappointment to me as I know it must have been to you my not being able to see you again last summer. No doubt I could have given you a call passing but only for a few hours at most and the pain of parting would have been so great that I thought it better as it was, besides which mother did not wish me to be absent more than could be avoided. I had hoped to have spent a much longer time at home and with you my dear sister but my stay in the medical establishment broke my plans.

I certainly enjoyed myself excessively where ever I went amongst old friends & acquaintances. In Toronto too everyone was most exceedingly kind. [...]

It was dull enough on the cars between Toronto & Winnipeg but there the three days that I spent passed quickly and pleasantly enough. [...]

I was very busy whilst in Winnipeg making preparation for my trip. I was glad when every thing was ready for a start as I was anxious to get home having not received a letter from Harriet all the time I was away. [....] [end missing]

W.E. Traill

FORT PITT *May 20, 1877*

My dear Mother

[...] I brought down Harriet and the children for a change and to see the old folks. Only Mrs. McKay however is at home. Mr. McKay has taken Mr. Clarke's charge during the absence of the latter in Canada, however he should now be back at Carlton & Mr. McKay may be close at hand— at all events we are expecting him. [...]

We will probably leave this place in a few days & return to Lac La Biche but for how long I do not know. I have made application for a change to some place where I can be near medical aid. My throat has not troubled me so much since I got my medicines but still I fear I shall

*William McKay family members at Lac la Biche. Back row: Angus McKay;
Joseph McKay. Front row: Gilbert McKay, who ranched in southern Alberta
around 1900; Thomas McKay; James McKay, who later became Justice McKay
of the Saskatchewan Court of Appeal, c. 1876–1879.* GAA NA–1010–6

*not be able to effect a perfect cure. I shall try your lime water cure when
I have convinced myself that my present treatment will not result in a
perfect cure. […]*

*I am in hopes that I shall be appointed to the charge of Battleford or
more properly speaking the HBC Post at that place.*

*The HB affairs, owing to the extremely low prices in the European
markets for fur, are in a very unsatisfactory state [nor] are things in this
country much better through mismanagement. Unless they keep faith
with me I shall very likely leave the service next spring, however I shall
I hope [to] know more of my own mind on this subject next month or at
longest after the Council.*

*The children are all well. They are all with us. We intend leaving
Master Willie with his grandmother, who wishes to have him. I told you*

in a former letter that Walter was going to school at the RC Mission. He has only been in attendance five weeks but promises to get on well. [...]

Willie is beginning to say a few words. I never in my life saw a child with such a mania for horses. He seems to think of nothing else and drives them even in his sleep. He is a very hearty boy for his age and tho willful has a good disposition. [...]

Our steamer has not turned up yet & I fear will not for some time as the water is very low. This is the day I left here last year for Canada. She (the Northcote) had passed up to E. [Fort Edmonton] and I embarked on her downward trip. [...]

I am glad that the Longman case turned out a mistake & trust you have rec'd some money from that quarter. [...]

27th Dear Mother. I am short of paper so must close. I leave for LLB tomorrow. [...] The steamer arrived on the 24th and landed a lot of my outfit and a good deal of private stuff I bought in R.R. nearly a year ago. [...] The steamer & Clarke arrived almost simultaneously tho one came by land. [...]

The steamer has a new Captain and will I trust do better than last season. The water just now is very low but she has gone on the Edmonton. [...]

Harriet is disappointed at not meeting her father. Mrs. McKay will probably pay us a visit in fall. [...]

We hope to feast on eggs going home as this is the laying season & there are plenty of lakes on the road. [...]

WE Traill

LAC LA BICHE *June 24, 1877*

My dear Kate

[...] I must help Mary and am at a loss to know how. If I had a Cr balance with the Co (which I have not) I could easily manage. I am at a loss to know whether it would be best for them that I should buy the place my mother speaks of and allow them to live in it rent-free or to let Mary have it as part of her interest in the Westove house and lot. At any rate I will buy it and leave it to mother which way it shall be settled. I suppose it would be a great relief to them to have a place that they could call their home & that so near to you. The rent they have to pay must be a great drag on their small resources. [...]

There will be quite an exodus from this place shortly. The people will all be going to Victoria to the Treaty. Of course they will all return. I should not grieve if they never did. [...]

The strawberries are beginning to ripen and I think there will be great show of them as well as berries of almost every description. There is certainly no fear of them ripening before full grown as we have seldom seen the sun since I returned from Pitt. [...]

The children have a new play fellow. What do you suppose it is— a tame skunk of which they are as proud as if they had a new baby brother or sister—But really it is a dear little fellow & very playful. It is cleaner than a cat and follows them all over even outside. They set up a doleful howl yesterday when they thought they had lost him when they were picking berries. I am sure my niece Katie would like to play with it. [...]

The flies especially the bull dogs are very troublesome. The cattle & horses never leave the smoke during the day. [...]

WE Traill

LAC LA BICHE *July 11, 1877*

Dear Mother

[...] I herewith enclose a Bill of exchange on Mr. Smith for $200.00 to buy Todd's place for Mary.

You will please explain to her that it will come out of her share in the Westove property as agreed upon between us last summer. I wish I were in a position to make her a present of the money but as I have before intimated my funds are very low just now and our prospects very blue indeed. I must keep enough money to buy up the Westove house tho God grant it may be many years before I am called upon to do so. [...]

WE Traill

[...]

LAC LA BICHE *April 28, 1878*

My dear Mother

[...] If I can get every thing ready I will start for Victoria[9] and probably Edmonton in about 8 or 10 days time.

I am thankful to say that we are all well. The baby growing fast—as dear a little pet as I ever saw tho I say it myself. He very seldom cries— indeed he is almost always crowing & laughing. He is smart for his age and strong. He catches hold of everything and, tho he cannot sit quite well, if placed on his back turns at once. I wish you could see the little fellow as he now lies on the bed in a beaded moss bag sucking his thumb & laughing at me. Willie is at his side & says papa look at your boy, he is laughing at you. [...]

Mr. & Mrs. McKay are now off to Carlton where they will remain almost all summer. This makes little difference to us as my post has been transferred to Mr. H's Dist so I go no more to Pitt with my returns.

Master Walter still goes to the R.C.M. School and gets on well. I don't think much of their system of teaching but for all that he makes fair progress in reading, spelling etc. He also reads French but is very shy about showing of his accomplishments. The Nuns assure us that he understands all that is said to him in that tongue. [...]

I am sometimes at a loss what to do as regards my future means of livelihood—no doubt the service presents a livelihood so long as the concern holds out, but if the price of furs does not rise I don't suppose the shareholders will continue to invest their money in such a hopeless speculation. It is now over two years since the commissioned officers received a single cent for their services and still the price of furs falls. If the state of affairs in Europe don't come to some settlement soon there will be no market whatever for furs so there is no very pleasant prospect in store for junior officers.[10]

I cannot however make up my mind to launch out for my self. I suppose I will be called upon to decide when I go to Edmonton. If I decide upon remaining in the Service I must send my children to school. It will cost not a little if I send them to Winnipeg. I have been thinking (I think I mentioned the subject to you in one of my last) that perhaps it would be cheaper for me to send them to Canada for two or three years.

To send Katie to the ladies school at St John's would not cost much less than half my wages. Of course it is only an idea. What think you of it my dear mother? Unless either Kate or Mary could take charge of them W & K it would not be practicable. It would be an understood thing that I should pay for their clothing & board & schooling. Would it be a help to Mary & Katie at least would have to attend her school. [...]

My throat keeps about the same way. I don't think it gets any worse. I am still applying the remedies I got in Philadelphia. They keep it from getting worse at any rate. [...] [end missing]

W.E.T.

EDMONTON *May, 21, 1878*

My dear Mother

[beginning missing] The Mail is just starting so I will have to close my letter with a brief note. I wished very much to write to all three of my sisters but have been kept so busy that I can scarcely find time for this note.

I left home on the 9th. Harriet & the children were then quite well. I stayed 3 days in Victoria attending to my packing etc, & then drove up here in one day, 75 miles. [...]

Here is some excitement about the Sioux but I think there is no occasion for any apprehension for some months or possibly for years. That the Sioux will lead to some complications with the Americans seem to me probable but I trust our police will keep them in order for some time.

As for the Crees they are too closely related to the whites & half-breeds to cause any trouble altho some may be discontented. [...]

Will

VICTORIA *June 11, 1878*

My dear Annie

[...] This is my second trip out here this spring. The first time I was absent from home 21 days. I had only been home six days when I got orders to come out here and [relieve] the officer in charge who has gone to Fort Saskatchewan upon business. The steamer Northcote is hourly expected and some one must be here to receive the cargo and see to the reloading of her etc. [...]

I am sure you find it a nice thing to have a piano in the house & above all to have a daughter able to play it and teach her brothers & sisters. [missing] Harriet learned a little music at school but has forgotten all about it. [...]

I suppose it will be a long time before I can afford a trip to Canada. I spent too much on my last trip—my trip from Ft Garry to LL Biche cost me as much as my expenses from Ft Garry to Canada & back. [...]

I am anxious to see the steamer [when] she turns up. I could not [leave at] once as my horses [had wandered] off, a common drawback in this country. Sometimes one loses horses more than 100 miles from home or the nearest habitation and then there is nothing for it but to tramp it. You can understand how inconvenient that would be. However, I won't be so badly off as that, as I can get other horses to go home with.

I often call to mind my promise to Clinton to send him a pair of robes. The truth is I have been in debt ever since I returned from Canada & have been trying to get out of that very disagreeable situation. Another thing is the difficulty of getting any thing forwarded through without losing it. Some things I bought in Winnipeg & forwarded before I left to go to Canada only reached me last summer & some things have not yet turned up and I suppose never will. [...]

Willie

LAC LA BICHE *October 6, 1878*

My dear Annie

[...]This country is changing very much. Every time I go out to the frontier I find it getting more and more civilized—that is to say I see a great deal more of the white man and his evil ways & hear more blasphemy and wickedness in a day than I used to hear in the course of a year. You know that it is always the roughest class that first find their way to a new country.

I have just returned from Edmonton where I stayed about ten days. I had by no means a pleasant trip. It snowed the night before I left home. I got drenched before I got 6 miles. The trees were loaded down with snow so that we could hardly force a passage through. After the snow melted we had rain almost every day I was on the road—sometimes snow. The road was as you may imagine any thing but in a fine state.

My saddle horse once broke through a bridge and could not get out. I hitched another horse to his neck by the tail and hauled him out. [...]

Harriet left me for a month on a visit to her parents at Fort Pitt. She had a pleasant trip and just got back before the bad weather set in. She has just heard that her brother Henry met with a serious accident. He was going out duck shooting. At the Fort gate he met an Indian and stopped to speak to him. He set his gun on the ground holding his hand on the muzzle. A child came along and pulled the trigger the charge passing through the palm of his hand and carrying off the brim of his hat and one of the bones of his hand striking him on the eyebrow. He will probably lose the use of his hand. [...]

Little Harry who I thought was going to be the smartest is not walking yet altho nearly 11 months old. He is a good little fellow. [...] He is very much like me, every one says. He is almost too good so he don't take after me in that respect.

You were right in supposing that Harriet has her hands full with all the children. She seldom has anyone to help her but a little girl about 12 years of age. [...]

WE Traill

LAC LA BICHE *February 16, 1879*

My dear Kate

Mr. Clarke has been very seriously ill of heart disease. Kate has had a son, her third child. She was very much grieved at our loss. She certainly loved little Katie as one of her own. [...]

There is a great deal of sickness in the neighbourhood, chiefly scarlet fever—There is not now a family that have not had it or have it now. There [are] sick in every house in some dwellings there are only one or two on their feet.

There have not been many deaths as yet 6 or 7 but I fear more will ensue.

Had it not been for the great kindness shown us by the Sisters of Charity I know not what I should have done. They nursed my darling wife & children and cared for the poor little Willie as if he was their own—in fact Sister Youville calls him her grandson. She showed the greatest sympathy with us in our bereavement. She had been attending on Harriet and my dear Katie but was obliged to go to the Mission to look after things. She told us to send for her if any one was worse. When she bid little Katie good by the dear child said to her——"Why are you in such a hurry". The last words she ever spoke to her. When she came again it was to see my darling a corpse.

She loved my darling Harry as her own child. When he died she said to Harriet "Dear Mrs. Traill I shared your love for that child, now let me share your grief' and she was sincere. He was the only child that would ever go to her and not seem afraid of her. [...]

Will

LAC LA BICHE *February 17, 1879*

My dear Annie

I am your debtor for your kind and interesting letter of 26 July finished 1st August. It is indeed a long time since it was written having been long on the road but still it has lain a long time unanswered. Doubtless you have heard through mother or Kate that I have gone through a very severe trial. God has taken from us two of our darling children, Katie, the delight of my heart, and our sweet little Harry. They were taken from us within ten days of each other. Since that time I have had no heart to write to anyone. As you may not yet have heard from Lakefield I will try and tell you of this very severe trouble that has come upon us.

On Dec. 12th my darling Harry who had been ailing for some time was attacked with the scarlet fever, which had been in the neighbour-hood for some months. On the night of the 14th Willie & the dear Katie were attacked. On the following morning Harriet was very suddenly taken ill. I was obliged to send for the Sister Superior at the nunnery, who came at once and rendered every assistance in her power. We had the greatest difficulty in keeping Harriet from choking. The children too got rapidly worse and I thought I would have lost them all at once.

I slept with my darling girl all the time. She did not seem to be in so much danger as her brothers till the morning of the 18th when she rap-idly grew worse and before night I saw that she was to be taken from us.

Willie Traill's family. Back row: Walter, Jessie, William, Ethel. Middle row: Harriet Traill (née McKay), Maria, Mary, Harriet, William Edward Traill. Front row: Annie, Barbara. Photo by Clifford Brothers, Prince Albert, c. 1896.
PAC C55562 Willie Traill 3

The baby also was at that time very low indeed tho he lived for several days after.

My darling girl was so very good throughout her illness never giving any trouble but taking the medicines without a murmur never failing to thank me. Dear dear child it was very touching the forethought and tenderness she evinced. She cried nearly all the first night that dear little Harry took ill. Little did I think that they were so soon both to be with their Saviour. The evening of the 18th she was very delirious altho she always knew me. The dear Mother was too ill to render her any assistance. Shortly before her death when the death film was on her eyes I asked her "do you know me my darling". She replied "don't ask me that again—of course I know you" dear child it was the last word she said to me.

We feared to tell Harriet but she perceived it at once but was quite resigned. She did not however fully realize the dread reality at that time. At the same time my darling Harry was lying at deaths door. The Sister Superior came to me and told me that we must have him moved to the next room as he had but a few moments to live and that she would not answer for the result on the mother who was in great danger.

We had the dear little fellow removed. I went out shortly after expecting to find that he too had breathed his last but was surprised to find that he was still alive. By this time they had laid out my darling girl and were making grave clothes for my darling boy. Again I went into the next room & was told that he had taken a turn for the better. He continued to improve and I began to entertain hopes of his ultimate recovery but next day his throat began to swell. Walter then took ill and was very ill indeed. He gave more trouble than all the others as he appeared to suffer more. Little Willie was getting better when the dear Katie died. Poor little fellow. He was very ill for 3 days during which time he did not taste food of any kind—after that he rallied and was no further trouble.

I had still Walter & the dear baby to attend to. They both required the closest attention, Walter being very restless. He did not stand pain well.

I sent off for Mrs. McKay as soon as I could find a messenger. She arrived on the 28th having left Fort Pitt on the 25th, Christmas morning. Christmas day was a particularly melancholy day with me. True, Harriet was somewhat better but Walter was very ill and that night my darling Harry was very low. I watched by him till after midnight expecting every moment would be his last but after midnight he rallied and my hopes were again raised it so continued till the evening of the 28th. Every night he appeared to be just dying and would then rally and appear so very much better. That evening just before dark Mrs. McKay arrived. She was pretty tired having come from Fort Pitt in 4 days & nights, a distance of 170 miles in rough weather & no road.

She appeared to think my child might recover. Shortly after her arrival the Sister who I had sent for arrived. She sat with me while Mrs. McKay had a sleep. He appeared no worse that night than usual so after Mrs. McKay awoke about midnight I lay down being very weary.

About 3 they awakened me to say that my darling child was much worse. He had taken a sudden turn for the worse. He died in a few minutes after. I am thankful to say I was spared the pain of seeing either of my darlings in convulsions.

It was such a comfort to have dear Mrs. McKay with us at that most trying time. Harriet was still too weak to realize her loss. She was unable to shed a tear for some days after. She did not shut an eye to sleep for four days & nights. Her sense of hearing was remarkably acute. I never saw anything like it. No one could speak even in very low tones in any part of the house but she heard it distinctly.

I trust we are both resigned to the will of our Maker, but as you know my dear sister by sad experience[11] it is hard to bear. Of the five children born to us we have only two left now—no wonder then if at times we feel our loss very keenly. Remember there are no kind friends and neighbours to come in and console us.

We often say that we will grieve no more knowing that our darlings are so much better off, still there are so many things that bring our loss to remembrance but I will no longer dwell on these things. [...]

I am now writing before any one in the house is stirring so as not to disappoint you again.

I am very much concerned to hear that your health is in such an unsatisfactory state. I trust that the remedies you have been taking have been very beneficial to you and that you may speedily recover. [...]

Walter has been obliged to remain at home since the middle of Dec-. We cannot part with him now. The house would be unbearably dull. Little Willie is the life of the house—He is very amusing. Sometimes he begins to tell some romantic story and if checked for telling stories he says "perhaps it is true perhaps only."

We had the pleasure of a visit from Mr. McKay who came for Mrs. McKay about a month ago.

He was looking very well. Harriet's sister Kate had a son a few days ago.

There is a great deal of sickness throughout the country this winter.

There have been 8 or 9 deaths in the neighbourhood this winter and still there are a great many sick. [...]

WE Traill

FORT PITT *August 3, 1879*

My dear Mother

[...] I came down here on the 28th Ultimo to see after some business and pay a visit to my dear wife—I am thankful to say I found both her & the children quite well but I cannot take them back with me but will leave them here according to my first plans until Harriet's confinement which will make her return to me very late in the fall. I trust I may have the delight of seeing her restored to me all right with a dear little child to fill in a measure the blank in our circle. [...]

The dear boys are very happy here having nothing to do but play. [...]

Their uncles who go to College in R R came up for a visit but only stayed two days—a long distance to come for such a short stay. They are both doing well and the eldest carries off a great many prizes. Mr. McKay has quite a nice little library composed of the books that his children have received as prizes at different times for the last few years.

I have had two or three letters from Walter this summer. [...]

He is about selling a piece of ground he bought for me when I was at Grand Forks in '76, and which has turned out a very good speculation.

I believe my chance of promotion is pretty good as I am first on a list of thirteen who have been proposed and of whom about six will probably be promoted. All the officers in these parts—I mean in this department voted for me so my chance is fair but I must not be too sanguine—indeed there is no great reason to be elated for at best it will only be a Junior Tradership which will not bring me a fortune but at worst is worth £150 per Annum. [...]

I had quite made up my mind to try my fortunes at stock raising or something else at the expiration of my present engagement which terminates in '81. [...]

We had the steamer "Lily" here on the first and had the honour of a visit from Lt. Governor Laird & suite. [...]

I believe we will see more or less of the surveyors this summer. They are going to explore the country near Lac la Biche for a railway route. I am acquainted with the head surveyor Mr. King who is from Port Hope and an exceedingly nice & gentlemanly fellow. I met him at Edmonton two years ago. [...]

There is more content just now among the Indians than for some time past altho I don't know how they are to be tided over the winter for there are no buffalo and government cannot afford to feed them all on flour & beef. I don't think they will do any harm so long as they see the whites willing to help them a little. [...] [end missing]

W.E. Traill

EDMONTON HOUSE *May 28, 1879*

My dear Annie

[...] Now that there is a railroad to Winnipeg we ought to be able to communicate in one half the time that we could formerly.

I have brought Harriet here for a change of scene and air. I could not bear to see her moping so. We left L L Biche on the 7th and came here staying a day at Victoria. We had a pleasant enough journey till we reached the latter place where I caught a bad cold which troubled me not a little. However I am all right again. [...] Harriet stood the journey very well, and the children enjoyed it as they generally do. Walter rode the whole way on his pony "Bob."

[...] Master Willie is supremely happy when other children are at home but when they are off to school he don't know what to do with himself.

Cree men and traders at Fort Pitt during autumn of 1884. Angus McKay, son of C.F. William McKay, is pictured holding a beaver pelt. GAA NA–1323–4

Harriet is going to go down to Fort Pitt and will probably remain there for some months. [...]

There was considerable excitement a few weeks ago about an anticipated Indian rising, but it has quite died out. I think the Indians are perhaps more content now than they have been for some time. [...]

It seems the past winter has been an unhealthy one all over. [...] Fish & buffalo were very scarce. Rabbits are a great stand by in this country when other food fails but they were very scarce the past winter. The Indians starved miserably on the plains & in the woods. One Indian was apprehended yesterday within a few miles of this for having eaten up his wife & family during the winter. There was a similar case last year, only the man merely ate two of his sons. In this case he ate his whole family.

We have just heard from Rev. Geo McKay, H's brother. He is stationed at Bow River a couple of hundred miles from here. He had a narrow escape from perishing in a snow storm. He says 'I was out 2 days and a night alone without food or fire. I nearly despaired. I got so weak I scarcely reached home after the storm was over.' I believe he is very popular with the people over there. He is putting up a church. [...]

WE Traill

[An undated letter to an unknown recipient]

[beginning missing] *I don't remember if I mentioned a horrible case of cannibalism that came to light at Edmonton during the time we were staying there. It was perhaps the most horrible affair of the kind I ever heard of. The wretch ate no less than eight of his relatives: his mother, wife & brother and another grown person besides four of his children. He had not the excuse of dire necessity as he was not more than two days march from the nearest settlement where he could have obtained relief. He must have killed the four grown persons at once as it is not likely that they would allow themselves to be made away with one at a time. From the appearance of the camp he must have remained there for some time till he either ate or converted into dried meat the afore-mentioned four and then pitched off and probably killed and devoured the children one at a time.*

On the plains great distress prevails. We hear of many cases of star-vation. All the plain tribes are said to be flocking to Battleford and if not liberally assisted will no doubt take the law into their own hands, as necessity has no laws and the government is very ill able to resist any demand that is backed up by force and are not in a position to grant a supply of provisions having nothing but a very limited supply of flour and ten thousand bags would not hold a ravening host like that long in provisions.

However reports may [be] and no doubt are greatly exaggerated, but Mr. McKay who is about as good a judge as I know of Indian affairs says that he thinks the Indians will give trouble.

Why I could ration a small town on dog's meat alone. I think I have told you before that the popular prejudice against dog meat is very groundless. A good dog is as dainty a morsel as could be set before a king. It is far to be preferred before bear & next thing to a good skunk. [end missing]

W.E. Traill

My dear Mother

[…] I am anxious in mind about my darling wife. Last night I lay awake for hours thinking about her. I could not sleep till near daylight and such a night it was. It rained torrents and was so dark that lying in bed without light I could not distinguish the windows. The beat of the waves on the shore just below the house was oppressive. My thoughts were very much on my darlings who are now in heaven. Sometimes I dream of them. […]

I count the days as they go by till I shall see my beloved ones again.

Surely I am blessed in having a wife who is one with me absent and present. Others would find her no doubt a very common place woman and so no doubt she is in many ways, but only those who know her spirit as I do can ever know her real worth. I can conscientiously say that we never disagree in any thing.

Her heart is ever tender towards any one in distress and her hand is also liberal. […]

There was a birth in our neighbourhood and all the women as usual collected. Harriet as she usually does [sent] some chocolate & sugar etc. etc. The ladies were regaling themselves thereon when one began to sigh and appear very dejected. When her neighbours enquired the reason she said "I wish that I too was going to have a baby". "Why you have lots of children and you are getting old."

"Yes but when ever I had a baby Oke mas quao (The lady) always used to give me chocolate, sugar, flour etc. but as it is I never taste such things."

I suppose her confinement will take place about a month hence. As there are no telegraphs I shall not hear a word till I go to meet her in November. So you can judge how restless I shall be till that time. [end missing]

W.E. Traill

LAC LA BICHE [*late summer or early fall, 1879*]

Dear Mother

[beginning missing] [...] *I have just seen four nuns who have lately arrived at the mission from Montreal. They had arrived with Mrs. McKay and Harriet at Fort Pitt about two weeks ago. They were very much taken up with Mr. Willie and his comical ways. He told them that he could speak French very well when he liked but did not wish to show off his accomplishments. [...] We asked him for a word only and he said one but I am sorry to say it won't bear repetition, however he was quite ignorant of what he was saying and seemed very pleased with his accomplishment. [...]*

I was unfortunate in money that I invested some years ago. Owing to the great depreciation of bank stock the $1000 that I then invested is now only worth $700. However the land that I bought has been a good speculation. [...]

You ask if I have still my farm at P. Albert. Yes, and I think I shall get a better house built but I hardly think I shall go to live there for some time at least.

Don't be in the least alarmed about the Indians. Should anything ever transpire it will be the fault of our rulers and the Indians would not hurt us. They look upon all half-breeds and those who are related to them by marriage as their own relatives. Our tribes are not like the blood thirsty tribes further south. I think the Sioux are too politic to fall out with the Canadian government. In fact if any difficulty arose between our government and our Indians the Sioux would espouse the cause of our Govt if they were permitted to do so. [...]

I don't know when I shall be able to send Walter to St John's. I hardly think to send him till he is 12 years of age if God spares him to us so long. [...]

W. Edward Traill

[...]

My dear Mary

[…] I wrote Mother lately and enclosed a small present for you in the shape of an Order for $50.00 which I hope you have already received. […]

I am sorry my dear sister that you have been so hard up, at the same time you need not go into ecstasies of thanks for a paltry $5.00 or even a $50.00 for that matter. If my means were as large as my heart I would be able to help you more than I do—as it is I suppose every little helps. […]

Fish have been very scarce all summer & we have received no imported provisions as yet so we have not been too well off although we have always had enough for ourselves.

We can always kill beef when too hard up but of course when not actually starving I don't like to do so. […]

This has been a remarkably wet season & the last few days have been intensely hot with severe thunderstorms & in some localities heavy hailstorms & hurricanes.

One storm that occurred last month when Harriet was on the road caused me much uneasiness till I heard that she was safe. The storm did not pass near them although it raged over an extensive piece of country making a clean sweep where it passed.

The rivers are all high and the roads nearly impassable. The lake is higher than ever seen by the "oldest inhabitant" and horses have to swim two creeks between this & the Mission.

The steamer on the upper Saskatchewan i.e. between Carlton & Edmonton is running well this summer but there seems to be something wrong on the lower River navigation as the "Northcote" had not arrived at Carlton about 10 July.

The murderer who killed his son and who I caused to be apprehended last winter has been sentenced to seven years penitentiary.

I was asked to attend the trial at Ft. Sask. but did not go. [end missing]

W.E. Traill

LAC LA BICHE *July 25, 1880*

My dear Mother

[...] Harriet & the children are off to Fort Pitt on a visit. They left me a few days ago and will be away more than two weeks yet. I had a note from Harriet yesterday by the man who brought the letters. Harriet's man had killed a moose. They expected to reach Pitt today. The children were quite well when she wrote & little Ethel[12] very good. Mr. & Mrs. McKay will be so glad to see them. Ethel was only 8 or 10 days old when H- left last fall. Mr. McKay is just as fond of his grand children as he is in his own and that is saying a great deal as he is quite wrapped in his family. So also is Mrs. McKay.

I will go and meet them at Beaver River when I expect them home. [...]

The rivers are all high so H- has to carry a skin canoe—two hides sewn together which are converted into a canoe on a framework of 2 cart wheels and a few willows. The construction of such a craft seldom occupies more than half an hour and when well made will float a cargo of 800 lbs or more.

I only lately returned from Edmonton. I was about 29 days. The rivers were all flooded so we had to carry the skin canoe and use it frequently.

I did not even carry a tent. I enjoyed myself well enough at Edmonton but the trip to & fro was a very rough one. The Company's steamer was laying high and dry waiting for high water. The Saskatchewan was not high tho all the streams running into it were flooded. The Saskatchewan takes its waters from the mountains and it is only extremely hot weather that causes a rise worth speaking of.

Last night we had a tremendous storm of thunder & lightening with hail and the heaviest rain I ever experienced. It came through the roof like a sieve. The fences were blown down and everything flooded. I hope it did not pass where Harriet was (Harriet was en route to Fort Pitt) as it was a tremendous storm. No tent could have stood before it for a minute. My garden was beaten as flat as a floor and some plants buried & others washed out by the roots.

Two of my men are out on a trade & should be on their way home. If so they must be nearly drowned as they have no covering but their blankets. [end missing]

W.E. Traill

LAC LA BICHE *January 3, 1880*

Dear Mother

[beginning missing] The telegraph is now [in] operation between this and all parts of the world so to speak. I was on the point of sending you a telegram on new years day to wish you a happy new year to say that all were well at home when I thought it would be better to save the money which would be a few cents under $4.00 and send to Mary as a New Year's gift so I [do] accordingly by enclosing $4.00.

The weather since I left home has been remarkably severe. The first night out was the coldest I have experienced in my 16 years residence in the N.W. Here the thermometer registered 56 degrees which is colder than the coldest I have known by 4 degrees. The weather for the month of December was cold throughout except the last two days. New Years day was beautiful weather. We had a good deal of fun: snow shoe races & sack races, old woman's races, blindfold races & tugs of war & firing of cannon.

The population of Edmonton is fast increasing. I see a great many new faces since I left in June last. No doubt this will be a very fine place when once communication is opened with the East. No word of a Commissioner. I believe no word has been received as to who are the recipients of promotion. [end missing]

W.E. Traill

My dear Mother

[...] The last mail brought me no Canadian letters but I had a short note from Mr. Clarke congratulating me on having received my commission. I have not seen it yet but suppose it has gone up to Edmonton and will come to hand the first chance. Clarke has seen it or had been officially apprised of its having been awarded me before he wrote. It is true that there have been no dividends for some years but the share holders have given a guarantee of $750.00 per annum in case there are no dividends so that sum may be set down as the minimum salary of a Junior Trader. Not only so but that $750.00 is equal to twice my former salary of $500.00 because I get my supplies at a much lower percentage & have a considerable increase of allowances i.e. groceries.

Of course in the event of the Company realizing a profit my salary would increase in proportion and we may reasonably hope that when the present financial depression in Europe is at an end that our affairs will improve and that the good old times of profit may return. At any rate I will be thankful for present mercies.

We have a little Indian girl that we have adopted. She is a little older than Willie. Willie plays with her when his brother is at school. He is always so glad to see his brother when he comes from school. He is always speaking of what he will do when he is big, but I am sorry to say that smoking is one of things he aspires to when he is a man.

I got the Peterborough papers you sent me and the card that Katie sent to little Ethel. I cannot say that she expressed any great amount of joy when Willie held it before her nose. It was a very pretty one however

& no doubt Ethel will think so when she is big enough to judge for her self so in her name we thank Miss Katie for it.

There is a general scarcity of fish about the lake & of other provisions throughout the country except in the settlement, where the settlers depend upon their own resources & not upon fish or buffalo.

I had a letter from Tom McKay who lives at Prince Albert & who is doing very well. He has the largest farm there & is Capt of an Infantry Corps. He is building a college for Bishop Saskatchewan who resides there when at home but he spends most of his time abroad begging. If my boys are spared to us we will send them there instead of sending them farther from home. [...]

WE Traill

EDMONTON *November 7, 1881*

My dear Mother

[beginning missing] [...] Since I began this letter there has been no chance of mailing it and I have been so busy that I have not had time to finish it. The very day after I began it something occurred that has caused me some trouble & annoyance and has resulted in my having had to leave home when I should have been there.

On the night in question a light was observed in the shop. On entering it we could see nothing but on producing a light and after a search we found a boy concealed in a pile of blankets. He had about him a considerable quantity of goods and a large quantity parceled up ready to be conveyed thence. We found that he had entered by a gable window that had not been properly secured. I immediately sent off a dispatch for the police at Victoria 100 miles distant. A few days after a Corporal & interpreter were sent to apprehend the young scamp. He was on an island with his father fishing. The weather was rough and no large craft so we had to wait several days. When the wind went down they secured their game and took him off to Victoria but before going subpoenaed myself and two others to appear at Fort Saskatchewan to testify what we knew about the affair. Altho I was daily expecting Harriet to be confined I was obliged to leave her with her mother and shut up my shop and off we came.

The first night we slept at W F Lake. [...] The second night at Victoria where we stayed half a day and then came on to F Saskon where I was most hospitably entertained by Captn Jarvis. The trial took place the day we arrived. He was found guilty and a true bill being found against him he was remanded till the arrival of a Stipendiary magistrate who is competent to try criminal cases.

We had to enter into recognizance to appear when the Judge comes but as it may be some time I have come here to wait for the trial. This is very provoking but I have to submit. [...] [end missing]

W.E. Traill

LAC LA BICHE *January 3, 1881*

Dear Kate

[...] I will be starting for Fort Pitt in two or 3 days. Two of my best horses have gone home. They came originally from Pitt. I am going for them unless by any chance Mr. McKay sends them back. [...]

We are just weaning Miss Ethel who is not very troublesome but at the same time I have no chance to write in the evenings. Willie has a sore throat and Harriet is complaining a little.

I expect to go to Slave Lake next spring but don't congratulate myself on the change. We will be out of the way altogether there. You need only expect to hear from us once in a while, say three times a year.

I never send for any books now, but get The Witness & the paper you send me & the Manitoba Free Press & two Saskatchewan papers. So I have no time to read more than all those.

The Witness is a really good family paper. [...]

Willie Traill as Clerk and later Junior Chief Trader in Charge at Lac la Biche from 1874 to 1881. Photo by Ewing, Cobourg, and Peterboro, c. 1876.
GAA NA–1010–43

I am afraid Harriet cannot go home (to Canada) till the P.C.R is finished. The papers speak of it being complete in three years. Surely in that time they will be able to give me a furlough. [...]

I never meet with any of my old friends in the country but I suppose some of them will find their way to Saskatchewan. Captain Hershmer of the police knew poor Harry very well. He is a very gentlemanly fellow but I fear he is very fond of the bottle. He promised to pay me a visit this winter. [...]

Whooping cough has been very prevalent in our settlement. I am thankful to say my children have escaped so far and as there are now few cases of it I hope they may escape altogether. [...]

WE Traill

Dear Annie

[...] I have been told by Mr. Hardisty that this will probably be my last winter at Lac La Biche. He did not intimate where he intended sending me but from other sources I learn that it is to Slave Lake, Lesser Slave Lake to distinguish it from G.S. Lake which is very far north. L.S. Lake is about 300 miles north of Edmonton so you may be sure I have no great reason to congratulate myself on the change more especially as I am only now beginning to make myself comfortable here—however, perhaps I may be more comfortable there if I really go but of course nothing is determined as yet.

I regret the change for Harriet's sake. There will be no society at all there. Here we have the nuns and one or two besides. We also have a chance government official or police officer. There we will see no one. [...]

Walter is not going to school this winter. We try to teach him a little ourselves but I am sorry to say we are by no means regular and he does not learn much in consequence. [...]

Willie does not know all his letters yet. He does not seem to care about trying to learn. He is not dull however but can pick up anything quick enough. I think he is quicker in that respect than his brother. He speaks like an old man, but nearly all his funny sayings are in Cree.

I enclose you a specimen of the Cree syllabic writing. It is a letter I got from one of my traders. Of course there is no real Cree characters except the hieroglyphics that are in use amongst almost all Indian tribes. The enclosed is a specimen of a system of syllabics that was invented by a missionary in this country each character representing a distinct syllable and it is used by all missionaries irrespective of creed or denomination. [...]

WE Traill

FORT SASKATCHEWAN *March 3, 1881*

Dear Mother

I have been up to Edmonton having left home 10 days ago & I am now on my way home. [...]

I reached Victoria my 3rd day but my horses fell sick there. I found that they were expecting Mr. Hardisty on his way to Lac La Biche and accordingly I remained two days waiting for him, but as he did not turn up I went on to Edmonton. Whilst waiting at Victoria there fell a deal of snow so I had very heavy roads from that place to E-. I slept here my second night, leaving at 10 next morning, reaching Edmonton at 3 P.M. distance 19 miles. [...]

I got through all my business with him next day (yesterday) and am now on my way home. I shall wait here for old Colonel Stewart (ex H B Factor) who is going to accompany me to L L Biche where he will spend some days with me. He is a very fine old gentleman and has seen a deal of service & hardship in the North. He is or was an "expedition man" and is most excellent [at] camping. He kept me awake till one o'clock this morning telling me of his adventures in the north. It is by no means the first time I have met him. He was at L L B with Hardisty last winter. [...]

It is all arranged that I go to Slave Lake. It is much further out of the way than L L Biche but as it is because the former post has been mismanaged and I am appointed to try & put things to rights. I have no reason to complain. It shows that they have confidence in me.

I will be leaving in all probability about the 10th June. The ice only leaves Slave Lake about 1st June or sometimes later.

Harriet is going to visit her parents at Fort Pitt before leaving. She will start as soon as wheels can run and will perhaps go as far as Carlton & Prince Albert returning before the time appointed for my departure from L L Biche...

My Walter is getting French lessons from a French man who is working for me at L L B. [...]

Little Ethel is very funny. She tries to speak. She tries to imitate the cock & the pig. We had a visit from Mr. & Mrs. Youmans, school teachers at W F Lake. We went with them to visit the nuns. The nuns played the organ & were delighted & amused with Ethel who insisted on dancing to the music although it was sacred. It was very funny. [...]

WE Traill

Six

LESSER SLAVE LAKE
1881–1885

AFTER SIXTEEN YEARS WITH THE COMPANY, having been in charge of eight posts or forts on a regular or replacement basis, Willie would finally reach the first rung of the commissioned officer's ladder in 1880 when he became Junior Chief Trader at Lesser Slave Lake.

The history of Lesser Slave Lake is typical of many HBC posts in Western Canada. The NWC arrived first (in 1802) and selected a prime site for their post on the west end of Lesser Slave Lake. The HBC arrived in 1815 and, atypically, elected to erect their fort on the east end of the lake. Usually the late arrival built as close to a competitor's post as possible.

After amalgamation in 1821, the HBC abandoned their post and occupied the NWC's. In 1816, the "Post was partially destroyed; employees imprisoned"; it was re-established in 1818, abandoned in 1827, reopened in 1829, rebuilt in the early 1880s, and destroyed by fire in 1933. Fire was a potential peril at all posts and, unfortunately, a reality at many.[1]

Fortunately, the Traills were some distance from the battles during the Northwest Rebellion of 1885, though their former post of Lac la Biche was sacked and the post master narrowly escaped with his life.

My dear Mother

My first leisure time on my arrival here I now dedicate to writing you, knowing that you will be glad to hear of our safe arrival.

We left our old home at Lac La Biche on Sunday morning the 12th Ultimo—not that I ever travel on Sunday when avoidable but all our crew being Catholics were anxious to attend Mass at the Mission where we remained over night. We were very kindly received by the good nuns & priests who professed great regret at our departure.

We had to take some cargo for the Mission so it was noon the next day before we got started. The kindness and attention we received from one and all could not have been greater and we left the nuns in tears. They were very much attached to Harriet and the children. They followed us to the waters edge amidst good wishes & kind words. Several of my old opponents took the trouble of riding to the Mission several miles to bid me good-by and one and all appeared sorry for our removal. One old Indian woman who had been asleep when we left the Fort walked all the way 9 miles to bid Harriet good by. And yet I meet with people that will not acknowledge the feeling of gratitude in an Indian.

Our boat was very heavily loaded and over crowded there being 21 souls on board an otherwise overloaded boat of 30 feet keel (open York).[2]

We had good water and consequently a fair run down the winding and rapid Riviere La Biche by which the lake empties itself into the waters of the Athabasca. The upper part of the stream is quite broad and the country a dead level of swamp & muskeg but further down it resembles very much the upper waters of the Red River except that the banks are less heavily tho more densely wooded & the timber is less valuable consisting almost entirely of spruce, poplar & birch. There are also a great many rapids which are somewhat dangerous on account of boulders and the sudden turns which the stream takes. The first rapid is the longest & worst so we sent all the women & children to walk over land across the portage. I remained in the boat & poled—for the men

Tripmen poling a York boat on the Athabasca River. (Edgelow Family Collection) Edgelow 1

use their poles more than their oars in descending and ascending rapids. We got stuck on the 1st rapid but managed to get the boat off without breaking. The rapid was not more than half a mile and at the foot we took in the families. I am glad H- was not on board as not being used to boat work she would have perhaps been nervous.

We lost a good deal of time owing to wet weather but our 5th day at noon we reached the broad Athabasca which I found to resemble the Saskatchewan in size but the banks are lower & wooded heavily with pine & poplar to the waters edge. Our last few miles down the Riviere La Biche was a succession of rapids which in low water are very bad but owing to the high water we ran without difficulty only rubbing pretty heavily on several rocks on the last rapid which was the worst of all.

The Athabasca at the junction of the La Biche is very tranquil & broad but we found some pretty stiff currents before we got into the Little Slave River.

On entering the Athabasca our crew had to exchange their oars for the tracking lines and collars. We had to take turns at tracking, 3 men hauling the boat while the other 3 sat on in the boat and amused

Tripmen using a line to draw a boat on the Little Slave River. (Edgelow Family Collection) Edgelow 3

themselves at the expense of their companions who were hauling the boat, one sitting in the bow & clearing the line when it fouled on trees & snags.

This tracking is hard work as there is no tow path, as on a canal, but the men have to scramble along the edge of steep & muddy banks sometimes through brush and heaps of drift wood, sometimes through mire and now and then falling into the river. They are wet from morning till night but are happy and full of fun & horse play as they can be. They are very good natured with each other and altho they sometimes push one another into the water they never get out of temper.

We ate 4 times a day—before starting or about 3 or 4 a.m., breakfast at 7 or 8, dinner about noon another meal at 3 or 4 p.m. and supper at night. We never stopped till about 8 unless it rained.

We were 4 days ascending the Athabasca to the Edmonton [Landing] where there is a warehouse of which I had the key. It is 100 miles north of Edmonton & is used to store all the freight going to Peace &

Athabasca Districts via Slave Lake. I had to take on some cargo there. We lost a full day owing to heavy rain while we were at the landing.

From the 'landing' we were another four days to the mouth of Slave River.

The Slave River is a stream larger considerably than the La Biche and were it not for the lower portion being broken very much by rapids would be navigable for small steamers. The rapids however are not nearly so long or so bad as on the La Biche.

Like the later stream it is very crooked. Sometimes we walked across points little more than a hundred yards that took the boat an hour to round. We caught plenty of gold eyes & perch and some jacks which were a great addition to our bill of fare, which consisted mainly of flour & bacon with a few dried fish we traded on the River from some of the L La Bichers we met.

We were 4 days in the Slave River. As we were running short of provisions I decided on traveling on Sunday which I had reason to regret for when we [end missing].

W.E.T.

SLAVE LAKE *September 4, 1881*

My dear Mother

[...] All my energies being required to conduct the transport both by land and water to a successful close, besides which I have to renew every building in this very dilapidated establishment and to provide hay for the cattle for the coming winter, which is no easy job as all the hay grounds are several feet under water & have been so all summer. Several of the cattle died last winter from starvation which my predecessor was pleased to call "Hoof & Mouth disease". I now belong to Peace River District, this post having been separated from Edmonton Dist by the Act of last Council. I cannot say I like my new Bourgoise as well as I do Hardisty altho Mr. McD seems very liberal in many ways

York boats under sail on Lesser Slave Lake, c. 1886. GAA NA–2283–10

and not disposed to crimp his officers. He advised me to make several alterations in the house which will add materially to the comfort thereof. His head quarters are on the Peace River about 150 miles N.W. of this post. [...]

What do you think of taking charge of Walter and Willie? If you would undertake the trouble, I might send them home next summer with their mother. It would do Harriet a great deal of good and she would like very much to go. The boys however you might find noisy or troublesome. Walter is naturally quiet but Willie noisy. I do not think they would be worse than two girls would be. I would pay for their board and washing. Of course I am not certain of [telling] them even if you consent to take them. I shall be glad to hear what you think of the project.

You will be glad to hear that the share holders at home have agreed to raise the guarantee for the last two years from £150 to £200 which they were not obliged to do. Nothing is certain for the present year but it is understood that the same will be granted. [end missing]

W.E. Traill

My dear Mother

[...] I am much distressed like yourself at Walters studied silence since his marriage.[3] You always ask me for particulars but all I have learned about him and his wife I have gleaned from what I have heard from yourself and the girls. I have not had a single line from him altho I wrote him shortly after hearing of his marriage. I can hardly suppose that he is ill as it would be mentioned in the Winnipeg or West [Lynne[4]] papers. [...]

Since writing you I have been down to the 'Landing' which is a warehouse we have on the Athabasca a hundred miles north of Edmonton where all the freight that I have to forward is left. One key is left at Edmonton & I have the other.

I went down to arrange some business matters by correspondence with Mr. Hardisty which I could only do by going down there. I went down with 3 Boats. We had a fair wind to the other end of the lake after which it was all down stream. We ran the Slave River in one day and drifted down the Athabasca all night, tying the 3 boats together & all hands sleeping. We did not touch on sand bar or stone and next morning found ourselves at the Landing by ten o'clock. We loaded the boats that day & I finished my correspondence and packed off the man who had been waiting for the letters.

About 4 in the evening I started home with 2 men in a birch canoe leaving the boats to come behind. We travelled hard but lay by on Sunday when the boats over took us in the morning & we passed the day together. Next morning we made another start not expecting to see anything more of the brigade but they came in sight the following evening but did not catch us. The weather was wretched raining or snowing night & day the whole time. I had to paddle to keep warm. One of the men hauled the canoe with a line, the other steering. These fellows are a hardy lot as you would think if you saw them tracking barefooted & bare headed in rain. [end missing]

W.E. Traill

Rafting on the Peace River. (Edgelow Family Collection) Edgelow 9

LESSER SLAVE LAKE [*early fall, 1881*]

[Addressee unknown]

[beginning missing] [...] We have just bought out our principal oppo-
nent in the fur trade[5] at this Post, and as the season is getting late I am
hopeful that no great amount of opposition will present itself this winter.

I shall have a trip to Peace River in early winter or even sooner. [...]

Fish are not so numerous as could be desired. We have an abundance
of potatoes and I intend to kill two or 3 beef cattle 'to save their lives'.
This is one of the best passes for water fowl in fall & spring. I have little
time for such recreation but when the [larder] is rather badly stocked I
take a canoe and gun and so replenish it. [...]

Mr. Clarke,[6] Kate's husband, has been elected to the North West
Council and is consequently an Honourable, a title which I look upon
much as I do on the title of Colonel & General in the American Army.

The boats are off to the Landing for a cargo. When they return they
will surely have a packet box & I hope to hear once more from my dear
mother and sisters.

The Landing is on the Athabasca 4 days ascending, below the mouth of Slave River. The Edmonton carts bring all the stuff and store it in our warehouse there & I send for it by inland boats such as I came in from Lac La Biche.

The trip generally takes 15 days but there has been so much rainy weather that I fear the present trip will be much longer. I have still another trip for the boats before winter. [...]

The fall promised to be an early one, we have had several white frosts which have cut the potato tops but which will do no harm to the crop. [...] [end missing]

W.E. Traill

SLAVE LAKE *November 20, 1881*

Dear Annie

[...] First I must tell you of the birth of a fine little daughter on the 15th. Harriet is getting along well and the baby is very good and we are all happy in consequence. Baby is the biggest and fattest of any of our children at that age. The boys are very fond of her & as for Ethel she is delighted with it. She thinks however that it has been got up expressly for her amusement and wants to have it all the time. [...]

December 19th I have allowed a month to pass since beginning this letter but as [a] month make little difference where there is no mail it matters little, but now I must set to work in earnest to be ready for the packet which will start in a few days & which will be the only chance till the beginning of March.

I have been away for 17 days to Dunvegan which is head quarters for this District, and since I came back have made a short trip of 4 days and when at home have been busy as a nailer so some of my nieces will, I fear, be left out in the cold when the Packet leaves.

I enjoyed my trip to Dunvegan very much. Both Mr. & Mrs. McDougall were extremely kind to me. I am quite in love with the place which

Floating down Peace River on a raft. (Edgelow Family Collection) Edgelow 8

is I think the prettiest I have seen in the Country. It is in the valley of the Peace River which is a fine river like the Saskatchewan only the banks are more precipitous & the current swifter & the river itself deeper than the Saskn. Dunvegan is shut in by hills 600 feet high so that at this season not much is seen of the sun. I traveled about 70 miles up the river and was delighted with the scenery the whole way.

I was only on the prairie once and that was just above the Fort. It is a beautiful country & nearly all prairie, clear to the foot of the mountains which however are too far off to be visible, but for all that there are mountain ranges so [-called] which enhance the beauty of the view.

No doubt Peace River will some day boast a dense population, but not I fancy for years to come as the means of getting into it are very limited. In fact it is about impossible to get there with an outfit for farming as this is the only route to it at present and as there are no traveling facilities except such as the Co. possess. I think private parties would find it very inconvenient & expensive to go there at present.

When on the road to & from Dunvegan I was much delayed by the extreme mildness of the weather. I have often told you I am sure that dogs cannot travel well in warm weather. It rained the day I left here and the next 3 days were very mild so that we could only make about 15 miles per diem but when the weather got a little sharper we got along better & when we returned the weather tho colder than going was still too mild for good traveling.

I am thankful to say that I found Harriet & the little ones quite well. Baby has grown a great deal. [...]

We have not yet given her a name but Mrs. McD. as good as asked us to call her Jessie after her and as it is a pretty name & so to speak uncommon I think we will call her by that name. [...]

Perhaps in a couple of years if I am spared my rotation of furlough may come round—at present I could not really afford a trip to Canada even should I be able to get away. I have a deal of work to do here for the next two or three years if I am spared & retain my present charge. [...]

W Edward Traill

[...]

LESSER SLAVE LAKE *July 2, 1882*

My dear Annie

Your kind and very welcome letter of 9th Feb. came to hand about a fortnight ago and as the boats will be starting in a few days I shall try and have a few lines in readiness. [...]

Your letter you see was a long time on the road. In winter it will always be so but in summer there are parties going backwards & forwards so that we get many chances of sending letters. It may be that some of your letters go astray but I think they all come to hand sooner or later. It is little matter about address as so long as they are directed to care of HBC or HBC Service they are bound to find me sooner or later. [...]

As you are perhaps aware I am alone. Harriet & the children are off to Winnipeg. Walter is to go to school there.[7] I had as you know intended sending them to Lakefield but the first reply I got from Kate gave me no encouragement and before I could hear again I had to come to some conclusion so decided to send Walter to St John's & keep Willie for a year or two longer.

As you can imagine I feel pretty dull without them. We have no neighbours and were it not for the amount of work I have to do I should be intolerably dull but they have now been absent a month and I have not found the time wearisome. [...] I hope H- will be able to join me this fall but am by no means sure. [...]

If I go home to Canada in a year or two I must really get one of my nieces as a companion to Harriet. It is very dull for her to be shut up all the time without company more especially if Walter is not with her. She frets about the children when absent. [...]

In a letter that Harriet got from Mrs. McMurray she says "You will be surprised to hear that Walter Traill who used to be such a friend of the family never comes near us now. All his old friends make the same complaint of him."

Many people are making money very fast in this country speculating in land etc. I am not one of the number but it don't fret me in the least. I do not think that Walter's wealth has added to his happiness. So long as I can give my dear ones a fair education and provide for them while they are dependent on me I shall be content and if I have good health I have not a doubt of being able to do that. [...]

W Edward Traill

LESSER SLAVE LAKE *December 10, 1882*

Dear Annie

My second who is an English half-breed is a very nice fellow and the children are very fond of him, especially Ethel who calls him her old

man. We miss him very much when away. He is absent just now at Dunvegan. We are expecting Doctor MacKay[8] from Dunvegan. He promised
to come and pass Xmas with us—and was to bring with him Mr. Brick a
missionary and by far the best preacher it has been my privilege to hear
since I left home. […]

   Willie

LESSER SLAVE LAKE *April 22, 1883*

Dear Kate

[…] Willie is going to school to the priests for an hour a day. He does
not learn well at home although it is not that he is stupid. He will learn
well & fast with strangers. I suppose we shall have to send him to school
with his brother soon but it is expensive paying $200.00 apiece for boys
of his age besides clothing them. I propose going off in day or two on a
beaver hunt but whether I kill a beaver or no means to be proved. I will
go overland about 20 miles to Heart River whither I have sent a canoe
and will float down to this lake which will take me 3 or 4 days as the
River is very crooked…

   The C P R will be at least 600 miles from this place for many years till
there is a branch running to Peace River.[9] […] [end missing]

   W E Traill

LESSER SLAVE LAKE *July 9, 1883*

My dear Mary

It was very kind & brotherly of Walter to act as he did. As you say his
behavior to you cannot be want of affection, but he always was queer.
   His silence to me grieves me but I must wait patiently & hope that
times will mend matters. You will be glad to hear that we have now
heard twice from our son Walter. The last was written on the 1st June

and I am proud of it. He is so thoughtful & affectionate——I will give you a part of it just as he writes misspelling and all.

W.E. Traill

My dear Mother

I hope that you are quite well and my dear brother & Sisters. I will soon be over with my examination. I am glad that the hollidays are coming. We will set off on the 7th of June.

There are a good many boys at College just now——Alex McFarlane is sick (son of C F Mcfarlane[10]). I will go down to Mrs. McMurrays tomorrow because it is Saturday. I saw Mr. & Mrs. McDougall they came to see me and they promised to come and see me again before they left. I have two big scars one just above my eyes and one below but I don't feel them now. I got a book from my dear Grandmama Traill that she wrote. It is called lost in the back woods——it is a verry good but I dont know what her address is and so I can never write to her. I wish you would tell me her address; I hope that my dear little sisters Ethel & Jessie are quite well it is nice now to look at the boys playing cricket but I cannot enjoy myself when I play it the boys had a nice time on the 18th of May because it was the Bishops birthday they had all manner of sports but I was very lazy to play. I am going down to Mrs. McMurrays with three Boys, Ned, Fred & George Camsell they are all brothers & I like them very much. We will have an examination on Monday both morning & evening. I am expecting a letter from you it is about three months since I got a letter from you the male is going off tomorrow and this will be the last chance of writing for three weeks there is going to be a match but at Stonewall against the Stonewall Club. We have no Study this evening and so we have lots of fun. I only wish to have Willie at this College now I can never forget him when I see the boys playing and my dear little sisters Ethel

& Jessie give them my love and many sweet kisses for me. I
hope that dear papa's throat is getting better. I hope that this
letter will reach you in safety and now good by my dear &
sweetest Mother. I always think of your words & I do all I can
to fulfill them. from your dear Son W Traill

The erasures are all mine. Don't you think it is a nice letter for a boy
with so few advantages as my Walter. [...]

I was very foolish to speak so confidently of my chances of getting
away this coming fall. I fear there is little chance. Unless my turn comes
up by rotation, there is none. We are badly officered in this district and
it is not easy for anyone to get a furlough unless in his turn. [...]

Willie is beginning to learn better. He is growing amazingly fast. I
shall have to send him to College next year I suppose but I am against
parting with him so young besides which the strain on my pocket will
not be light, as Walter costs me about $300.00 per annum including his
clothes. [...]

W E Traill

[...]

LESSER SLAVE LAKE *July, 15, 1883*

My dear Mother

In a week or two more we will hear from Council. I fear there is no
chance of a furlough for me [...]

We have not heard from Walter since my last date but I had a letter from the Bishop enclosing College report. He speaks of Walter in
the highest terms. And the report is very favourable. The Deputy Head
Master wrote me a kind note speaking very highly of my son. He says he
gives the greatest satisfaction both in conduct & progress & that he is
one of the nicest boys at St John's. He took one first prize for progress
in religious instruction.

HBC office at Lesser Slave Lake. Photo 1906. HBCA 1987/363–L–20/3

I have just written to the Bishop & have applied for admission for Willie next year.

I hear that Mr. McDougall have been appointed to Edmonton so he will not come back to Peace River. Dr. MacKay I presume will be in charge of the Dist—It little matters to me as I am left almost entirely to my own resources & devices. [...]

WE Traill

[...]

LESSER SLAVE LAKE *August 26, 1883*

My dear Annie

[...] I am quite alone just now. Harriet is off on an excursion down the lake about 50 miles—We have no fruit of any kind in the neighbour-hood and she has gone with the children to try & get cranberries etc. She left on Wednesday last & will not be home for a week yet. I was to have gone with them had I had time but I found myself unable to absent myself even for a day. [...]

I think it is probable I shall send Willie next year but can hardly afford it as the two would cost me well on to $500 per annum not to speak of the expense of sending them down & clothing them. [...]

It is very strange that we have not heard from Council who is to succeed McDougall who has taken the place of Hardisty at Edmonton. [...] These things are of great interest to us HBC people as also the appointments throughout the service & before all the promotions [...]

Could you manage to get and send to me a little wild rice for seed? I am very anxious to try it in this lake which has a muddy bottom and just the place for it—I would be glad even if a pound which could come by express but of course it must not be parched. I will enclose a dollar to buy it with & pay postage. I should like to have it as soon as possible so as to sow in fall or early spring. [...]

W E Traill

LESSER SLAVE LAKE *February 10, 1884*

Dear Annie

[...] I do not know what I could have wrote that made you all think I might have been going home last summer. The will is not wanting but to get furlough out of rotation is another thing. At any rate no furloughs are granted in the summer nowadays to those whose lot is cast in the interior districts. I find that there is no chance of my getting away till the fall of 1885 when my turn should come by rotation. Unless sickness compels me to go before which (God forbid) there is no other chance of my visiting Canada before. [...]

The Packet brought us the sad news of the very sudden death of my worthy father in law.[11] *He came up to Edmonton to spend Xmas & New Year and take home a daughter of Mr. Clarke who was spending some time with the McDougall's. On Xmas day he was invited to dinner down at the Fort along with Miss Clarke. After dinner they walked up the hill to Mr. McDougall's house. He was talking about Mrs. McKay all the*

Chief Factor William McKay, Willie Traill's father-in-law, in charge of Fort Pitt, c. 1883. He died the same year during a visit to Edmonton. GAA NA–1193–5

way. On entering Mr. McDougall's room he lay down on the sofa. Mr. Hardisty noticed something wrong with him and went to him & found that he had great difficulty breathing & that he could not speak. They laid him on the carpet beside the sofa & sent for the doctor but nothing could be done for him. He expired without being able to utter a word. His son Joe was at the Fort but I presume was not by when he died.

His death is a great blow to Harriet who was very deeply attached to her father—indeed all his children were very devoted to him as well they might. I never came across so kind and indulgent a father.

Poor Mrs. McKay will feel her loss very keenly. They had lived together nearly 30 years & were very much attached to each other.

I can enter in deep sympathy with the whole family as I was very much attached to Mr. McKay.

To turn to more cheerful topics, the children I am thankful to say are all well except for a cough which is prevalent just now and of which old and young are getting a share.

The baby is now two and a half months old and very big and healthy.[12] She is much more amiable than at first. The others are all very fond of her. Jessie soon got over her jealousy and is as fond of baby as the rest.

We did not hear from our son by the packet but we had letters from Mr. McMurray & the Bishop. We also received a packet of his photographs which are very good but all are expended. He appears to have grown a deal since he left us. [...]

The account you gave of our nephews Dick, Tom & Earnest I am glad to hear that they are growing up so steady. [...]

I am much concerned to hear that Clinton's health does not improve. I fear he has to work too hard. If he could afford a holiday, a trip to the northwest would do him good but I fear farmers are like HB officers— they can ill afford to leave their work.

You must enjoy a visit with Clinton Jr. I envy you in the musical talents of your family. My children have no more ear than I have myself which as you know is not saying much.

Harriet too has very little ear. I hope my sons will grow up as steady as yours. [...]

I am going to start for Dunvegan in a few days—I will be absent about a fortnight. Harriet is very dull these times and will be very lonely while I am off. [...]

My dear Annie Your loving brother
WE Traill

2nd March I have just returned from Dunvegan. Had a very cold trip for a week, the thermometer never rose above 40 below zero. Sometimes it was down to 56. Found H- & the children all well.

LESSER SLAVE LAKE *September 8, 1884*

Dear Annie

[...] We seem to be more cut off from the world now than ever but I suppose it is only because it is only here that things are altogether at a standstill, for elsewhere the country is filling up and getting more civilized daily but after all I do not think we lose so much as we are apt to suppose.

So far as I saw when at Edmonton the class of people that are coming to the country are not such as we care for as neighbours. Our Canadians are well enough at home but as a rule the farming and mechanical class are not desirable society when from home. Even the word Ontario when spoken with a nasal twang irritates me. I never could reconcile myself to the change from our Canada of old. [...]

We have just heard from our son Walter. He has won two prizes at St Johns; one for French, one for religious instruction. He also won a prize for a foot race. No doubt he is prouder of the later prize than of the others.

There is a good deal in the papers about Indian troubles. I do not think there is any great fear, certainly not for HB people. If an Indian war ever takes place, I think the Govt officials & Police Officers & Indian Department officials will be the cause & will be the first & greatest sufferers.

Our dear mother seems to keep her health & memory remarkably well. I cannot perceive any falling off of either. [...]

W E Traill

LESSER SLAVE LAKE *May 24, 1885*

My dear Mother

[...] We have just received startling news from the Saskatchewan of a half-breed and Indian uprising[13]—news that no doubt is old to you, but which we have only just learned and that only by rumour as not a letter has been received.

I hope you are not in any way anxious for me or mine because there is no cause.

Any disturbance in the Saskatchewan will not affect us more than perhaps to interrupt communication for a short while. The Indians may for a short while commit depredations but the whites are a power now in the land & with the facilities that they now have for the [movement] of troops any trouble must be shortly quelled. We can bear hardly a guess as to what has been going on, as they have cut all the telegraph lines and all kinds of rumours are afloat in the upper Saskatchewan. It is said that some of the RC Clergy have been killed and others in the hands of Riel. I expect to receive a packet in a few days when I trust we will learn the truth.

Harriet is naturally anxious about her mother & brothers & sister who being in Prince Albert are likely she thinks to suffer, but I cannot think that the Prince Albert settlement are not able to defend them- selves and Mr. McKay's family were so well known & very popular both with the Indians & half-breeds that I think they should be quite safe.[14]

I am pretty sure that had Mr. McKay been alive he would have been able to restrain Big Bear from any excess.[15]

So many rumours have been started in the past that it is hardly pos- sible to [give] credence to half of what is said.

It is singular that Mr. McDougall in Edmonton has not sent me any word, which makes me think that he does not credit in full the reports flying about.

Enough about a subject on which you are doubtless better informed than I am altho so far distant. [...]

I have put off finishing this from day to day expecting to hear definite word from the seat of war. [...] I have to send off my boats tomorrow which I did not count upon which entails a considerable amount of work. [...]

I am greatly relieved to hear that the report concerning the murder of William my brother in law was untrue. You have no doubt heard of the pillage of my old charge Lac La Biche and the flight of Mr. & Mrs. Young & family. Young had a narrow escape. He was absent at the time of the sack of his Fort and was watched by a band of my old Indians for three days. They at last thought he had taken another road & so left. When he passed the place their fire was burning still brightly altho it was raining at the time.

I might remark that he was very unpopular with the Indians there.

I hardly think my life would have been in danger had I been there but it is hard to count on Indians when once their blood is up.

I am most thankful to God that I was removed more especially on Harriet's account as she is very much afraid of Indians. [...]

I have not yet had time to look at the papers more than to glance at the very latest. By it I see that Riel has given himself up but that will have very little effect on the war. He has started a fire over which he had no control from the first. I hope that he may reap the just reward of his crime. Were it not for a corrupt government and an intriguing church he would never have got clear the first time & this war would most likely have been avoided.

The Government is greatly to blame for not redressing the wrongs of the half-breeds before. As for the Indians they have been treated pretty well, but there have been a great many promises made them which have not been fulfilled, not treaty promises but promises made from time to time since. I do not think that the agents are guilty parties as some correspondents write. I have watched the Indians & their agents pretty closely and am sure that the agents were blameless. Dewdney & Wadsworth are the parties who should be saddled with the blame but that will no doubt be fully demonstrated later.

I fear this disturbance will drag on most of the summer but as to the final results there can be no question. The chief brunt of the affair falls on the settlers and private individuals who are forced to abandon their homes & property. The Indians themselves will bitterly rue the

HBC post on *Lesser Slave Lake. Photo by McConnell*, c. *1888.* GAA NA–1162–2

day even tho the government grant them a free pardon for all their
misdoings.

I fancy had Mr. McKay been alive he would have been able to sway
Big Bear as he had a great influence over him and all his band, but perhaps it is a mercy that he was taken before this outbreak. It would have
grieved him much on account of the Indians whose welfare he studied
& strove for. There was more than one occasion where the Police &
the Indians were nearly breaking the peace where Mr. McKay used his
influence with both parties. No doubt had the police fired then on the
Indians, they would have precipitated the war that is now raging & fire
they may have done had it not been for him.

[…]

WE Traill

LESSER SLAVE LAKE *September 20, 1885*

My dear Kate

[…] I would have written more often this summer but was always in
hopes of obtaining furlough, but now that there is little hope of my
being able to leave this winter I will write to let you know I always

entertained good hopes until lately but avoided saying so as I know how much disappointed you would all be if I failed to get away.

I have leave from the Commissioner subject however to Dr. MacKay's approval, but altho he authorized me to apply to the Commissioner now he tells me that I cannot go. I will however most likely get leave in spring. I need not say how disgusted I am as I had set my heart on going this fall. Harriet too is very much put out, however it may be for the best as she certainly could not have gone with me to Canada this winter as if all goes well she will add one to the population of the North West sometime during the winter.

Owing to the shabby way that Dr. MacKay has treated me[16] I have been obliged to make application to be moved from this district. Of course I will only receive the Comr's reply in winter and I cannot get a change of appointment until next summer.

It is too bad to have to shift camp after having the trouble of building a good house to live in, but I will put up with anything sooner then serve under such a man. [...]

You will have learned by the papers all about the State trials of Riel & his confreres long before we do. True we know the results of Riel's trial but do not know whether he was reprieved or not. I rather think he will not be hung although I think he deserved it. [...]

We never hear from our son Walter which is very strange but we continually receive flattering reports of him from the Bishop & Head Master and others. He took 1st prize in French.

The Bishop says he has not brilliant talents but has perseverance & industry with a good disposition, in fact all the attributes that build up the character to a good & useful man.

The McKays you read of in the papers are my brothers in law. Cannon McKay is George William, who rescued some of the women [and] is the one who was reported to have been found murdered soon after the outbreak. Thomas & James are all Harriet's brothers & Joseph the interpreter is either their uncle or cousin. [...]

WE Traill

Seven

FORT VERMILION
1886–1889

IN 1886, WILLIE RECEIVED A FURLOUGH—his second holiday in twenty-two years. With more than six months leave he was at last able to enjoy some long-awaited visits with family members. The first letters in this chapter were written near the end of his journey.

Willie had applied for a new post because of his poor relationship with Dr. MacKay. He arrived, albeit somewhat reluctantly, at Fort Vermilion, on the north bank of the Peace River, on August 27, 1886, to take up his new post as Chief Trader in Charge.[1] He found the post to be in very poor condition.

Fort Vermilion was the Traills' penultimate post. Notwithstanding its dilapidated state and remote location it would be, in many respects, their best posting. Two more daughters—Marie ("Yummie") and Harriet—joined their swelling ranks. The family withstood another whooping cough epidemic.

Willie's devout religious faith and the frequent wish for sympathetic and convivial neighbours was more than fulfilled by the presence of Bishop Young and Reverend Scott and their charming families. To his delight, Willie was invited to act as a lay delegate to an annual Anglican Synod. Willie's wish that son Walter might join the missionary service lay on fallow ground.

During Willie's tenure, the region experienced reasonable fur harvests. Paradoxically, mild winters with little snow had an adverse effect on moose hunting. In addition, the post survived a major flood in 1888. The success of Willie's performance at Vermilion is evidenced by his subsequent transfer to Fort St. James, in charge of New Caledonia District.

My dear Kit Kat[2]

I received your kind and interesting letter yesterday and will drop you a few lines in reply. I only got home yesterday by the train. I enjoyed myself very much at Ottawa but am glad to be home.

I was down at Montreal & saw Clin who is quite well again. We went together to the Browns and had teas & stayed till 8 o'clock and then went to the Hutchisons and spent the rest of the evening, only going home at midnight.

I fear I cannot go down to the sale as it is too far to walk and I have no other way of getting down. If your father wants me very much he could send up Clin or Mr. Drayton for me & then I would drive your mother up, but I do not see what good I could do and I am sure you will have plenty to cook for without me.

I am pleased to find the girls all here & looking so well. I walked up yesterday with Annie & Bapsie and we all came down together.

I believe Eva is to be up next week.

I shall be so glad when you are all here together. […]

I have very little more than a month to remain in Canada now. I regret the time I lost when in Ottawa & Montreal. […]

I was at the theatre three times when in Ottawa. The Mikado which is a comic opera by a Japanese troop was splendid. I also went to an Oratorio "Handel's Messiah" but was disappointed in it.

I was at one party when in Ottawa. I went in full dress. You cannot imagine what a pompous looking old cuss I looked. […]

Believe me my own dear little Kitten Katten Your loving old Uncle.
WE Traill

Dear Annie

[…] Walter left yesterday for Crookston where he has a contract but was to have been home today. He did not return but wrote to say that the manager he went to see had not come. He promises to be home tomorrow. I propose going to Winnipeg on Monday unless ordered sooner. […]

We had a couple of nights hard frost here, but luckily the oats are not yet up & the barley not sown else they would have sustained considerable damage. […]

I am sure everything looks lovely with you. Here there are no trees but oaks & they are not yet in leaf. South of this the country is almost under water. Lots of settlers houses standing in water so that they have not a dry foot of ground near their houses. The river here is rising fast but I do not think there is any danger of a flood as the land here is pretty high.

I like Mary very much. She makes Walter an excellent wife. If he were half as careful as she is he would be much better off. He makes lots of money but does not take the best care of it. He is very happy in his domestic affairs and very fond of Cora & Hardisty [Mary's children, Walter's stepchildren].

Cora is very lively. I fear however she is not strong. She is very slight and pale.

Their house is very small. I sleep in the servant girl's room and she sleeps in an invalid's chair. Mary is a marvel as a housekeeper & gardener. Walter does not kill himself with work altho he is kept pretty busy. He is very domestic. […]

I see by the papers that the HBC are intending building a steamboat on the Athabasca this summer. I did not think they would do anything toward it until winter. I hope when I next write to be able to say whether I go back to my old quarters or elsewhere but I presume it will be the same old Post. […]

W E Traill

The Queen's, O'Connor & Brown, Proprietors
Dear Kit Kat

[…] I have now to tell you a piece of news which will not be so agreeable. I have just got orders to take charge of Vermilion which you will
find is about 200 miles further north than my last charge and about 3
weeks farther off as far as time is concerned. I fear Harriet will not be
overjoyed at the change however in our service there is no help for it.

[…]
W.E. Traill
P. S. I saw Hargrave today for a few minutes. I am staying here with
several other HB Officials one of whom succeeds me at Slave Lake. Mr.
Moberly who has been in charge for many years at Vermilion goes out
on furlough and I do not know where he will go afterwards. My address
will be Vermilion Lower Peace River.

WE Traill

FORT VERMILION *August 29, 1886*

Dearest Kitten Katten

[…] At the same time I have no leisure for letter writing just now as
I only arrived the day before yesterday & this being a new place my
whole time is taken up in interviewing the natives and looking into
business matters: besides which I have to leave tomorrow for Fort
Chipewyan[3] which is the head of the District & is about 300 miles from
here. I expect to be absent at least 25 days. We go by canoe. I shall have
the company of a brother officer & a Bishop. […]

Our present quarters are very wretched. The roof does not keep out
the rain and the floor is rotten & uneven & the windows patched & dirty
and the plan of the house which is only one story is the most inconve-

nient that ever was constructed. To go from the office to the kitchen you must pass through every room in the house.

I intend to build a new house as soon as I can do so, but there is much to be done before I can commence & I have no carpenter.

This was at one time the best post in this part of the country, but through mismanagement it has run down to one of the poorest and I am sent here to see if it cannot be pulled out of the mire. If I succeed it will be to my credit but the job is not one that I like & will be attended with many discomforts. I do not mind for myself but your aunt will be the chief sufferer. She is reconciled on account of being near a school & Mission and there are a few English speaking people in the neighbour-hood. The Bishop is a nice man. So also is Mr. Scott a missionary.[4] We have not heard from Walter since we left him at P. Albert and conse-quently are anxious to hear from him. [...]

Bishop Young came out in the same ship with a gentleman going to Lakefield. I think it must have been the young fellow who came to the Lefevres. Ask him. I forget the name. [...]

Address your letters from this time until spring via Carlton & Green Lake so that they may not be sent to Slave Lake where they would remain until next summer. In spring they had better go via Calgary & Edmonton.

I must now close as I promised to visit some of the missionaries this afternoon as it is my only chance before leaving for Chipewyan.

With much love to you all and to my dear Willie believe me Your loving Uncle
W E Traill

FORT VERMILION *August 29, 1886*

My dear Mother

[...] We had a fair passage from L S L to Forks and from thence we came by a flat boat heavily laden so much so that we had very little room to stow ourselves. We fortunately had fair weather. Had the weather been wet, we would have been most uncomfortable. We floated down the stream only using the oars to keep in the current. Where the river was safe we floated at night. We killed two bears on the trip and found the meat very acceptable after living on salt provisions for a long time.

We found this establishment wretched in the extreme so that I have to go to work and build as was the case at LLB & LS Lake & I suppose when I get things into ship shape I shall have to leave for some other tumble down place to set it in order. [...]

We all went to church today & met our future neighbours. I think there are a few with whom we can associate.

My brother in law Joe accompanied us and will either remain here or at some outpost in the neighbourhood.

I hope to have some sport going down to Chipewyan as there is a good chance of bear, moose & other game. We go by canoe, I say we for Mr. McKenzie a brother officer goes with me. He is good company but is somewhat of an Indian. [...]

The weather is getting cooler and there have been one or two light frosts already. You will see by the map that I am far north of my old Post and consequently winter will be earlier. The crops of barley & potatoes are good this year but there is no vegetable garden this year. It is not fair for an officer to leave his post so bare for his successor but I have been treated in the same way before. [...]

WE Traill

[...]

FORT CHIPEWYAN *September 14, 1886*

Dear Kate

[...] The distance between this place and Vermilion by water is nearly 300 miles & the opportunities for forwarding mails are not frequent. If letters come here after June there will be no chance of forwarding until fall so that after 1st May any letters you write must be addressed via Calgary & Edmonton. […]

We had anything but a pleasant trip down from Vermilion having to [lie] by three days with wind. The last day we were lying within sight of the Fort. We had no sport to speak of. I killed a few geese & white wavies or brants which were an agreeable addition to our bill of fare.

I expected to remain here not more than a couple of days but Mr. Ross is not at home & will not be here for a week yet so that I am constrained to wait for him. I have only once met him and that was for a few minutes 10 years ago, so that I do not know how I shall like him. Mrs. & Miss Ross are here. I like Miss Ross very well. She is a nice lively girl & very amiable.

I did not stay long enough at Vermilion to see anything of our neighbours. Lawrence the Mission farmer is a married man & so is his brother. Both of them Canadian farmers and altho not just the kind of society we would desire it will be agreeable to have English speaking neighbours. Mr. Scott the Missionary is also a family man. Bishop Young's family will only join him next summer.

Vermilion was at one time one of the best Posts in the N.W. but has been allowed to run down to such an extent that it is at present one of the worst. If however Mr. Ross gives me my own way I hope in a few years to work a change and make it a profitable & desirable Post. In the meantime however we shall have to endure a deal of inconvenience & possibly privateness. […]

I suppose you know that we have a steamboat on the Athabasca which runs up to Fort McMurray & down to Smith—it can & has been up to the foot of the falls 60 miles below my Post but it will seldom go there as my outfit comes in by way of Slave Lake—the route I followed this summer. We have also a steamer on the McKenzie running from Salt River or Ft Smith down to the coast if necessary.

Next year we are to have one on the Athabasca at the "landing" down to Grand Rapids so that we will soon have all the waterways open, when it will be no great undertaking to come from Ontario to any part of this country & not a whole summer's journey as has been the case with me. [...]

My own health has been excellent. I have entirely got over my illness of last summer.

H- is in very fair health. She has stood the fatigue of travelling very well indeed. She will be getting anxious for me long before I get back for I did not expect to be so long from home.

I have gathered a few ferns on my way—will enclose some. I have no way of pressing them so they are in a rough state. I hope by damping them you can press them as they should be done. Perhaps mother will find some with which she is unacquainted. They are all rock ferns. [...]

This summer has passed away like a dream. I must now settle down to hard work after nearly twelve months holiday. With fond love to mother believe me my dear Kate

Your loving brother
WE Traill

FORT VERMILION [*September 1886*]

Dear Mother

[...] Harriet & I are not a little exercised as to the future of our boys. It has been my earnest desire that he [Walter] should have studied for the church as a missionary but so far that does not seem to be his desire. We can but commend him to our Heavenly father. If it is in his counsel that he should be a Missionary he will no doubt call him to the work. [...]

The spring as you know was late & seeding backward but on the whole we have splendid crops & a beautiful garden. We have had all the vegetables we could use including peas, carrots onions, lettuce, beets, radishes etc. Pumpkins & squash & beans were frozen on the 2nd of August. The potatoes were touched but we have a splendid crop for all. Our cauliflowers would make your mouth water. [...]

Harriet is busy as usual. She is a great favourite with Mrs. Young &
the Scotts.

Mrs. Young says of Harriet I believe Mr. & Mrs. Traill's whole
thoughts are on in what way they can give pleasure to others. Certainly
this is true of Harriet as she delights in doing little kindnesses to all
whether they be rich or whether they be poor. She has received much
benefit from the recent revival amongst us. [...]

W.E. Traill

FORT VERMILION *October 8, 1886*

Dear Mother

Just a line by the present unexpected chance to say that I got back from
Athabasca yesterday from a tedious trip of 3 days to find all the children
down with whooping cough and little Maria[5] very dangerously ill with it.
We are both very much afraid that we are going to lose our little darling,
but we are not without hope in the mercy of our heavenly father who
will assuredly do what is right.

The week after I left they all caught it, first the two elder ones &
later on the two younger. The two eldest were pretty bad & still cough a
great deal but they are evidently improving. Little Mary is also we think
improving but little Maria is in hourly peril—still we hope for the best.

I do not know what H- would have done had it not been for her
brother Joe who is with us and who sat up night after night with
her attending to the little ones. They are all very fond of Uncle Joe.

I had Bishop Young & A. McKenzie for my traveling companions to
Chipewyan & back. I like the Bishop exceedingly. His wife will join him
next year which will be very nice for H-. The Rev Mr. Scott & his wife
are both very nice people & we find them good neighbours. [...]

We have just heard that the whooping cough is very bad at Slave
Lake & that a great many deaths have already occurred.

On my way back from Chipewyan we were delayed two days by a heavy snow fall. We had to shovel away about a foot of snow whenever we went ashore to cook or sleep. [...]

While staying at Chipewyan waiting for Mr. Ross I went out for a couple of days shooting and killed 75 geese & wavies. Altogether myself & two men killed 94 and a few ducks. It was the best sport I ever had in my life. The gun I had with me at Lakefield is the best I ever shot with.

We have fair prospect of a comfortable winter as regards grub as moose are unusually numerous & we have some flour & 300 bags [of] potatoes & some barley. Starvation for years past has been the rule here and the grossest mismanagement has reduced this Post, which with exception perhaps of S.L. was the best in the North West to a perfect ruin. [...]

WE Traill

[...]

FORT VERMILION *December 10, 1886*

Dearest Mary

[...] Since I last wrote you we have had a world of trouble. The whooping cough broke out but a week after we got here and gave us a hard spell of it and just as the children were recovering the measles broke out so we have hardly ever been able to undress. Little Maria was very low with the first but recovered. The measles with her led to bronchitis. She lay for about 10 days on the balance between life & death, but I am thankful to say she is mending slowly altho far from being out of danger.

We have had to watch by her cradle night and day for about 3 weeks hardly expecting her to see morning—in fact several times we thought she was just expiring. Surely we have great cause of thankfulness for her recovery. We will always look on her as restored from the dead—if she recovers.

At Slave Lake there is hardly a family if there is one who has not lost one or more members—some families have lost all their children. When we last heard Dr. MacKay had lost one of his youngest and one of the others was very ill. Things have been going from bad to worse since I left there. [...]

You are right in saying that my Willie's greatest fault is want of reverence. It seemed born with him in that he closely resembles his Uncle Gilbert. I am so pleased that you are all so fond of him. Had I known a little sooner that [we] were coming here I do not think we would have parted with him. There is a school here, but I fear it is not one that would have suited Willie, and as for leaving him at Prince Albert to go to school neither of us would have thought of it. His cousins the Clarkes' and Tom McKay's children are a lot of badly trained youngsters. In fact they all run wild and would soon have made Willie as bad as themselves. Whereas with the Atwoods I know he will be well taken care of and his morals and manners closely watched.

I am glad that his Majesty acquitted himself so well at School.

There is not a house or tent in the neighbourhood where there is not measles so you can imagine that our Society is not very lively just now. [...]

WE Traill

[...]

FORT VERMILION *January, 20, 1887*

My dear Mother

[...] It is a very hard winter for the Indians as all fine winters are in this country as they are unable to hunt moose for want of snow & wind. [...]

We have had a pleasant winter so far. The greatest cold was -44 degrees. Very little snow till last week but now we have quite a lot. We have not received a pound of moose meat since Septr. We had to kill a horse today to feed the Packet dogs upon. I fear other horses will have

Cree or Beaver tipis at Fort Vermilion, where Willie Traill was Chief Trader in Charge from 1884 to 1889. Photo taken c. 1899. GAA NA–949–37

to go ere long. Don't be alarmed for us as we have lots of flour and cattle. […]

WE Traill

FORT VERMILION *January 21, 1887*

Dear Mary

[…] Mary is as fat as a seal and full of chat as a magpie. She is most amusing. She remembers everything she hears and can repeat whole verses of hymns and sings them in a fashion. She [jumbles] them up together in a most comical way. She is evidently the cleverest of them all.

I never told you about a little episode that took place in my journey from Winnipeg to [Qu'Appelle].

I was in the smoking car with Hon. John Norquay, Mr. Bridges and a lot of others when a young Englishman, evidently just out, turned to Mr. Bridges and said to him

"Did you hear of that most atrocious act of the HBC? The most cruel & atrocious thing I ever heard of. I mean killing & stuffing of Eskimo Dogs to send home to the Exhibition" with further comments not complimentary to the HBC. I felt riled but kept cool & turned to Mr. Norquay & said to him, "Mr. Norquay do you know what the Company's real intentions are in that matter? I am now underway for Peace River where the Beaver Indians are all heavily indebted to the Co & cannot pay. My orders are to kill & stuff two of them to send home as drivers to complete the outfit."

Our Englishman began to study the country through the windows while the Company enjoyed the joke exceedingly. Our friend evidently very uncomfortable and finally disappeared and I never saw him again. [...]

WE Traill

FORT VERMILION *March 27, 1887*

My dear Mother

I have a chance of sending off a letter or two by a priest who leaves on foot tomorrow for Dunvegan. As every ounce makes a difference to a man carrying his bedding and provisions for a distance of nearly three hundred miles I can only [send] two or three letters. [...]

It may be that this letter will only reach you about the same time as there is no communication between Slave Lake & Edmonton before 1st June as a usual thing, but as they are building a steamer at Athabasca Landing I think there may be a chance of forwarding letters. [...]

I find that I am obliged to withdraw Walter from College. He will leave about the 1st June after examinations. As he cannot get through until fall he will stay in Winnipeg part of the time & spend the rest of the time with his uncle at Pembina until Bishop Young leaves in August when he will accompany the party. [...]

I intend to keep Walter at home for one winter, during which time I must interest some of my friends in his behalf to find him a situation. He has had a pretty fair show and if he can get a good place I doubt not will do well as he has great steadiness & perseverance which is all that is wanted to ensure success.

I wish I could afford to send him to you on a visit, but I must retrench for some time to come. [...]

Little Yum Yum is quite smart now & fat.

She creeps all over and will walk soon if not thrown back—She is the first of ours who has not walked under a year, but then her sickness kept her weak so long. She is full of fun but cannot speak a word yet whereas Mary talks enough for three. Her memory is something more than ordinary. She knows several hymns and learns her Sunday school lessons almost as well as Ethel & better than Jessie. She can count in French but neither she nor Jessie knows Cree although Jessie was a thorough Cree before leaving Slave Lake a year & a half ago. [...]

Your loving son Wandering Spirit [...]

FORT VERMILION *May, 15, 1887*

Dear Annie

[...] You cannot believe how full my hands are just now as I have taken the roof off my house and have added another story above which will greatly improve the house & give us double the room we had formerly.

Just as soon as the roof [was] off we had a spell of very bad weather. Rain & snow which put us out very much & at the same time delayed the work, however I have just finished the roof and now I do not care what weather we may have, but it will be a long time before I finish the inside as I must be my own carpenter. [...]

I had a long letter from Uncle Walter yesterday. He writes in good spirits. Cora was ill again but recovering. He has sold his interest in the

Northcote farm. His crop was 18,800 bushels wheat from 1000 acres or 18 B's per acre. On the whole it was good for such a dry season. [...]

WE Traill

Dear Nan [Annie][6]

[...] I am much concerned at mother's continued ill health. I trust the spring weather will do her good as it generally does. The severe winter you have had seems to have been very hard upon her.

Kate is so thankful for your giving her so much help either by your own presence or that of her nieces. She is as ever [loud] in their praise, in fact if she did not temper her admiration by more or less advice in which she delights she would run a great chance of spoiling them. Dear Kate she has a hard time of it. I am so glad that she has had better health of late, otherwise the anxiety of mother's illness would be too much for her. [...]

I am sure Clin misses his son very much. I hope Willie will be most attentive to his uncle who seems to be fond of him. [...]

I think after all I will allow Walter to remain still at St Johns. He desires it so much & is getting on so well but what to do with him I do not know. He talks of going in for Modern Languages. I believe that is his strong point as mathematics is his weak one.

Harriet was looking forward to his being with us this winter. [...]

Bishop Young has a family but he only proposes bringing out the two youngest. [...]

There has been a dreadful case of starvation & cannibalism at Little Red River 60 miles below this. The whole camp was reduced to such straights [straits] that some died & the survivors ate the dead from which they went on to kill & eat one another until there were only two women left out of a camp of 29. At last one killed & ate the other. She is now a prisoner & I think they have most likely taken her on board the steamer & will take her out to Edmonton.

The Commissioner, his staff passed here a few days ago. The steamer Grahame came up to the falls to meet him. Mr. McDougall left the boat there & came here to meet the C C.

It was he that was in charge of Peace River when first I took charge of Slave Lake. [...]

I am glad that Walter has written to mother again. You must all remember that he is very busy & is from home much of the time. [...]

Little Mary does not like her sisters going to school. Yum Yum is too small to amuse her much and she mopes a good deal during their absence & is quite delighted when they return. [...]

W E Traill

FORT VERMILION *June 20, 1887*

Dear Mother

[...] The Commissioner has just passed down and will go down the McKenzie as far as Resolution.

Since he passed I have heard that I am to pass the summer at Fort Chipewyan in charge during the absence of Mr. McDougall who will go out to council at Winnipeg—this is a great nuisance. I have much work to do here to get things in trim for the winter and now to go away & leave it all undone is too bad besides having to leave wife & weans behind me. As yet I have had no official notice of this as the packet has been left behind but I will know ere closing this. I shall have more time for letter writing and will write a few lines by the Commissioner as he goes out. [...]

I am glad to hear that Aunt Sarah sent you some money. I hope that you may not be disappointed about the pension. It was very kind of the Marquis to interest himself in your behalf. [...]

Your loving son
W E Traill

My Dear Mother

[...] We had pretty severe frost a week ago which has cut the potato crop in some places. I hope it did not extend to Vermilion.

I am anxiously looking for the steamer which is due not later than the 20th at the latest. When she comes she will go onto Fort Smith and return making the trip in four days. Mr. Simpson should be up on her to relieve me and then I shall be free to start home. I need not say how I wish to be back with the wife and weans. I have been reading D'Aubigne's History of the Reformation which is a work of great interest. I do not know how I should pass the time but that I am well supplied with books just now.

20th I am now anxiously looking for the steamer which is now due. When she comes she has to go down to Fort Smith and will bring up from there Mr. Simpson to take my place here. If she turns up tomorrow and is able to cross the lake I ought to be able to get away about the 29th or the 1st Septr at latest. But if she is later than tomorrow I shall be delayed. It has been blowing a gale from the north for six days past so that were The Grahame in the mouth of the river within sight she would have to wait until it calms but it cannot always blow such a gale. [...]

I am not sending all the ferns I have gathered although I am sending a few of each variety so if I have not sent you enough of each you can let me know. I intend trying to set up some for myself. In your last you say nothing about your prospects of getting the pension you wrote of in a former letter from which I fear that the Marquis has not been successful, but there is always a good deal of delay about these things so I trust that I may yet hear that you have received some encouragement.

28th The steamer arrived from Fort McMurray on Sunday last and has gone down to Fort Smith. She has been due three days now and I am beginning to get anxious about her as any mishap would prevent me from leaving for home at once as I hope to do. I have everything ready for a start and will probably get the captain to run me up a day with

S.S. Wrigley, one of three steamers built in Fort Smith by the HBC in the 1880s. (Edgelow Family Colletion) Edgelow 23

the steamer which would be a great help. The weather today is very rough—rain and boisterous wind which would prevent the steamer coming in were she close as there is no shelter for the steamer as the wind is now. [...]

29th The steamer came yesterday but did not bring Mr. Simpson to relieve me. She goes on again to Fort McMurray and I have to stay until she returns which will be on Thursday or Friday so that I will not get off until the 6th instead of the 1st. I had a chance of writing Harriet today. I saw nuns who were at Vermilion in July. All were then well.

Good by dear mother and Kate and God bless you all.

WE Traill

FORT CHIPEWYAN *July 15, 1887*

Dear Kate

[...] I suppose you will have heard through others that I had to leave home on the 20th June without a days notice & come down here for the summer charge. I need not say how much it went against the grain & how disgusted Harriet was at my having to leave her & the children so long. I had one letter from her since, written only a week after I left. I am not at all likely to hear again from her during my absence.

The children are all so accustomed to my going away that they don't make any fuss but no sooner am I off than they keep asking for me and wanting me back. [...]

I am not yet sure whether Walter comes home yet or not. It depends upon what he decides to do for a livelihood. If he wants to enter the Mission Service which I would prefer or adopt teaching as a profession he is to stay on otherwise he is to come home until I find him something to do. [...]

I may be able to get away from here in September. I hope so for I am quite sick of this and wearying for the wife & weans.

Give my love to my son Willie. [...] I am very much pleased to see that he is getting on so well & that he is in favour with all. [...]

I am glad that you all tell me so much about him in your letters. I had no idea that he resembled me in the least as he is much more of a McKay being very much like his grandmother. [...]

We are expecting the steamer at any time. She has gone down to meet the Comr & take him as far as she can go which is up the Clear Water River a few miles from Fort McMurray. [...]

W E Traill

FORT CHIPEWYAN [*Early Fall, 1887*]

[Dear Mother]

[...] It is nearly a year since I mailed those ferns to you & only now I learn that you received them. I have not been able to collect any so far since my arrival on account of the mosquitoes which keep me shut in but soon they should be getting their quietus & then I will see what I can do. I shall try and send some too to Mr. Fletcher when I get his address or else send them through you.

I think I shall be able to press them this time altho I have plenty of time to sit on them as you recommend.

Tell all my correspondents to address all my letters from the date of receipt of this until March next via Qu'Appelle & Prince Albert.

Is your book on Canadian flowers[7] out of print? I would like to get a couple of copies, one for Commissioner Wrigley & one for Bishop Young. The Bishop is a great admirer of your work & Mr. Wrigley seemed [end missing]

W.E. Traill

FORT VERMILION *September 18, 1887*

Dear Mother

Just a few lines in acknowledgment of your very welcome letter of the 10th July, which I got on my return on the 15th. [...]

I had on the whole a pleasant & speedy trip up. The steamer brought me a day & a half and dropped me at the foot of the Rapide des Boyar from whence I came in 9 ½ days steering my own boat and acting as guide as none of my men know the river.

At Little Red River I picked up Mr. McKenzie. Black McKenzie as he is called who helped us get the boat over the chute. [...]

If Walter is coming he should be with us in three weeks time. I have not heard from Walter J.S. this summer. I believe he has left Pembina but do not know his address.

We are always so glad to hear of our Willie through you all & to find that he is a favourite with all. [...]

I shall have my hands full until well on in the winter getting my house habitable.

We have no garden this year. The grasshoppers destroyed everything but the potatoes & they are poor owing to summer frosts & the hoppers. It is well that I have a large stock of other provisions which makes me independent of the garden. [...]

WE Traill

FORT VERMILION *October 9, 1887*

Dear Clinton

[...] When men come down from Smoky River we cannot get them to stay for more than one day & then we have a lot of correspondences—business & private and so some are left out in the cold. [...]

I know how hard he (Willie) is on clothes & boots. I am much concerned that he still wets his bed. I was in hopes he would get over it before now. I hope the medicine you were giving him will be of some benefit. It will be a terrible drawback to him if he does not overcome the habit. [...]

We hope to get Willie's photo by next packet. I am glad to hear that he is a good boy & obedient & that he learns well at school. We have not heard from him once this summer but I suppose the letters will all come in a batch. [...]

I am very busy getting my house ready for winter. I have also to make furniture—We have no furniture shop to run to and if we want to eat anything in the way of game I have to take my gun & go out for a night. I have killed over 200 ducks since I returned from Chipewyan, made & put in five windows in the upper story of the house besides doing a lot of work that does not show. I have also made a new dining table. I am the fisherman of the establishment also so that you can see that my excuse of being too busy to write is not an idle one. [...]

WE Traill

[...]

Dear Kit Kat

[...] You must have all been delighted to have your brother Clinton
with you again even for a short time. I know how you dote upon him.
Happy is any young man who has such a loving welcome awaiting him
on his return home. If there is anything I admire it is to see such attach-
ment between members of a family and it is even more delightful when
it extends to uncles who have been exiled for years. It is worth while
enduring years of separation just for the pleasure of such greetings as
you all gave poor old Uncle Bill, but then the worst of it is that partings
come after & spoil all. [...]

We too have had the great pleasure of having our son Walter with us.
He came with the Youngs on the night of 15 Octr. just a month after my
return from Chipewyan. We could see the light on their scow for an hour
at least before they came to the landing before the Fort. The children
were in great glee & on the tiptoe of expectation. They could not wait
until the scow landed but called out "Brother Walter, are you there?"
The answer was yes & then what a chorus of little voices some calling
one thing & some another. We had a pile of shavings etc. which we lit
as the scow was about to land & it made a grand bonfire.

Walter has grown very much since we parted with him at Prince
Albert a year & a half ago & he is quite manly having quite outgrown
his extreme shyness. The children all are very fond of him. They all call
him "Brother Walter".

Mrs. Young is a very superior person very tall & amiable & very grey.
She has her two youngest children with her, Walter & Irene. The little
girl is a dear little chatterbox like Mary. The boy [is] the image of his father. Coming through to avoid confusion they called Walter, Walter Major
& the little fellow W- Minor but they both called our W- major Walter.

The Youngs have just moved into their new house which however is
in a very unfinished state. They had a house warming on the 1st Instant.

We had a dinner, speeches & music. Mrs. Young is a capital performer on the piano but they have not got theirs through yet. The Scotts lent them their organ for the occasion. There are two organs on the neighbourhood and I hope there will be a third next year, for Mrs. Young says I must get one for the benefit of Ethel and of course I cannot refuse. Ethel is learning and Mrs. Young says she will do so readily. [...] [end missing]

W.E. Traill

My dear Mother

In a few days we will be sending off the Packet so it is high time that I should set to work and get my letters written. [...]

I have not much to write about as our time has passed by without any event worth recording except the arrival of my dear son Walter on the 15 Octr just a month after my return from Chipewyan. [...]

He [...] had a sickness towards the end of the term Canon Matheson writes me which put him back in some of his studies so that he gained no prizes last term which says the Canon has somewhat discouraged him. [...]

Mrs. Young is teaching Ethel music. Of course she has not made any great progress yet but she says she will learn readily & so I must send for an organ. It will be very nice to have in the house as there are several in the settlement who can play and in a year or two Ethel ought to play a little. I am going to order it now. [...] I would have sent for a piano at once were it not for the difficulty of freighting it out, the expense being nearly equal to the original cost.

Walter cut his leg about a month ago rather a nasty cut about 3 inches long and quite to the bone but I dressed it so that he never took the bandage off for a fortnight and then it was quite healed up. He was only confined to the sofa one day & to the house for a week. He makes himself generally useful and attends my traps. So far he has been pretty successful. He walked 25 to 30 miles one day not long after he got on his feet again.

The river froze two days sooner than last year i.e. 17 Nov. [...]

The weather has not been very severe so far. Cold enough however to freeze quite a few ears & noses. H & I both got frozen on Sunday last coming home from church. The church is about a mile and a half from here. Ethel got her face frozen the other day coming from school but I thawed it out with snow & then greased it which prevents the skin from being discoloured. [...]

Altho the house is far from being finished it is very much more comfortable than last year. I have altered the arrangement of the rooms. We have the sitting room nicely carpeted with a handsome Brussels carpet & the bed room with "Ingrain."

[...] Ethel [is] very womanly for a child of her years. Jessie is improving in looks we think. Mrs. Young takes great notice of her. She is very much amused at her odd ways & sayings. She says she never knows what Jessie will say next.

The children eat their lunch at the Scotts or Mrs. Youngs as we do not care for them mixing more than possible with the Indian children who are neither too clean not too well mannered. [...]

Mr. McKenzie who has charge of Red River 60 miles below left two of his boys with us to attend school so with our own 4 and the two McKenzies & Jemima we have a large family of little people to look after. There are 11 of us to sit down to table. My Second & his young wife live & mess apart.

We are doing pretty well in spite of the failure of the crops & scarcity of meat. We have lots of imported flour & some bacon. I killed two cattle & salted a barrel of ducks & another of fish so that with porridge for breakfast & some kind of animal food for dinner & bread & butter and often some kind of jam or fruit for supper we manage to [keep] body & soul together. [...]

Believe me to be your loving Son
WE Traill

My dear Mother

I am just sending off the usual Feby Express and have delayed until almost the last moment that I might give you the very latest news about H-. I could not write before. I can now tell you of the birth of another daughter yesterday about 12.30[8] while the rest of the household were off to church. Both H- & the little stranger are doing well. Baby is very fat & healthy looking & weighs ten pounds without the moss bag. She is very good so far but when she cries she makes herself heard I assure you. [...]

The baby is very fair. Hair not so dark as the others when born. We have not yet determined the color of her eyes. We all think her very much like Mary.

I believe her name is to be either Harriet or Henrietta. [...]

Jessie was very loath to leave as Mr. Spencer told her he would take the baby as they have none. [...]

Mrs. Young finds Jessie the most original of them all as she is always saying queer things. She says she will prove the clever one of the family. We thought she would not learn quick but she reads very well for her age altho a year ago she hardly knew her letters. She reads fairly well in the testament. [...]

The great Council took place in Winnipeg in August but I have not heard any definite Official news only that they succeeded in getting somewhat better terms for us out of the "board".

I have been well but very busy fitting up a couple of rooms upstairs & making some furniture which makes us much more comfortable the wee [end missing]

W.E. Traill

My dear Mother

[...] I was very glad to know that you were then enjoying good health considering your years. I was however grieved to learn through Kate's of a much later date that you were again suffering from the old neuralgia [affliction]. I trust however the spring brought with it a change for the better. [...]

We have had a remarkably late spring the latest I have ever experienced. There was no thaw during the month of April. The thaw set in on the last day of that month. The river broke on the 7th May, but the ice jammed below & caused the water to rise rapidly. I was afraid to go to church that morning but allowed Walter & Mr. Spencer to go but the water began to surround the church so that they had to discontinue the service & every one go home & try & save their property. I had to send off Harriet & the children on foot as we had no horses in. I & my men had to go to work and pack up my fur & put everything as much out of reach of the water as possible in case it should rise over the banks. We had fright after fright for one jam would break and then the water would fall rapidly only to rise again as the new jam would form. I managed to get an ox & cart off all our furs & some of our own effects to the hills beyond reach of the flood. Sunday night H- & the children were in the tent on the hill about a mile from the Fort but Walter & I and all the men remained in the Fort in case of anything transpiring. On Monday morning the water was almost up to the brink of the bank but as we did not like the looks of things I kept working packing & removing every thing we could. There was a jam about a mile above but we could not tell how far back it might extend. I took a walk down to see our Missionaries and ascertain how it fared with them. I found them on a rising piece of ground about a mile below the Fort. I only saw the ladies their husbands being down at their houses trying to secure their property. They however seemed to think all the danger was over. I assured them that such was not the case & told them on no account to go back to their houses until the jam above broke. I then went back and took up my carpets & prepared for the worst.

About sundown we heard a noise up the river which we knew to be a sign that the ice was giving—in a few minutes the whole [body] of ice began to move & such a crash of ice & timber you cannot imagine. On the island above the large spruce & poplars were falling as grass falls before the scythe & a cloud of dust like smoke rose caused by the falling timber. Trees two & three feet in diameter were as stubble. The water rose very rapidly—it had fallen many feet before but now it rose at a rate of several feet in a minute.

We now thought it time to move as I was afraid that the river would burst its banks about half a mile above & cut us off from the higher ground on which the families were camped. I would not then have given a ten dollar bill for the whole establishment, however when the water had risen a little higher than the level of the foundations of the Fort & was beginning to pour over the embankment both above & below the Fort, it suddenly began to subside without doing any damage at all to the establishment.

It was fearful to stand on the bank & see the immense mass of ice bristling with trees & debris of all kinds rush [past] at a speed that was simply terrific & to know that the rise of another foot would have swept the Fort & settlement out of existence.

I am sorry to say that all our neighbours did not get off quite so well as we did, for with the exception of the Bishop's house all their dwellings were flooded & their farms were several feet under water so that they were unable to put their crop in but had to break out other ground.

We found out afterwards that Bishop Young & family & the Scotts returned to the Bishop's house on Monday evening seeing the water subside, and when the jam broke above they found themselves surrounded by water without means of escape. They passed a terrible night with the water all around them and the ice sweeping past them in the river & between them & the higher ground which they foolishly left. Fortunately the house was on the highest ground about there &

the water rose just to the foundations & no further but they must have
passed a night of horrible suspense & fear shut up in the loft of their
unfinished house without windows & listening to the swirl of water
& the grinding of the ice & the crush of timber as it swept past.

Mrs Scott who is a martyr to rheumatism stayed with us for a week
until the house was cleaned out & dried so as to be safe for her to live in.
The Lawrences had quite a job to clean out their house and get things
out to rights after the flood. Luckily there was no great loss of property
except in fire wood & lumber etc. [...]

Harriet joins me in fond love. [...]
WE Traill

FORT VERMILION *June 8, 1888*

Dear Kate

[...] Monday night we did not sleep much as we were carrying
everything moveable to our camp. We laid in a good stock of grub &
ammunition in case of the whole establishment going down stream,
but towards morning the water began to fall and we were soon out of
all danger. Such a sudden exodus put everything to Sixes & Sevens and
caused a great deal of extra work, to everyone especially to the women
of the establishment.

Our Missionary neighbours had a much worse experience than ourselves as with the exception of the Bishop's house all were flooded and a
flood of Peace River water means a deposit of mud in proportion to the
depth of water & the length of time the flood lasted.

The church was in a frightful mess and will never be as it was before
the flood. Altho it has high foundations the water was six inches deep in
the seats. [...]

We have not seen much of our missionary neighbours since the flood,
in fact everyone has been put about so by it that they have not yet got
things in order.

We have ten cows milking. Harriet & Mrs. Spencer do the milking &
butter making, to do which they have to rise at six.

Our diet just now is wheat porridge & cream & bread & butter for
breakfast. Bread & butter for dinner with ducks fish or moose meat &
bread & butter for tea. Of course we have some extras—for instance
Mary tells me that we are to have a big plum pudding for dinner.

We have plenty of water hen eggs just now. H & I went out to Bear
Lake the other day & brought home 300. Walter was out the other day
& brought nearly as many & we get some from the Indians so that on
the whole we manage to keep the wolf from the door.

And now dear Kate I must close.[...]
W E Traill

FORT VERMILION *June 17, 1888*

Dear Kitten Katten

[...] The flood upset us greatly and put me so much back in my work
that I have never been able to catch up with my work. We were never
in any personal danger but we ran a great chance of losing a great deal
of property & of having to live in tents all summer, as some of our neigh-
bours living on the opposite bank of the river are now doing their homes
having been crushed & floated off. [...]

Walter will be leaving us now in a few days. We shall feel his going
away very much as we are quite in the dark as to what he will do & of
course do not know when we shall see him again. We are not in a land
of railways so that there is no chance of us seeing him for years. Such
is life.

He will most likely go to the Commercial College for a six month
course after which he will have to look for something to do. He says he
will ask his Uncle Walter if he cannot find a situation for him. If nothing
better offers I will apply for a situation for him in the H B Service but
the prospects are not good now for young people. [...]

This summer my second, Mr. Spencer, has to go but as he takes his wife he will not feel the change. I fear however that they will not be back. I feel it more on account of his wife who is a great help & comfort to your aunt! However we can better afford to lose her than [when] we were without other friends. Here we have Mrs. Young who is a delightful person & to whom we are all greatly attached. Then there is Mrs. Scott & then all our neighbours are English speaking whereas at other places we have been all our neighbours have been Cree or French speaking people.

There is to be a local synod held at Vermilion about the 1st July. We will have the Revd Holmes from Slave Lake & A.C. Garrioch from Dunvegan & Arch Deacon Reeve from Athabaska. The latter is here now having come up with Mr. McDougall. The latter is off again but the Arch Deacon remains for the Synod & is now waiting the arrival of the others. The Bishop has asked me to attend as lay delegate which I intend doing.[9] [...]

The flood has seriously interfered with Ethel's music as Mrs. Scott's organ was spoiled by the flood. I believe only the bellows were spoiled and I hope I can mend them but have not even had time to examine them hitherto.

I hope I shall hear from you shortly about the organ you were to get for me. I made a great mistake in forgetting to tell you that it should have been done up in a watertight tin lined case as it is very apt to get injured by wet en route.

I am so pleased to hear that your Grandmother is so well & on the other hand am much concerned to learn that your mother & father are both far from well. I hope that the summer brought them better health & spirits.

Do I remember the apples we used to eat? Well yes rather & the weeks we used to have & the way my cruel nieces used to tease me & tickle me with hairs & torture me in every way they could devise & not sing to me when I asked them to (some of them) and pretend (?) to be sulky. [...]

We are entitled to a furlough every seven years. Two have already passed since I submitted myself to the tortures I have just enumerated and I suppose I may be weak enough if I am spared to go back and suffer a like affliction but four more years will turn my head as white as a badger or as bald as a billiard Ball so possibly my nieces who I trust are growing wiser with increasing years will reverence my grey hairs and not tease so much [...]

WE Traill

VERMILION *October 24, 1888*

Dearest Kitten Katten

When last I wrote I could not say anything about the organ as it had not yet come to hand, but it duly arrived early in the month & is much admired for neatness and good tone.

It came through without a scratch or damage of any kind but some of the keys are a little swelled with damp so that they will not rise when pressed down. The Base Knee swell too is a little out of order but I trust that when it gets all the dampness out of it that it will be all right. Mrs. Young who is the most critical judge of such matters pronounces the tone to be excellent. One could not wish for higher praise. It is still in the house but we are to leave it with Mrs. Young all winter so that she may be able to give Ethel her lessons regularly. Mrs. Scott's organ got damaged by the flood and I fear will never be the same as it was. [...]

We are all very well indeed. True my throat just now causes me a good deal of annoyance, but that is nothing new. All the children in the settlement had colds and ours among the rest but they are all getting better. Ethel & Jessie are off to school.

We have a new clerk; a son of late Bishop McLean. He was at Chipewyan last winter but through bad behaviour got into trouble. Since he came here he has behaved very well & says he has made up his mind to turn over a new leaf. I think he is a trifle simple. Jessie has undertaken to teach him to read. She is quite earnest about it & schools him every night.

Walter only got to Winnipeg about Sept. 1st altho he left here in June. He had a very hard trip from Chipewyan to Athabaska Landing. Had to walk 95 miles through swamp & brush with scarcely anything to eat. In fact they were nearly starving & their companions who they left behind were 3 days without a mouthful.

With my fond love to Willie your father & mother and a big hug and countless kisses for your wee self. [...] [end missing]

W.E. Traill

FORT VERMILION *December 11, 1888*

Dearest Kitten Katten

[...] Well if you had seen this old ruin of a house when first I took charge & were to see it now you might think otherwise when you came to understand that I am my own carpenter & blacksmith & plasterer and paper hanger & all the other trades boiled down into one, besides being at time fisherman & hunter & cowboy & gardener. [...]

Well my house altho not finished is getting quite comfortable & I can tell you what a house you build tho it be a mere shanty becomes a palace and a chair you make altho hardly such as you see in illustrated advertisements become something very luxurious to which no Turkish divan could hold a candle either for elegance [or] comfort & so you can see I ought to be a very contented man—at all events I am not likely to find fault with my tradesman or dispute their "bills" altho your aunt might find fault with her "bill" & sometimes does. [...]

We are to have a Christmas tree here and the organ is to be brought up & there will be high jinks. The children are full of expectation but poor dears they will get few presents.[...]

We have not many friends here but some of them are very dear to us and we have all been drawn together much closer this year than ever

Three of Willie's nine daughters who survived childhood: Ethel Bigg, later wife of Frederick Johnstone Bigg; Mary Traill; Jessie Drever, later wife of William Rothney Drever. (Willie Traill Family Collection) Willie Traill 4

before by a revival of religion among us—not from the work of any evangelist coming amongst us but by the earnest preaching & labours of our own minister. The Bishop was away all summer but was much rejoiced at the good work among his flock. I wish you had among you an earnest man such as Mr. Scott instead of a listless lifeless man like your parson who is a very good fellow as a private individual & a very good whist player but as a minister of God is by no means up to the mark. [...] I would sooner see my son breaking stones on the road than filling a pulpit merely for a living. Believe me my dearest that religion if it is to benefit a person must be from the heart. Christ as the Saviour of the world & your own personal saviour are very different persons. [...]

Willie I trust is well. His mother has written to him & so has Ethel. I wish you could see my dear girls. I know that you would make a good deal of them. Ethel is growing quite tall & has a good deal of judgement for her years. Jessie is very bright & reminds me of my favourite niece in expression & some of her ways. You may be able to guess who that young lady is. Mary reminds me more or less of Florence more in appearance than manner. She also reminds me very much of your dear grandmother.

Your Aunt is very busy preparing for the Xmas tree. She always manages to come in for the lion's share of the work in anything like that, and I expect most of the presents too will come from her & Mrs. Young. They are great friends. With them both it is much more blessed to give than to receive. Your aunt suffers a good deal from her back but she still works on.

Good by dearest Kitten Katten. [...] Merry Xmass & happy New Year to you & a big hug such as we used to have with a perfect shower of kisses & blessings.

WE Traill

FORT VERMILION *December 10, 1888*

Dear Willie

Lest I should be pressed for time when the packet is about starting I will write to my boys first. I have just done writing to Walter.

We are all quite well. Your mother has no doubt told you all about the children. Ethel & Jessie are growing quite tall & go to school with their writing but they both [do] very well, and are also getting on well with arithmetic.

Ethel is getting on well with her music but Jessie is only just beginning.

I have been very busy since the hard frosts set in trying to make the house comfortable. I have just finished the upper story—4 rooms.

Your mother has a sitting room up stairs & our bedroom is also on the 2nd floor.

I have made a staircase a very good one but not quite so good as the Ashelworth [stairs].

As you did not see the house before we lived in it there is not much use me telling you about the alterations. Next summer, if I remain in charge, I must take up the lower floor and put new sleepers & new floors & new partitions. I am always hard at work. I suppose when I get this house fit to live in I shall be sent to some other broken down establishment to rebuild it.

Little Harriet is just the picture of what you were when you were a baby. She is rather cross as were you. [...]

I had to take all the keys out of the organ before it would work well. We are much pleased with it. It is down at Mrs. Young's just now on account of the girls music lessons.

We like the Youngs & Scotts more & more the more we see them but as we are all busy at all times we do not see as much of them as we would like. [...]

We have not heard from Walter since he went away from Edmonton but we heard of his arrival in Winnipeg. [...]

We never forget you & Walter even for a day or an hour. I trust my dear son that you will continue well and that I shall hear the same favourable accounts of your conduct & progress.

I have not had time to trap until last week. I had occasion to send my Interpreter & clerk off on a trade so I accompanied them two days and made traps along the road. I came home alone in one day. I got two martens & when they were returning they brought another.

Some of the Indians are starving already. I fear they will see hard times before spring.

Young McLean would like to be a dog driver but I fear he will never be much at all. He was one of Walter's school mates, but Walter says he was always a bad boy. I think he is a little wrong in his head. [...]

Your uncle Joe is still at Chipewyan. He would like to be with us again.

I am going to try and write to all the Atwoods this time. I suppose they think I treat them badly.

Trusting that you are well & happy believe me my dear son your loving father.

WE Traill

Dear Kate

[...] I have already in former letters spoken of the increased interest in religious matters among us. [...] Instead of our Bishop throwing a damper on the movement which began during his absence he has entered fully into it himself.[10] As for Mrs. Young she has always showed great interest in it & has indeed been a prime mover in it. Harriet who you must know is one of the most conservative of beings and who looked askance on what appeared to her to be something new has changed her views entirely and is herself greatly changed. When I am from home she now conducts prayers and takes a great interest in her own children & with such others as are thrown in her way. [...]

Instead of two services on Sunday we have a prayer meeting in the church after the Sunday school is over. The days are so short that we have hard work to get to the Service at half past ten back to dinner & Sunday school at 2.30——It is sometimes quite dark when we come out of the prayer meeting.

We still keep up our Thursday evening prayer meeting altho very often there is no one there but the Bp & Mrs. Young, Mr. & Mrs. Scott & either Harriet or I for we cannot both attend.

It is the greatest privilege to know a man like Mr. Scott. The only trouble is that he works too hard & I fear his health will give way—— indeed it is not good at any time. [...] [end missing]

W.E. Traill

My dear Mother

There is a packet of letters before me recently received from you & my sisters & nieces ranging all the way from August last until 9th April. There are at least 15 of them all together and I am quite unable to answer one of them just now as the Inspector (my old friend Hardisty) is here & Dr. MacKay & family en route for Chipewyan and have not a spare moment and besides which I have just got marching orders. I leave this in a few days for Fort St James, Stewart's Lake, New Caledonia B.C. to take charge of that District. We will go down the Peace by boat to Chipewyan & by Steamer up the Athabasca to Athabasca Landing & Edmonton. Calgary by C.P.R. to Ashcroft—thence by stage to Quesnel from thence up Stewart's River to Fort St James on Stewart's Lake my future station. I am too much unsettled to write anyone but will do so on my way out. It is within the bounds of possibility that Harriet may part with me at Calgary & go east & winter with you. We cannot make up our minds as we have only just heard of this change & there are many things to be taken into consideration. She is very anxious to go & see our son but if she goes she cannot rejoin me this year. I am somewhat backward about sending such a lot of them to invade your quiet house more especially as there will be an addition to the family about New Year's time. So I hope you will not be disappointed if she does or does not go out.

I know nothing of my new home more than that it is a long way from here & that it will take us about 5 or 6 weeks travelling but it is more accessible than this place. There is I believe a monthly mail & it is a beautiful place in the mountains & a good place for living. [...]

You can tell all my sisters & Clin & Tom that I will write them all as I go up the Athabasca as I cannot write just now. [...]

W.E. Traill

Dear Clinton

I learn with regret that there seems to be a "hitch" somewhere as to the payment of Willie's board. In case that I am in your debt I enclose an order on Sir D.A. Smith for $100.00. If you have already received payment in full you can place it to my credit for the year which begins sometime in June. You ought to have let me know at once if I am behind as I have made it a rule through life to "owe no man anything".

When you received the money for the organ you wrote me that the balance that was over cleared up Willie's a/c since then I have sent you I think first one hundred dollars for his board for the year beginning June 1888 and afterwards fifty dollars extra. If I am mistaken I am extremely sorry for it. I learn with regret that you are hard up. I trust that the present year will enable your tenant to pay up all old scores.

When I come to think of it it is possible that I did not send the hundred dollars last spring. As I […] find no memorandum of it I will make the bill $120.00 as I must owe you for Willie's clothing. If I am still due you anything counting from June 1889 backwards, don't scruple to let me know & I will square with you at once. […]

Walter has I suppose by this time left the Business College, but whether he has yet got anything to do is another thing. He seemed hopeful of getting a situation in the C.P.R. when I heard from him in Jan.

I have no doubt when he gets a situation that he will do well.

We are in the middle of farming & gardening & fur packing & accounts etc. The river broke first on the 11th Inst but only cleared on the 27th. No flood this year.

Now dear Clinton I must close. Hoping you will overlook the inconvenience I have occasioned you.

Believe me Ever yours faithfully
W E Traill
[…]

FORT VERMILION *April 30, 1889*

Dear Mother

Your very welcome letter of 9th February reached me the day before
yesterday. [...]

I am glad my dear mother that you mentioned the matter of my
being behind hand in my payment of Willie's board. The fact is I had
the idea that I had sent him money that I never sent. [...]

I have written to Willie quite lately and little more than a month ago
to your dear self & Mary (I think) [...]

Harriet is off on a visit to the parsonage. I was invited but could not
as I am very busy; all the children are off with their Mother. [...]

We are going to lose our good Bishop & his most estimable wife. They
go to Chipewyan. [...] [end missing]

W.E. Traill

ATHABASCA LANDING *July 29, 1889*

My dear Mother

[...] By letters I wrote as soon as I knew I was to leave Vermilion
you will now learn that I have been appointed to the charge of New
Caledonia Dist. [...]

We left Vermilion on the evening of 24 June—took ten days to Fort
Chipewyan, stayed there part of 4 days, there by Steamer Grahame to
Fort McMurray. Part of two days there. From thence five days to Grand
Rapids. This part of the River is a succession of rapids. We travelled by
open boat. Beautiful weather but rather too hot. Few mosquitoes but
lots of bulldogs. At Grand Rapids we met Joe McKay who had had a very
narrow escape from drowning a few days before. We stayed there part
of three days. From that place we reached here day before yesterday a
month & three days from Vermilion but we did not travel on Sundays.

I held morning service every Sunday which was attended by all the
Protestants in our brigade. We had a nun in our company who held a
short Service also attended by her own people who made a hideous row
all the rest of the day.

She was the greatest coward I ever came across.

We are now getting ready to resume our journey to Edmonton by
wagons that arrived yesterday with freight. We will probably take 3 days
to Edmonton a day or two there to look after some business matters &
then on to Calgary. [...]

You see my dear mother there is another addition to our little family expected about Xmas and she is naturally averse [to] going among
strangers to trouble them And yet she is most anxious to take the children
down to leave them at School. I cannot speak more definitely at present
but I suppose ere we get to Calgary she will have made up her mind.

H. & the children are all well. We are invited up to dinner today
at Mrs. Woods. Woods the H B officer in charge here & his wife a sister
to Mrs. Hardisty.

We meet here lots of people we know but none that we care much
about. We are not favourably impressed with our first taste of so called
civilized life. We could not sleep on Saturday night for the row caused by
a dance close to us in which the "Spirit of civilization" was very freely
indulged in.

Harriet joins me in much love. [...]

Excuse haste & believe me my dear mother your loving son
W E Traill

FORT EDMONTON *August 4, 1889*

Dear Mother

Harriet has quite decided on going through with me to our new home.

We arrived here on Thursday the 1st instant and leave tomorrow.

Walter has not yet found employment so I have telegraphed him to join me at Calgary on Saturday next. He will go with us to St James—in the meantime I must try & find something for him to do. [...]

Every one here is very kind. Mr. Hardisty told us to go to his house but we did not like to impose so are at a hotel. We would have been wiser to have stuck to our tents.

Harriet is tired of her trip & is rather too lame to go about. We have only called on Mrs. Hardisty & her sister, but several have called on us.

We leave tomorrow afternoon. The children are disappointed at not going to see grandmamma on which they had quite set their hearts. [...]

I enclose a slip from bulletin announcing our arrival & shall ask Oliver to send you the next issue in which will be a notice of the address & presentation to us on our departure from Vermilion. [...]

Walter in his last asks where he could get a couple of copies of the Traill genealogy. I do not know what he wants with them but I would be glad if you would let me know as I forgot the address Kate gave me. [...]

Believe me as ever Your loving son
W E Traill

CALGARY *August 13, 1889*

Dear Clinton

As Harriet has decided not to go east I will as I promised enclose you a check for Walter's board for the current year. I presume that if I send you the amount of his bill for clothing & sundries at the end of the year [that is] next May or June it will be all right—if not let me know.

I have been at considerable expense lately else I should have added $50.00 for Willie's expenses. [...]

I should have been off on Monday but got a letter from Wrigley asking me to wait for him. We will travel in the same car to Ashcroft. [...]

*Excuse haste. My love to all my nieces & Willie in which Harriet joins.
Ever yours faithfully*

> *W E Traill.*

> [...]

Dear Kate

*[...] We arrived here last Saturday evening & spent the Sunday in camp.
I walked into town intending to go to church but was too late.*

*I met Walter on the bridge. He was looking out for us having arrived
in town two days before. He has grown a good deal but is not so tall as
I am. I do not think he ever will be. As he failed to get employment I
had to telegraph to him from Edmonton to join us at Calgary. I had
arranged to go on at once but found a letter from Mr. Wrigley asking me
to wait & join him on the train Friday night so we are all here at no little
expense to the Company. The children all take very kindly to civilization.
They are greatly disappointed at not going to see grandmama. Walter is
to teach them this winter. I am buying a typewriter for him to practice
on as he will have to keep up that & phonography so as to be prepared
for whatever may turn up. He is a fine manly fellow & is greatly praised
by all who know him. [...]*

*I am put to considerable expense for one thing or another having to
launch out a hundred dollars here & 200 there—no wonder I cannot
save a cent these times. [...]*

*You can well understand that my salary of $1500.00 quickly goes. I
will if I have time give you some account of my trip later. The air is so
full of smoke that we have not been able to see anything of the country.
We should long ere this have had a glorious view of the Mountains but
cannot for the smoke. I fear we shall not get a good view even in passing
through & over them.*

I must now close. Harriet has been nowhere except to call on the Thompsons. He is the officer who took Willie through to Peterborough. He is a very nice fellow & his young wife a very nice person. She is from the Orkneys & knows lots of Traills. W- tells me that Sir D.A. Smith's head man at Silver Heights is a Traill. I do not know of what branch. [...]

Excuse haste & believe me dear Kate Your ever loving brother
W E Traill
[...]

Eight

FORT ST. JAMES
1889–1893

IN 1889, WILLIE AND HIS FAMILY JOURNEYED TO FORT ST. JAMES.[1]
Visualize the Traills' journey there from Fort Vermilion. They travelled down the Peace River to Fort Chipewyan; up the Athabasca to
Athabasca Landing; overland to Edmonton and thence to Calgary; by
train to Ashcroft, British Columbia; and via the Fraser, Nechako, and
Stuart Rivers to Stuart Lake and Fort St James. Much of the time they
traveled in open York boat or canoe. Harriet was pregnant, and their
five daughters ranged in age from sixteen months (Harriet) to nine
years (Ethel). The entire trek would take 88 days.

With respect to the fur trade, Willie faced insurmountable problems at Fort St. James that were beyond his control. His predecessor's
reckless behaviour, coupled with poor fur yields and mediocre
prices in the European market, made it impossible for Willie to turn a
profit in the New Caledonia District.

Though it lacked the compatible society the Traills had enjoyed at
Fort Vermilion, Fort St. James was not without its redeeming features.
The fort was in a beautiful location, and its buildings were in excellent condition. For once, Willie wasn't faced with the need to make his
family's living quarters inhabitable.

While at the post, Willie and Harriet were blessed with the arrival of two more girls—Annie was born in 1889 and Barbara (Catherine Barbara) in 1892.[2] Harriet must have secretly welcomed the end of her child-bearing years, for she apparently suffered from morning sickness with every pregnancy.

In 1893, Willie was faced with bleak prospects in the fur trade. At the same time, he and Harriet wanted to give their children a proper education in an environment that would allow them to develop friendships with peers. They decided it was time for Willie to leave the HBC.

Dear Kate

As I have written mother from Edmonton & Calgary I will address these few lines to you, not that it makes any difference.

As you are aware we left Calgary on the night of Friday the [20th] or rather at 1.25 O.C. Saturday morning. Of course we took the sleeper & when we awoke we were in the Selkirks. Unfortunately the smoke was so dense that we could but faintly see the glorious sights that would otherwise have been visible.

At about 8 O.C. Mr. Wrigley turned out and I was occupied most of the morning in business with him.

The morning being cool we got the porter to make a fire but we had reason to repent having done so for the stove which was a coal stove smoked and sickened Harriet & the children—even Walter was quite sick so that not one of them enjoyed their ride on the train. Mary when asked afterwards whether she liked the cars & railroad said "Uncle Joe's railroad was the best". Now Uncle Joe's railroad was the very primitive wooden train way & truck at Grand Rapids on the Athabasca.

We had (Mr. Wrigley, Walter & I) breakfast at Donald; dinner at the Glacier & supper on the dining car. H- & the children had a lunch basket but ate little or nothing all day.

The scenery through the Selkirks was grand in the extreme especially at Glacier & for 40 or 50 miles beyond. Very little snow remains on the mountains this year as the snowfall was lighter last winter than ever before within the memory of those acquainted with the mountains.

At Revelstoke I was not a little surprised to meet Mr. McFarlane my predecessor in charge of the N.C. District—He came to have a long chat with me on the business of the District which he was leaving. Mr. Wrigley & he did not pull well and there was a decided change in Mr. Wrigley who gave McF- a very cool reception.

At Kamloops another old friend James Grahame got on board with his wife. That was at 22 O.C. so that I did not see much of them as we got off at Ashcroft a couple of hours afterwards.

The children behaved very well considering that they were wakened out of sleep at midnight and were surrounded by strangers and strange surroundings.

They were not at all troublesome on the train which was fortunate as Mr. Wrigley is a trifle particular. It was amusing to watch the old fellow. There was a young woman or rather girl who would insist on sitting down in Mr. Wrigley's seat & trying to engage him in conversation. The old chap tried to be courteous but it was evidently uphill work & his success was by no means unqualified.

At Ashcroft we were left standing beside a big pile of cordwood & were told that the hotel was on the other side. We managed to get the children round the wood & the train & then found the hotel. We were given rooms, & Harriet & the children were not sorry to get to bed for Harriet did not sleep much on the sleeper.

The beds were full of bugs & the children got up next morning all bitten up—That was only a first experience for we have been pretty well bitten up ever since at every stopping place but this.

We remained at Ashcroft all Sunday. I attended a funeral & Walter & I went to an evening service—a very good sermon not particularly well delivered.

Harriet did not venture out—I put on moccasins for a change but had reason to repent as in going to church I slipped on a lot of cactus & thus got a hint that I was in a different country.

The scenery about Ashcroft is rather fine. It is in the valley of the Thompson surrounded by bare hills covered [with] cactus & wormwood & sage brush. No trees to speak of except at a distance the hills are crowned with some kind of fir. Nothing can be raised there without irrigation. Water is brought from long distances in drains or sluices for that purpose—By irrigating they can raise almost anything including apples & grapes plums etc.

On the Monday we were awakened at 4 O.C. & started at 5 in the stage, H- & I and the 5 children as insides & Walter & two others beside the driver on the outside. At Clinton 32 miles we had dinner & changed stages & in so doing our three umbrellas were left in the stage we vacated.

There we were entertained by an old Scotch woman with an unmistakable beard only that she shaves. She was very kind & hospitable & gave us a good spread & did not overcharge. Here also the other two outsiders left by the other stage for Lillooet. So we were left as sole passengers.

We changed drivers here also—We changed horses & had supper at 83 Mile House (not 83 from Ashcroft) and went on over a rough road until 11 or rather 23 O.C. when we stopped for the night at Bridge Creek. H & the children thoroughly done out as well they might be after a ride of 85 miles. Next day we had only 55 miles to make but alas did not make it. After dinner at 134 Mile H- was feeling very poorly[3] but not wisely ate some dinner. After dinner she washed down some napkins in a creek. Just before getting on board again she felt very unwell but as the stage waits for no one she got on board. Before going a mile I was obliged to ask the driver to stop [which] he did at a creek. She had a violent fit of vomiting and felt a little better, but was shortly taken very much worse. I had again to ask the driver to stop [and] lifted H out. She was inclined to pains & had to dash water in her face. Fortunately there was a house close by. A man came out & finding what was the matter asked me to bring H in. I did so with his help & put her on the bed. She was alarmingly ill. The stage could not stop so I told Walter to go on with all the children but Hattie to the next station 150 M.H. as the man said that if H was better he would drive us to the station that evening.

For a while I was seriously alarmed, as H's symptoms were very alarming but gradually she got better altho weak. I found she would require rest & as the man McCarthy kept a sort of eating house I got him to go with me to 150 Mile House for W- & the children. They were just going to bed when we got there but were overjoyed to find that their mother was better & that they were going back to her.

We got back at 10 or rather 22 O.C. Harriet was better so we camped in an old house which our host had just vacated & which was used for a dairy. One room was placed at my disposal & we made beds on the floor having our meals over at his house. We remained there from Wednesday until Saturday at noon. I then hired a man & team for the modest sum of $60.00 to drive me here. This did not include board & beds which cost from the time I stopped at McCarthy's until my arrival here over 35 dollars without counting 7.50 for team to 150 Mile Station[4] to fetch back the family. I trust however that the Co will foot all these bills.

From [McCarthy's] we were all packed in a two seated waggon. The children sleep a great deal, sometimes all of them slept at the same time & as there was not room for all to lie some had to be held. As H- was not able to nurse Miss Hattie fell to my care. Walter got on famously with all of them but Hattie who does not yet take to him very kindly.

As I am writing to Annie I will close. At the present Harriet has a cold but is otherwise well & all the children as fresh as can be. Great notice is taken of them by all but Hattie comes in for the greatest degree of notice. We will I trust leave tomorrow.

With love to mother & Mary. Believe me dear Kate Your loving brother W E Traill

QUESNEL *August 28, 1889*

Dear Niece Annie

[...] We are pretty tired of travelling and will be glad to be quietly settled once more. I expect that we will have more comforts, as the house that we are going to is a good one & we have a Chinese servant. (cook & washer man etc.) But we'll miss our kind and sympathetic friends that we parted with at V. We find the people on this side very nice and quiet. [...]

I was very much concerned to learn that you had suffered so much last winter from a carbuncle or something of the kind. I hope dearest niece that you have quite recovered from the effects thereof.

We will take from 15 to 20 days to reach Stewart's Lake from this place according to the weather. My new address will be Fort St. James, Stewart's Lake via Quesnel B.C. which will fetch me every time.[…]

The children attract a great deal of attention especially Hattie. We could not get their photos taken as our luggage was ahead & nothing to dress them in & Ethel had a swelled lip.

I have written to Willie & sent him a parcel from Calgary. […]

Your loving uncle
W E Traill

QUESNEL *September 20, 1889*

My dear Mother

As the boat[5] which brought us up will leave on the 23rd for Quesnel I will drop you a line to let you know that we arrived here safe & sound yesterday after a very tedious journey of 21 days including three Sundays which we remained in camp. […]

As you may suppose Harriet was heartily tired of the trip as we were cramped up in a space about 6 ft square. To keep off the rain we had the tent pitched over our nest in which H- & the children were cooped up night & day. Walter & I remained on deck all day & Walter slept on deck with an oil cloth over him at night to keep off the rain of which we had a great deal. We ate on shore when the weather would permit, but where it rained too hard H- & the children ate in the hold. The river is very rapid with the exception of 30 or 40 miles on the Stewart River. There are several dangerous rapids but the men are very expert and we had no accident whatever.

From Quesnel we followed the Fraser to Ft George[6] where we spent one night, taking part of six days to make that stage on our journey.

A view of Nacausley, an Indian village at Fort St. James, from the shore of Stuart Lake, 1891. HBCA 1987/363–F–61/11

We left Ft George on Saturday the 7th but only got 2 ½ miles from Ft George up the Nechako River. We remained there over Sunday & were visited by Mr. Ogden who rode over in the rain to see us. On Monday we started again & continued up the Nechako to the mouth of the Stewart where we left part of our cargo which belonged to one of my posts up the Nechako. We made a few miles up the Stewart & camped passing Sunday the 20th. The Stewart from its junction with the Nechako is very rapid & some of the scenery very wild. The Stewart is a small river about the size of the Otonabee. The river is full of salmon coming up to spawn but they never take a bait so that we did not kill any, but Walter & I amused ourselves catching trout which we relished exceedingly. The farther up the river we came the more abundant the fish became. We passed many places where the Indians were fishing for salmon. They have very clever contrivances for catching them which I will describe at some other time. As we neared this place we met several canoes either fishing or hunting & they all followed saying they were waiting for me. The 2nd night before we reached here we travelled all night & all the next day only stopping to cook & eat. Our last night we camped about 6 miles below this at the foot of the last rapid.

Coming in sight of the Fort yesterday morning the men commenced a regular fusillade which was answered by a large crowd of Indians gathered round the Company's flagstaff on which the HB flag was flying, a reception which in the eyes of the natives was worthy of an Emperor.

I had been led to expect a fine establishment & a beautiful view but the reality exceeded my expectations. I would give a good deal to be able to sketch that I might give you an idea of the scenery. The lake is a beautiful sheet of water surrounded by mountains. There is a peak five miles distant 2,200 feet high above the lake but the more distant mountains are much higher. One peak distant many miles from the lake they tell me is capped with snow but the weather is too smoky just now to allow a good view of it. Just now the foliage is very pretty. Altho evergreen & poplar with some birch is the principal timber growth yet the tints are lovely. I never saw the foliage of the poplar so bright as here & on the Stewart.

The dwelling house is very comfortable & all the buildings are comparatively new, some of them quite so & good platforms all over. The Fort is on rising ground about 40 ft above the level of the lake. There are no palisades but neat picket fences. I will give more minute details when I write to the girls.

The Indians are a tiresome lot to deal with. Today we had a pow wow but they did not show their teeth at all. Mr. McFarlane who has a reputation for spoiling Indians[7] has not broken his record here. I would rather succeed any other man.

I trust to be able to send you specimens of the flora of this part of the country, but could collect nothing en route as we only had time to eat when we put ashore all the way up.

H-, altho pretty tired has been pretty busy getting things a little in shape today. The children are delighted to be on their legs again. Hattie especially is delighted. She chatters away at an awful rate. She looks the picture of health. The others too do not seem in any way the worse for the long journey.

As soon as we get settled Walter will begin to give the two oldest lessons an hour every day & he himself must take at least that amount of time to keep up his short hand.

I shall have my hands full & will I fear have less time than before for correspondence but however pressed for time I will never be too busy to write to you my dear mother. [...]

And now dear mother I must close. I may not have another chance of writing for some time, so do not be uneasy if you do not hear soon. In a country where mail service is uncertain one should never consider that silence means something wrong. [...]

Walter is looking well & very manly. He could raise a fine beard if he would let it grow but says he will not until he is doing for himself as he thinks it does not look well for a man with a beard to be depending on his parents. [...]

Believe me my dearest mother your loving son
WE Traill
[...]

FORT ST. JAMES *September 22, 1889*

Dear Annie

[...] We were put to an expense of between $80 & 90 having to hire a double team to take us on. The conveyance was an easy riding double spring buggy, but open with only two seats capable of seating 3 persons on each seat. Into this we 8 had to crowd as well as the driver. You may imagine we had not much elbow room. Fortunately as is generally the case with children they slept a great part of the time so that when asleep we were able to stow them under the seats. The weather was rather rainy and unfortunately when changing coaches at Clinton our two umbrellas were left in the coach we vacated & I forgot my

Facing transportation challenges as a pack train leaves Fort St. James. Photo by James McDougall, 1891. HBCA 1987/363–F–61–8

waterproof at another of the stations, so that things were by no means agreeable. We had however a waterproof sheet & H & W had water-proofs, all the others having cloaks we were thus able to keep pretty dry. Fortunately too the owner of the buggy who drove us the first day until he exchanged with a driver of his we met, forgot his waterproof when he turned back—an illustration of the truth of the proverb—"Tis an ill wind that blows no one luck". The first night we made about 13 miles & camped at a stage station & hotel where I met an ex C Factor, Gavin Hamilton. He however was rather under the "influence" & talked in a most extravagant manner of his own doing when in the service. He had been long in charge of the Dist to which I was on my way & gave me no end of advice as to how to manage the District affairs—men & Indians, but like this advice of all drunkards I did not take much stock in it and so "he wasted his sweetness on the desert air". [...]

Next days travel was through heavily wooded country with mountain range in sight at times. We passed the night at an hotel & stage station Soda Creek[8] [...] a place of great note in early mining days but which has not very little left of its former glory as all the buildings are going to rock & many untenanted. On arriving at that place the road descends for many miles into the valley of the Fraser which we came upon here for the first time. The road winds down the precipitous banks taking the most unexpected turns & twists, and often you can look down hundreds of feet on one side or the other. We were comfortably housed & well served as indeed we have been everywhere, but our new acquaintances, the bed bugs which first interviewed us at Clinton, were uncomfortably attentive & the children in the morning bore evidence of their attentions. One of Mary's eyes was quite closed up.

The servants here & else where are mostly Chinamen except stage drivers & hostlers who are all whites.

Next day our route lay along the Fraser. The road often left the river out of sight for long distances, but we were never really more than two miles distant from it. On our right were the mountainous banks of the Fraser & on the left the River—sometimes we descended within a couple of hundred feet above the river bed, at other times the road wound up the sides of the hills until we were hundreds of feet above the river & again we would descend. The opposite bank of the river was always in view & here & there we could see ranches on the terraced (natural) banks opposite and a few on the side our road lay upon. One of these where once stood old HB Ft Alexandria.[9] We had dinner where an old scamp McJuinus from the North of Ireland charged us double for our dinner which however was very good. His old wife had a heavy beard on her chin which however she kept pretty short. She is the second woman with a beard we met on this road.

One of the horses was sick that day & it rained a good deal. To keep the children dry we had to spread our Indian Rubber sheet over their heads.

We camped that night at the Australian Ranch owned & kept by two old bachelors from Australia. One an Englishman—the other a Swede. They were both very nice & took great notice of the children. The servants were Chinamen. The living excellent. We had a three bedded room all to ourselves, Walter sleeping in another room with our driver but not in the same bed.

We had intended going a mile & a half further to Bohanans Ranch as we knew Mrs B- through Mrs. Spencer who was a great friend of hers. Mrs B- is said to be a fine & good woman, but owing to the sickness of our horse as before mentioned we did not, but passed the ranch in the morning the road not running within half a mile of the house. That day there was no stopping place so we carried a lunch with us & made the 28 miles without stopping & drove into Quesnel or Quesnel Mouth about 4 P.M. & put up at McLean's Hotel. There is a HB establishment here but the officer is a widower without family, who lives in a little house with his clerk. There is a large HB dwelling house now uninhabited the floors having rotted away. We were again well housed fed & attended on, the host a miner being very attentive & helping his guests, looking after their every comfort. Here we stayed from the evening of 26th to afternoon of 29th.

Mr. McNaughton (HB) is a very nice person indeed. His wife died over two years ago after little more than a year of married life. He took us to see her grave which is beautifully kept being surrounded by a bed of flowers amongst which not a weed is allowed to grow. He says that he hardly ever allows a day to pass without visiting it. He then took us to his little house. His sitting room he keeps just as his wife left it. She must have been a very ladylike & superior person & very skilful in all ladylike arts & accomplishments as the specimens of her work testify. It was very touching to see how he cherishes her memory.

One thing which is new & interesting to me which I have not mentioned is the mining which is done along the Fraser. Chiefly placer mining but there are extensive flumes, which we first came across near Soda Creek. These flumes are built of boards & timber & are often miles in length bringing water from some creek or lake high up in the mountains, to wash out the gold & also for irrigating such crops as are raised in these parts.

On the Fraser after leaving Quesnel we saw quite a lot of China men washing out gold with the primitive rockers. These men generally work on pairs, one shovelling in the dirt (pay dirt as it is called) & the other with dipper in one hand & shaking the rocker with the other washing out the gold. They make but small tonges but [in] aggregate the output by these men throughout B.C. is enormous. We also saw old mines on the hill sides—tunnels running a long way under ground, but they have long since been deserted, as the pay was small.

As we passed along our Chinese cook [Ah] Chung used to hail his countrymen and ask them how much they were making. They invariably answered from 4 bits to one dollar six bits ($0.50c to $1.50) but Mr. Ogden assured me they were making from $2 to 5.00.

To go back to Quesnel we left that place on the afternoon of the 29th Mr. Ogden of Fort George having arrived from that place on the 26th. You should have heard the row that his crew made as they came down the river beating kettles & pans & singing their national songs—a row that we had to endure with little intermission for 21 days. They sang as they tracked the boat, they sang as they poled her where there was no tracking and when on shore they sang all the time that they were not eating, gambling half the night; such a din as none of you have heard. Some of their Airs by the way are rather nice & far ahead of the Cree & Saulteaux airs.

The Fraser is very rapid & we made but slow progress tracking first on one side & then on the other. [...]

Where the river was very crooked & extremely rapid we made portages carrying the two youngest children. On some of these portages we found lots of huckleberries & some other kinds.

After leaving Fort George which we reached on the 26th & where we bid good by to Mr Ogden we ascended the Nechako River, a clear & very rapid stream. The canyon of the Fraser is very wild & picturesque, and during high water is quite impassable for boats coming upstream. There are several very wild rapids on the Nechako, but it is not half the size of the Fraser & no great difficulty in bringing up a well manned boat. The boatmen are well up to their work.

On the evening of the 14th we reached the Forks of the Nechako & Stewart Rivers, the Stewart being the smaller of the two streams. Here we left 5000 lbs of our cargo for two of my posts up that stream & sent an Indian to acquaint the officer in charge of Story Creek of the same. We went on a few miles and camped. Next day we did not go far as it rained hard until noon after which we put up for the night. Sunday we lay by as usual. Monday we encountered some stiff rapids. Walter & I spent all the time we had while the men were cooking fishing for trout & kept ourselves in fish, as our provisions were principally corned beef & bacon.

On the 17th we reached slack current & the men worked hard & carried on all night half the crew sleeping while the others worked. They sang & poled all night while we slept in the hold as we had done all along having a space 6 ft square to sleep in at night, Walter sleeping on deck with an oil cloth over him when it rains which was very frequently.

18th We carried on & camped at the foot of the Stewart Lake [canyon] a few miles from the Fort. That day we met several canoes who all turned & followed us, the men sometimes coming on deck & working while the women standing up in their canoes poled their canoes along, keeping up with us. They use the pole more than the paddle. The paddle was unlike any paddle I ever saw before being longer & sharp pointed more like a miner's shovel.

We started later on the morning of the 19th than usual having breakfast before starting contrary to custom. The men decorated themselves in their best, one old man making himself look very ferocious by sticking into his belt a Bowie knife & revolver. They also painted their faces which I had not expected as nearly all spoke pretty fair English.

The rapid at the canyon is short but stiff after which there was about a mile of slack current & then another little rapid and then we came out into the lake. The river here divides into three channels, each channel being shut with a barrier of stakes & wicker work to keep the salmon from passing. There are gateways in this in which they set wicker basket traps for the salmon. The fishery is about over but these immense wicker baskets were lying on the low Islands on which are sheds for the storage of the dried fish.

Coming out into the lake we saw the R C Mission to our right & coming further we caught sight of the Fort which is nearer to the mouth of the river but hidden by a point.

We were received by volley after volley of musketry which was answered by the crew who must have fired far more than a hundred shots from rifle gun & revolver. The flag was flying & a crowd of Indians, men women & children assembled to shake hands with the new Master.

I must now close as I must write to Mary if I can find time. As I cannot go over all the ground again I trust you will tell her all of this long rigmarole if you think it worthwhile. Hoping you will have the patience to read so far & with much love to each not forgetting my Willie

Believe me Ever your loving brother
W E Traill

FORT ST. JAMES *September 23, 1889*

Dear Mary

The Fort is a very fine one, all the buildings being substantial & the dwelling commodious & containing many conveniences to which we have been strangers for some time. The dwelling is one story 45 x 33 ft with a wing 16 x 16 which constitutes our bed room which opens into a smaller one which we have taken for the children. The windows are large. The front door opens into a fair sized hall in which are deer & caribou heads for hat & coat racks & the skins of three large eagles not stuffed. This hall opens on the right into the sitting room fully 18 ft square & further on into the mess room a trifle smaller. On the left are two bedrooms of good size & at the other end there is a door & passage

Sir George Simpson Centennial Celebration at Fort St. James, 17 September 1928, some thirty years after Willie was the Chief Trader in Charge of Fort St. James. HBCA 1987/363-F-61/78

leading to the kitchen which is a separate building & in which Ah Chung our Celestial[10] lives & cooks.

There is a stairway in the hall leading up stairs but there is only one room in the attic that has been divided off and it is not finished. The rest of the attic is a mere lumber room or store room at present. There is a veranda in front of the house & platform leading to the office which is just opposite the hall door but about 60 yards away. There are also platforms or side walks leading to every building in the establishment. Under the same roof with the office is the Indian trading shop & some distance further on a large warehouse, a very substantial building of two stories.

Besides these there is a salmon store, interpreter's house, servants dwelling & provision store. These constitute the establishment. As I said before all these buildings are connected by sidewalks & divided from each other by light picket fences. The cattle byres & stables are behind at a respectable distance.

There is a good vegetable garden containing good potatoes, beets, turnips, cabbages, lettuce, onions & horse radish with a few roots of rhubarb.

The scenery is beautiful, the lake a beautiful 40 miles long & from 2 to 6 miles wide surrounded by mountains on every side. There is a peak about 3 miles distance nearly 5000 above the sea & a range on the other side of the lake fully higher. There is a peak beyond the other end of the lake which even now is said to be covered with snow but the weather is too smoky for the cap to show. The foliage just now is very beautiful & the contrast between the orange & yellow & green of the birch & poplar & evergreens is very striking. On approaching the Fort from the lake the most conspicuous objects apart from the Fort are the salmon caches which look more like stage graves of the Stonies & other tribes.

There are abundance of fish in the lake & creeks & Rivers. Salmon, trout of all kinds, sturgeon up to 1000 lbs weight and other fish which I have not yet made the acquaintance of. [...]

WE Traill

FORT ST. JAMES [*November 1889*]

Dearest Kit Kat

[...] I have just ordered from the company at Fort Simpson on the coast a barrel of oolachans[11] to be sent to your father. You will wonder what are oolachans. They are very delicate little fish not much larger than sardines & I trust that you will all like them. You will however give a few pounds to your Uncle Tom & if they like them at Westove a few pounds also.

To cook them they should be soaked all night in cold water & then taken & laid straight on a cotton or muslin cloth & rolled up & boiled for a short time. The cloth is to keep them from falling to pieces. They can also be fried or grilled—such good housekeepers will not be long in finding out different ways of cooking them. I don't suppose they will turn up much before Xmas so you must accept them as a family Xmas present. The greediest will therefore get the biggest present. [...]

The scenery along the lake is beautiful, mountains everywhere some blue in the distance, & along the foot of some we sailed. They are nearly all wooded but some crags are bald & bare & come down to the water's edge almost or quite perpendicular for hundreds of feet. Not a fern or plant and inaccessible. I am too stout & lazy for mountain climbing but must sometime get to the top of Major Pope's cradle—the highest peak within many miles where Major Pope was obliged to pass the night as he would not take advice & take his blankets with him as he was sure he could go & return. When he got to the top he could not return & slept or rather passed the night there without bedding. When you come to see me we will go together to the top & look for Arctic plants etc won't us? & I will give you the room where the grog is kept so that you can have a snifter whenever you like—won't that be nice & then we will fish for trout every day & sometimes for sturgeon, regular sharks of 1000 lbs weight. [...]

Your aunt likes Stewart Lake (I always spell Stwart wrong) but she misses the society we had at V-. Here there are none but Indian women & we can't understand their language. They all speak a few words of very bad French. Their own language is Porter or Currier.[12] They are a branch of the great Dene or Chipewyan family of which the Beavers of the Peace River are also a branch & the Slaves & Hare Skins & Louchoux & Copper Knives & a great many other tribes are also branches.

I suppose there will be no further chance of getting letters after the boat which is now daily expected from Quesnel & I know of no chance of forwarding letters until about Xmas.

Walter teaches Ethel & Jessie about an hour every morning & applies himself to his shorthand for about the same time. He ought to get his typewriter this week when he will have to practice it also for an hour daily.

Mr. Hall the Officer in charge of Simpson District has promised to try & get him something to do in Victoria. I hope he may succeed. [...]

W.E. Traill

[...]

Dear niece Annie

[...] This is such a pretty place & the house is so comfortable, compared with anything we have been used to for a long time. The only draw- back is that we have no society. We miss our kind friends at Vermilion, but then about the time we left nearly every one else left. The whole community was broken up, only Mr. Scott & the family & the Spen- cers remaining.

This is the first fine day we have had for a long time.

Walter was down on the ice skating for the first time this season. He goes very fast but is not a fancy skater.

It is very nice having him with us, but I wish I could get a job for him.

Ah Chung, our cook, is not the best cook in the world but when your aunt is better able to look after things I expect he will do better, as the Chinamen are all quick to pick up anything. His worst fault is extrava- gance. [...]

Now dearest Annie I must close or I will never get through all my correspondence. With every good wish & prayer for your happiness.

Believe me with much love Your loving Uncle
WE Traill

Dear Kate

[...] Hatty would be great fun if I could only write baby talk. She chat- ters incessantly but a great deal is Greek and Latin to us and I have not the art of writing baby talk. [...]

When she takes her place [on] her high chair she gives a nod to Mr. McDonald (the accountant) & says morning Donald, morning Murray *(pronouncing it Mully), morning Kenzie (McKenzie). They are all very much taken up with her.* [...]

She is great friends with our Celestial cook (who is very kind to her and gives her cakes & pies). She calls him Johnnie. We call him John. All Chinamen are called John here.

There are a couple of Chinese ladies at Quesnel. I did not see them but Harriet & the children did & report their curiosities.

Old Mr. McKenzie tells a rather funny story of Mrs. War Lee (one of them) and Mr. Alexander. They were all coming up from Ashcroft in the Stage together and poor Mrs. War Lee got very sick: Like Harriet and many other 'female ladies' she could not stand the jolting. Mr. Alexander got out at one of the places where they changed horses & Mrs. War Lee took advantage of his absence to lie down on the seat that he had vacated. It was dark and when he came in just as the stage moved on he sat down on Mrs. War Lee's head, but did not notice that he had done so. There was another Chinaman on the opposite seat who began jabbering & making signs and then they found out that Alexander was sitting on Mrs. W. He is a very heavy man, and had it not been for the Chinaman no doubt he would have killed her in a very short time. [...]

Our Celestial does the ironing but often scorches the clothes. The other day I gave him a blowing up about it. He said "not me burn clothes. You get too hottee and burn cloths not me".

He told me this morning that I will have to look for another cook for next summer as he is going to the mines. He is not a particularly good cook so I can easily replace him.

There is a day school in Quesnel & sometimes Chinese children go and learn readily.

When the present school mistress went there first there was a little fellow going to school. The first lesson he came to the word book and spelt it b-o-o-k. She told him that that was not right B-double o-K- He replied "B-o-o-k you bet." He had been taught to spell in that way and would not have any new fangled ways introduced. They are conservatives, are the Chinese.

I suppose this will reach you shortly before Christmas so I will wind up with a Happy Xmas and New Year in which Harriet joins me. We expect a young stranger about that time but you will not hear of it until long after. [...]

Believe me dear Kate with much love your loving brother
W E Traill
[...]

FORT ST. JAMES *January 21, 1890*

Dear Kate

[...] I have now to announce the birth of another daughter on the 28th December,[13] the day [anniversary] of the death of our darling Katie. H is all right but she was in dreadful low spirits for some time before. She was suffering from extreme nervous prostration. She suffered in the same way before Mary's birth, and again the spring of the late Indian War. I began to fear she would go out of her mind, but a dose of chloral hydrate[14] cured her like magic.

Baby is not much like any of her sisters at the same age. [...] The children are delighted with it. I suppose you will say What a pity it is not a boy. Now I do not think that is right. We are both just as pleased as if it had been a boy. Perhaps had it been a boy we would have been just as thankful.

I suppose it will be long before we have an opportunity of having her christened and so have plenty of time to choose a name, but I think she is going to be call Julia after Mrs. Young. H and the children wish her to be so named. [end missing]

W.E. Traill

Dear Annie

[...] We find this place dull after Vermilion. [...]

The winter so far has been not so cold as on the other side [of]
the "big Stone" but has been less changeable than I expected. Down
towards the coast it is abominable—rain & sleet & wind—hardly a
fine day all through the winter.

The greatest cold we have had has been 31° below o.

The Lake froze on the 21st Dec.—but Babine Lake they say is not yet
set in some places.

We have open water at the mouth of the river. I have been out three
times shooting lately and each time got a couple of ducks. We live more
or less on fish. That is fish for breakfast, beef or fowl or other game for
dinner and supper.

Walter who has been used to living where there are plenty of people
finds it dull. His time is more or less occupied in teaching his sisters and
in practicing shorthand but still he has a great deal of spare time which
he finds it hard to fill in.

He says that if he can't find anything else to do next summer that
he will enter the HBC if he can. I think he would make a very good
H.B. man but it would hardly suit him were he sent to an outpost.
Then indeed he would find it dull. [...]

I will keep the girls at home for a year or two yet if not longer. I think
the only way for me to do will be to get a governess. It would be much
cheaper than sending them out. I can do well enough for two years
yet but after that time I must really get some one. It would pay Carrie
Muchall much better than dress making. [...]

I believe we are going to have a steamboat on the Skeena River. The
Skeena as you may know is further north than Vancouver. The mouth is
just about the same latitude as Stuart's Lake, but its course is rather to
the north. It will aid very much in the transport and be an easier way of

getting out to Victoria but will not help so far as postal facilities are concerned. To get out either to Quesnel or Victoria is no trouble in summer but to get back is the great trouble, as whether by Skeena or by Fraser it is a very up stream trip and there is current in these mountain streams. […]

Your loving brother
W E Traill

FORT ST. JAMES *January 29, 1890*

Dear Mother

I will be starting off a couple of men on the 3rd with a packet for Quesnel, but the weather has been so bad of late & the snow so deep that I fear they will take a long time to reach their destination. For the last few days it has snowed almost incessantly. The cold had not been great— a few degrees below zero, but the wind has been very high. I pity those who are out among the mountains. I do not know what depth of snow may have fallen here, probably 2 feet of fresh fall—before there was not a foot on the ground, but here there never is any great depth of snow whereas at some places within sight the snow fall is double and in some places treble what it is here.

Mr Peters the young officer in charge of McLeod's Lake[15] is here— detained by the bad weather. He must however leave tomorrow no matter what the weather may be. He will have a bad time of it as at McLeod they had and always do have very much more snow than here. […]

The days begin to lengthen visibly and I trust next month to be able to fish through the ice. There is a very interesting little salmon on this lake. I do not think it is known to naturalists, at least I never came across a description of it. I have never seen them alive but have seen them floating dead in great numbers on the Lache River. They are about the size of Digby herrings. They appear to be a salmon having the appearance and all the habits of the real salt water salmon—they never however go to the sea. They ascend the streams, and perish just as do the real salmon, none of them returning to the Lake. I will get some next summer and preserve them in alcohol & send specimens to some naturalist. If they are known it is curious that I have never come across a description of them. [...]

I hear Ah Chung rattling the dishes in the next room (mess room) so will have to close for the present. [...]

Believe me dear mother Your loving son
WE Traill [...]

STUARTS LAKE *March 18, 1890*

Dearest Mother

[...] I was rejoiced to hear by your letter of your good health, but when Willie wrote (4th Feby) you and Kate were both recovering from an attack of La Grippe. I was most thankful to learn that you were both recovering, and trust & pray that you may be both now enjoying good health. [...]

I have just received a letter from the Smithsonian Institute at Washington requesting me to make collections of eggs etc etc which I will try to comply with. I have [a] copy of The Canadian Crusoes. The girls will enjoy it I am sure. [...]

I am so glad to hear that Walter has written. I am not surprised that he is rather disheartened at the state of affairs in Dakota but fear his going to Montana will be out of the frying pan into the fire. He would be much better off to come north of the line and once more become a British subject. On our side of the line we have not the blizzards & cyclones & vicissitudes of climate that they have in the States. [...]

The children will enjoy being free once more for they have been very much confined to the house. Ethel & Jessie are growing big girls, the younger promising to outstrip her sister. Mary is learning to read very quickly. She will soon be able to read to herself—indeed she does read little things to herself & says that when she is a woman she will write stories like grandmamma Traill. If any one of them turn out clever, it should be Mary. Yum is very like what Carrie Muchall was when I was with you in 1876. She is very slight of figure and promises to be the most lady like. Hattie is fatter than ever and as much of a chatterbox as ever. It is the greatest fun to hear her. I never saw a child speak so plain at her age. [...]

Our Chinese cook will be leaving in about a month's time. He is going to mine this summer. Harriet will have more work on her hands when he is gone. I will however try to replace him when I go to Quesnel.

The present winter has been a most unfavourable one for our trade, and the Indians have suffered a good deal from sickness which has prevented them from hunting. Furs of all kinds are scarce all of these circumstances combined against me in my first charge of a District.

I hope Clinton got the barrel of fish. [...]

Your loving son
W E Traill

FORT ST. JAMES *March 20, 1890*

Dear Kit Kat

[...] I am so glad to hear so well of your brothers. I do not wonder that you are proud of them.

I do not know what to say as to Willie's love affair. It is rather soon for him to be in love. Walter does not seem to be so susceptible, but as far as that goes he may be over head and ears in love with some of the girls in Winnipeg. [...]

The children did not get the books yet. The rascally men who went to Quesnel for the Packet would not carry anything but the letters so papers & books are there yet, but I am going there soon—in fact I have made up my mind to go on foot next week. It is a trip that I dread for I am not used to tramping it now altho I could do that kind of thing well enough when I was half my present age. A trip of 200 miles on snow-shoes is not just the kind of thing I like. [...]

At one of my Posts (Connolly),[16] the spring is always fully a month later than here and the fall at least a month earlier. There they have to wear snowshoes to go to the shop & the same to go to the water hole. We have no wells but get our water from the lake or river as the case may be. [...]

I was much pleased to hear that Walter J.S. had written. He has not written to me for years. [...]

So Emma Barlee has a daughter. I am sure I wish them every joy. Be sure and give her my love. You can do that every time even when I do not mention her name. She is as you know a great favourite of mine. So is Aunt Emma. [...]

Believe me dearest Kitten Katten Your loving old uncle
WE Traill

QUESNEL *April 3, 1890*

Dearest Niece Emily

[...] As you will have learned I left home on the 24th with a canoe. Walter & Mr. Murray brought me down the river 12 miles which is as far as it was open. We had some fun coming down spearing Loche with poles. We got 6 I think. We all had dinner together & then I put on my snowshoes and my men shouldered their packs, bid good by to W & M and off we came. I brought no clothes but socks & shoes & an overcoat in case it should rain. I had no coat only a cardigan jacket. My men carried everything but a small hand axe which I carried & found it quite enough. Their loads were about 60 lbs each but as a great portion of it was grub we got lighter every meal till at last they had not more than 35 or 40 lbs each. I did not even carry a knife & fork. I trusted to my pocket knife.

My Chinese cook came with us as he retired from the service of the HBC, because your Aunt looked too sharp after him. He too carried his bedding & some grub and a long handled miner's shovel as he is going to mine at Fort George. The little man never walked on snowshoes before & we all expected that he would play out, but not so. He always came into camp shortly after us, but "Hi you tired" He was a source of great fun to us but no little annoyance as he lost everything he could get his hands on. We had at the start 3 pots & 4 pocket knives amongst the 4 of us. He lost his knife at the first camp. Next spell he lost my cap. That night he lost my knife and the next day came into camp minus another pot, so that we were reduced to 1 pot & 2 pocket knives amongst us four but I have got ahead of time. I will now give you the order of our march.

25th We got up at 2 A.M. but it was 4 before we got off and good daylight. We footed it until 11.30 when we had dinner. Our road lay along the Stuart River & the walking was good on the whole, but there was water on top of the ice which had frozen but now & then we broke through the top ice. The weather was very warm. We only traveled till 3 P.M. as it got too soft. We left the river about two & took to the woods. Had to climb some very steep hills and go through a small creek which was open.

The snow was very deep in the woods—about 4 feet. On coming to a steep hill I slid down on the heel of my snowshoes which Ah Chung assaying to do came to grief & tore the seat of his inexpressibles if he did not do worse, however skin soon grows & is less expensive than cloth.

Ah Chung was very tired when he got in but entertained us in the evening with some of the most extravagant lies in his pigeon English. As we would not trust him with anything which he could lose he dropped his own hat & did not know it but I was behind at the time & picked it up.

26th We got up at 2 A.M. but having only one pot & two knives we were two hours before we could get out of camp by which time it was nearly daylight, which was as well as Ah Chung could not get through the brush fast enough & could not see our track till it got light so we had to wait for him now and again.

The country was very hilly & the snow very deep. I wish some members of the Snowshoe Club could have a few miles of such country &

such snow & through the woods. They wd think that it was not all fun. We had breakfast at 7. About 10 it began to get very warm & the walking very heavy, but we struggled on till 12.30 & had dinner quite tired. It being too soft to travel we slept till 4 & had a bite & started again. We did not get far before I got very weak & all over perspiration & thought we wd have to camp, but felt better after awhile, when the others began to feel the same way so we decided to camp. It was 6.30 when we stopped so we had a good nights rest.

27th. Started at 3.45. Breakfast at 7 & got back to Stuarts River after going up & down some of the highest & worst hills I ever crossed on snowshoes. In some places a slip would have sent us down perpendicular cliffs of far more than a hundred feet. We had dinner within 12 miles of F.G. but as it was soft we had to stop for a few hours. The last ten miles the road was very bad. We got in to F.G. at 6 PM after a rather trying day's walk, but I was as fresh as when I started. Not so poor Ah Chung who altho he kept up like a man, was quite done out & the next morning cd hardly walk.

I found Mr. Ogden quite well & as fat and pleasant as ever. He is a bachelor about my own age but awfully stout. He weighs 260 lbs or more. He is a very nice fellow & a favourite with all. I stayed all day with him attending to business & preparing for my trip to Quesnel. As no doubt you are tired of my journey—perhaps more so than I was I will burden one of your sisters with the next chapter as I must leave something to write about. So my dear niece I must say good night.

With fondest love believe me to be as ever your loving old Uncle WE Traill

FORT ST. JAMES *April 3, 1890*

Dear Mother

[...] I came on foot to Fort George, my man carrying bedding & provisions having no dogs. We came half way by the river & then struck through the woods that being the shortest. The snow was very deep in the mountains and the road—very rough & hilly. I expected that I would find the trip very hard, but arrived at Fort George fresh as a daisy. There I stayed one day and night occupied with my business & then left about sundown for this place by dog train. I was able to ride most of the way. Here & there we got among rough ice & deep snow which obliged me to walk a little, but on the whole I had a very good trip. We travelled mostly by night as it was too warm & soft in the day time.

We lay in camp all Sunday from 12 AM until about 1 AM Monday when we started again and would have reached this place but it got very soft & the men were too tired. As it was we camped only 4 miles short of Quesnel & as I said before were here before folks were astir.

Mr. McNaughton is from home so I have done nothing but read & answer letters which reminds me that I sat down to acknowledge your very welcome letter of the 8th & 10th March. [...]

Believe me dear mother Your loving son
W E Traill

FORT ST. JAMES *April 3, 1890*

Dear Annie

I am glad to learn that you received the oolachans at last and that they are appreciated. I was beginning to fear that they would not reach you. I sent them by slow freight as express charges are so high. I am much pleased to learn of Willies good behaviour & progress. It strikes me that he might do better in the way of writing but I do not say anything as it might discourage him. He has not the art of letter writing as have all his cousins. Walter writes a very fair letter. [...]

He is asking me for a cricket bat. I have no idea of the cost, but will send him what I think should buy one. If it is too little you will please pay the difference and put it in the Bill.

We had a shock of an earthquake at Stuarts Lake on Feb. the 8th (I think) I took a note of it at the time. I find that it was felt here also. I have not heard whether it was felt elsewhere.

I do not know what to say as to your enquiry when I may again pay you a visit.

Not at any rate before '92 if then. My regular furlough should be in '93. I can hardly afford to go before as then I can travel at less expense as the Co must in that case pay some of my expenses. [...]

Our China man left us and came out with me as far as Fort George. He was all right so long as he had everything his own way, but was very extravagant & where H- began to get about & look after things, he did not like to be looked after too closely especially as we had to lock up some of the groceries, so he asked to be set free which was granted him. They are industrious and with their own property exceedingly careful, but wasteful with their employers property. Their English is very defective & what they can speak is rather too plain Saxon. They know no politeness & are not aware that they violate the proprieties. Mr. Hall told me that Mrs. Hall had occasion to take her cook to task when he told her "You won heap damn foolee" for which he got kicked out altho he plead that he did not know what he was saying. [...]

Believe me my dear Annie & Clin Your affectionate brother
WE Traill
[...]

FORT ST. JAMES *April 5, 1890*

My dear Niece Florence

[...] Well I left Fort George on the evening of the 28th a little before sunset with the same two men I came with from St Lake, & a train of dogs. I had no cariole and when I rode I had to stick on to the sled as best I could. I had no great comfort having to hold on hard. Sometimes

I would doze off to sleep, when a piece of ice would tilt the sled & I would be thrown off on my back. I would then have to run till I caught up & jump on again to repeat the performance. Some places the sled wd run close along the edge of open water for the river, being very rapid, was open in places.

We made 12 miles & camped at the mouth of a creek on a bare place under some trees with a big hill just behind us with a big stone looking as if it might roll down on us at any time & flatten us out. Just as I was falling asleep I got a start from a slide of a lot of stones down the face of the bank but they did not come near us so I went to sleep again to be awakened several times in the same way.

We started next morning at 5. Breakfast at 8 below Fort George Canyon a very rough place. Of course we came up here in the boat last summer. It would make that long glossy hair of yours stand to look on such a place, perpendicular rugged rocks on each side & some in the middle of the roaring seething current. The ice was very rough here and I had to walk two or three miles. The river was open in places and it made me shudder to look on it.

My men being Catholics would not eat beef but pitched in to bacon & salmon. I had calf's head (canned) and was not sorry that they had scruples of conscience. An hour for breakfast for I had a stock of knives & pots to enable us all to eat at once. We carried on till 1.30 when it got too soft for the dogs so had a good sleep and started again at 4.30 and camped at 7.30 having made a portage of about 3 miles up a very high point. In descending again to the river in the dark I got into mud with my snowshoes. The mud stuck to them so that we could hardly lift our feet each snowshoe weighing 10 lbs at least. We tried to get the mud off but only partially succeeded & as we could not walk with them had to camp much earlier than we otherwise should have done. As it was we made fully 40 miles. Here we spent the Sunday as I have made it a rule never to travel on Sunday or do anything else that I can avoid.

On Monday morning I called the men at 2 AM and started at 2.30 and made 12 or 15 miles before breakfast which we had at 7. We passed

Black Water River where there is a village of 2 houses. This village was once populous which the "Bone Yard" hard by indicates by the number of graves it contains.

We had dinner below the Cotton Wood Canyon & thought to reach Quesnel that night & would certainly have done so were it not that we came to a place where the river was open and we had to pass along the edge of a big "slide". It was thawing freely & the water & mud was pouring down the side. We had great difficulty in getting along at the risk of being mired or slipping into the rapid current. The dogs & sled (on which besides our bedding & grub I had $1300.00 in gold) got into the river & we were at the risk of losing the whole thing: however we got them out all right and managed to get past the slide without either being drowned, mired or crushed by falling stone, but we lost so much time that when we got to the Chinaman's ranch 6 miles from Quesnel it was getting dark & the men tired. I could not ride from the Big Canyon so had to walk. [...]

With much love your loving old uncle
W E Traill

VICTORIA *April 15, 1890*

Dear Mother

You will see by the date that I am in Victoria. When I got to Quesnel I found that it was necessary that I should come on to Victoria to arrange business matters.

I left Quesnel last Monday by stage and had a somewhat rough trip in owing to the state of the roads which are neither good wheeling or good sleighing. The snow was pretty well off at Q and for some miles there was a good deal of mud with snow here and there in shady places. At Old Fort Alexandria the roads were dry & flowers in bloom. Plowing & seeding was going on and I thought that as I went south I should find a great change, and so I did but not the change that I looked for. We

soon got into a climate more like what I had left & found a good deal of
snow here & there. We passed the first night at Soda Creek on the Fraser
which we reached at 10 P.M. [and] started next morning at 7—Road
pretty good but an interminable hill to climb which winds round &
round on the face of a very high hill. We ascended for several miles
without encountering a great deal of snow, but when we got to the top
of Carpenter's Mountain we got into deep snow & got stuck. The horses
a 4 horse team plunged about for a while, and after a little trouble we
got out and soon got into a country facing the South & rattled down
the mountain at a tremendous pace & drove into the 150 Mile Station
at a brisk gallop. Here it was that I found that I must come on to V- as
I could not arrange with the freighters I had come to see owing to the
stupidity of the V. people.

Had dinner & started on. Good road most of the way. The scenery is
beautiful. The Fraser hundreds of feet below the road on the one side
and on the left the high mountainous banks, clothed with the Grand
Douglas pine & other woods. We reached Lac La Hache at 7 PM. Here
lives an old ex H B man who is blind. Of course I never lose a chance of
calling on old H B officials & old McKinley & his wife were very glad to
see me. Here we had a capital supper & then drove on 15 miles further.
We did not reach the regular station but camped at a telegraph station.
A miserable house kept by a miserable couple, the operator & his wife
(his bride) for he recently married a young lady of some 50 summers
who did not strike me as possessed of many charms except that of being
able to drink twice as much whiskey as her husband—which by the
by is no mean accomplishment. I believe they pass weeks without having to receive or deliver a telegram so that they have lots of leisure to
devote to each other & the bottle. We got to bed at 12 & started next
morning at 4. The road leads over a mountain & we found the winter's
snow lying deep & cold. The morning was fresh [and] as we climbed the
Mountain we got into a very wintry region & wintry weather. We were
in a wheeled stage. The snow 3 feet deep but the road well beaten—

too well, for a large band of cattle had been driven over it a few days previous. The day had been soft and the cattle had cut up the road so that it was like driving over corduroy or a ploughed field. Altho we drove slow I never got such a shaking in my life. We reached the next station at 2 P.M. The sight from the top of this mountain is grand as we get a good view of the Cascade Range.

Had a good appetite for our dinner, which we dispatched while the horses were being changed & off we went again.

At the next place we changed horses at a tremendous chasm which is close [to] the road but which we did not see coming up—I took a walk along the edge & was much struck with its awful grandeur. At the upper end is a small water fall which disappears at once. Hundreds of feet below my feet waved the tops of cedars & pines. The sides are perpendicular. It makes one shudder to think what might result from a runaway—which is not uncommon on that road. We reached Clinton that evening about sundown. The last few miles the road was beautiful & the de[s]cent rapid. We came tearing down the hill sides at a hard gallop & I enjoyed the ride immensely altho a nervous person might feel a little squeamish looking down on the right, hundreds of feet.

Next morning we started at 6—a lovely drive down a deep mountain gorge of 32 miles. The decent is 2400 feet in that distance or an average of 66 feet per mile. The country is superb. It would require the pen of an angel to describe it. The road is beautiful. The steep hills are covered with Douglas & other pines, set out one would suppose by the hand of man—No underbrush & bands of cattle grazing here & there. Deer are numerous but I saw none. It snowed heavily at times which ob- scured our vision at times. We rattled down the hills at a tremendous pace sweeping around the curves like a flash. [It] is all very nice when the road curves inwards, but when it sweeps round a rocky point where the road is either blasted out of the rock or built up with timber crib- bing one cannot but hope that the rigging is sound, but I could always comfort myself with the assurance that very few people are killed on the road. When stage robberies occur they never harm people who submit without a struggle.

I must now go to dinner so must close. I will try & write Mary in a day or two. I shall leave V- on Friday or Saturday. My love to Kate & Katie.

Your loving son
Caledonia

FORT ST. JAMES *June 18, 1890*

Dear Clinton

[...] In the first place I enclose [an] Order on Sir D.A. Smith for $200.00, one hundred and fifty being board in advance for Willie and the other $50.00 to buy clothing. You have not sent me his account for the last year. Let me know if I owe you anything on last year's a/c. I am much pleased to hear such good accounts of him, and also to know that he is such a favourite with you all. I am afraid that the $5.00 I sent him was not enough to buy a good cricket bat with. I did not know that they are so dear as Walter tells me they are. [...]

Thursday I start on horseback to Fort McLeod 100 miles distant. I expect to be back in 8 or 10 days. After my return I must then go to Connolly Lake nearly double that distance, by canoe. The trip will take me 3 or 4 weeks. I have also to visit Babine which is about 180 miles, but I hope I can arrange to pass that way going to Victoria in Septr. [...]

Walter continues to teach his sisters & practice on the type writer. I will not send him to Victoria until I go myself—if I go—if not he will have to go in September. [...]

Believe me dear Clin Yours very faithfully
W E Traill
[...]

FORT ST. JAMES *July 26, 1890*

My dear Mother

I have very little time for letter writing just now but will not let the chance pass without writing you. It is very seldom if ever that you have allowed my birthday to pass without writing to me when you have been in health which I pray & trust may be the case today.

I have just returned (yesterday) from Connolly Lake whither I went on what must be an annual tour of inspection. I had a pleasant journey but for the rain, and was absent from home 24 days. The scenery is delightful all the way & in many places magnificent especially at Connolly which is beautifully situated at the N.E. end of a Lake 14 or 15 miles long and 2 or 3 in width surrounded on all sides by mountains from two or 3 to 8000 feet in height and crowned with eternal snows. I took an excursion into the mountains but was unable to climb any of the highest peaks. I am getting too stout for such exercise which I very much deplore. [...]

I had some very good trolling for lake & salmon trout, but as I did not take a rod I did not have as much sport as I would had I done so.

I went into the mountains in quest of marmot or ground hog as they are here called, but I took a rifle instead of a shot gun and consequently only got one whereas I ought to have bagged several. I will send a skin some day for Willie who seems to be anxious to make a collection of curiosities and I wish to encourage him.

Tell Willie we got the photos all right and were very much pleased with them. Judging from them he has all the good looks of the family, but that you need not tell him.

Tell Mary that I have been longer in her debt than usual but cannot help it as I am too pressed for time, and will pay when I can. This is always a busy time as we are closing the accounts for the year. [...]

Ever your loving son
W E Traill
[...]

FORT ST. JAMES *December 8, 1890*

My dear Mother

[...] I wrote you from Hazelton since which time I have had but one opportunity of sending off a letter & then I had not time. I only stayed two or three days after my return & then started to Fort George so that I had only time to write one or two letters.

The season was far advanced and I was afraid I might get frozen in, but the season has turned out a very open one and so I got back long before it froze up. The river is now frozen in part, but the lake is quite free of ice yet except in the Bays. [...]

I find my time so much taken up with travelling, and when I am at home with business that I am unable to keep up my correspondence as of old so that my nieces must be content with a letter now & again.

The days just now are very short altho not nearly so much so as at Vermilion. We rise about 7, Breakfast at 8. At half past nine I give the three eldest girls a couple of hours of schooling: besides them I have two boys 13 & 11 years of age. They are sons of one of my officers & are only now learning to read. I have only been teaching two weeks & they can read in words of one syllable. The lessons are very rudimentary—only reading, writing & a little geography & arithmetic. Ethel is quick in figures. Jessie is not dull. They both read much better than they can write but even in that respect they are both improving & as for Mary she promises to read better than either of them. The two eldest have so much nursing & home work to attend to that they have not much time to their lessons out of school hours. [...]

We think of getting a governess for them next year, as I can not find time to teach them & their Mother is overworked. We have no servant. I thought to get a cook at Victoria, but as I turned from Hazelton I had no opportunity. It is very hard on Harriet.

We have had a very bad cold which carried off some of the Indian children at the outposts & one at least in the village here, but I am most thankful to say all my dear ones have been spared to us.

I found a long cheerful letter from W.J.S. awaiting me on my return from Hazelton but altho I have written him in reply my letter is still here. Harriet however wrote him as soon as she received his.

I hope he may visit you as he intended. He spoke of paying me a visit, but I fear he will find it too tedious a trip. [...]

We have just learned of the death of Lawrence Clarke. His health had been very precarious for years. He had a heavy insurance on his life & I trust has left Kate well off. They have 5 boys & one girl. [...]

I wish you could send me a book of short sermons suitable for our services. I often read Talmage's sermons, but altho they are very clever they hardly come up to my idea of sermons such as we require to lead sinners to the Saviour. Indeed in some of them His name is hardly mentioned and in very few, are we taught how to come to Him. I think too much is taken for granted. There are many sermons suitable for believers, but few for seekers & fewer still for those who require to be roused to seek.

I had a book of Rainsford's sermons which Harriet gave to her Mother. They were excellent. We hear occasionally from our most excellent friends at Vermilion & Chipewyan. Their letters are full of interest & kindly enquiry after our best interests. I am sorry to say that Mr. Scott meets with many hindrances, from the activity of the R C Priests & from false brethren & from the indifference of my successor. [...]

Believe me dear Mother Your loving son
W E Traill
[...]

FORT ST. JAMES *December 19, 1890*

Dear Willie

On my way home from Hazelton I met Walter at Babine. We were there together one night. The next day he started for Hazelton & Simpson & I left for home. Since then I have not heard any word of him, but trust

Willie, Harriet, and a number of their relatives. Back row: Mrs. Livingstone, school teacher; Harriet Traill; Barbara Morrow (neé Traill) and her son Dick; Phyllis Bigg; Harold Morrow, Barbara's husband; Winnie Bigg; Percy McKay; Jack Bigg; Ethel Bigg (neé Traill). Front row: Ted Bigg; Willie Traill; Walter Bigg; Harriet Traill (née McKay); Helen Bigg. Hattie, Barbara, and Ethel were daughters of Willie and Harriet Traill. Phyllis, Winnie, Jack, Ted, Walter and Helen Bigg were children of Jack and Ethel Bigg, c. 1914–1917. (Willie Traill Family Collection) Willie Traill 10

he is all right at Simpson. No doubt he will write you. I trust we shall all have letters from him by the Packet.

I had head winds coming home from Babine & reached here my sixth day, being Sunday.

Ethel & Jessie had gone down the Stuart River to meet me as they expected me from that side. When they returned that evening I hid from them. Their mother asked them why they had not brought me. They were quite put out that they had not met me. All of a sudden I popped out from my hiding place & then you should have heard the laughing and fun.

I only stayed a few days & then went to Fort George. I was away nearly a fortnight. Since my return I have not been away from home excepting one night when I went out across the lake to look for some timber. I slept out & shot some partridges & three rats & an otter. I also got one large trout.

Your mother and I went out shooting one day & got 12 grouse & would have got more only I ran short of cartridges. We went out again on Monday to make snares but a snow storm came on. We only made 4 snares but shot three grouse. The snow fell so deep that it covered all our snares so that we have not even gone to visit them. [...]

I suppose you will be having good fun at Xmas. I hope my dear son that you are well & that you still gave your aunt & uncle as much satisfaction in your behaviour as formerly.

We all join in wishing you a very happy Christmas & pray that the New Year will be a happy & prosperous one. [...]

With much love your affectionate father
W E Traill
[...]

FORT ST. JAMES *June 30, 1891*

Dear Annie

Your letter to Willie dated 25th May reminds me how very remiss I have been in my correspondence to you and my nieces, but my dear sister you must remember that I have been on my travels ever since I left here on 8th April & altho I was 16 days in Victoria my time was fully taken up with business matters so that I could not possibly do more than write to say that Willie had joined me & that he was well. Since that time until my arrival here I could not write a letter & after so long an absence I have arrears of work which occupy my time—indeed I find less & less time for letter writing as the years go by. I will now try & devote an hour or so to writing you. [...]

In the first place I must thank both yourself & Clinton for all your kindness to Willie. I do not know what we could have done with him, as owing to his unfortunate failing[17] he could not well have gone to a public school. You will I am sure be glad to hear that he appears to have quite got over that. I wish for your sakes that he had got over it years ago.

You seem to think that I am dissatisfied with your care & management of Willie—I am a poor hand of expressing thanks, & feel quite unable to express how much I feel that we owe to you. [...]

We left Victoria on the 15th May by Steamer Danube for Simpson. We had a delightful trip up the Coast. It is hard to suppose ones self on salt water as the channels are so landlocked that one would suppose oneself on some of the Inland lakes such as Babine, or Tattla. The scenery is fine but the mountains are no higher than they are in the interior. We were always on the lookout for whales & seals, but saw none of the first & only one or two of the last. On the 3rd day early we arrived at the mouth of the canneries where we spent more than a day unloading at different canneries. The fishing season had not commenced but they were making cans at a tremendous rate. In the manufacture of the cans, only Chinese & Japs are employed as they work much faster than whites. It is amazing with what rapidity & mechanical precision they handle the sheets of tin. About 10 men make 30,000 cans per diem or 3,000 cans per man. It would take much longer to describe the whole process than it would for one of the workmen to make a thousand cans.

At each of the canneries we unloaded hundreds of tons of tin & solder. One can hardly conceive that all this tin is used in a single season.

After cruising about nearly two days we steamed on to Simpson which is 40 miles north of the Skeena, altho we had to ascend that river later, but we found that the Caledonia had gone up to Hazelton & so we had missed our chance of getting up to Hazelton.

We found Simpson very dull as Mr. Hall & family had moved to Victoria & Clifford had not yet moved down from Hazelton. Mr. Lockerby, the gentleman in charge is a very nice fellow but his wife is a "klootchman" or Indian woman & is no companion for him. His sister is living with him as housekeeper. His wife will not do anything.

Mr. Robson is a very nice fellow & a particular friend of Walters. He is married but his wife being in bad health is living in Victoria. We employed most of our spare time in fishing from the wharf. We did not get many fish, but some of them were queer critters. We got dog fish, flounders, devil fish, star fish—some with 5 rays & some with 19. They are horrible looking creatures when alive but when dried have nothing repulsive about them.

Willie at Simpson & also at Victoria seemed to be a great favourite.

I forgot to say that I called on the W. Gores. They invited me to spend the evening with both my sons which I did. Both Mr. & Mrs. Gore complimented me on my sons. Willie however seemed to be the favourite. Walter is so much more reticent but he too is a general favourite & the Gores insisted that he should come to see them at least once a week which Walter promised to do.

Willie went there several times & Mrs. Gore trotted me round at a great rate & took me to see the Lieutenant Governor and also to Higgins, Speaker of the House & she would have taken me to call on a dozen others had I felt inclined. I must now go back to Simpson.

We stayed there from Monday till the following Monday. The steamer "Caledonia" arrived on Friday having made two trips to Hazelton, but the Captain did not expect to be able to get up again until after the high water & in that he was not mistaken.

On Monday we steamed out of Simpson taking what freight was lying there, which freight was to be stored at Kitselass Canyon which was as far as it was thought she could ascend. We took a lady passenger aboard at Simpson. She is a missionary (Methodist). It was expected that we would reach Essington at the mouth of the Skeena that night which was her destination, but it blew up a gale & we had to put back (not to Simpson) & anchor in a bay. As there was no accommodation for passengers so Miss Beavis was rather in a queer predicament. She seemed to be quite put out when she learned that we could not reach

Essington, but I assured her that we did not usually eat ladies, and as we were well provided with grub at that time she had nothing to fear.

The Captain very kindly gave her up his room so that she was quite comfortable. I was suffering from an attack of neuralgia which prevented me from paying her as much attention as I should otherwise have done.

At Essington where we "wooded" I met Mr. & Mrs. Fields from Hazelton. They seemed delighted to see me, & Mr. Field made me promise to hold a service in his church at H- en passant, which I did. I also made the acquaintance of several missionaries, Mr & Mrs Gurd, Mr Price, Mr. Pierce & several others. I saw Bishop Ridley for a few minutes.

I forgot to say that from Victoria to Simpson we had as fellow passengers two missionaries (CMS) Rev. Collinson & Dr. Adah. The latter a very nice fellow but a trifle conceited & fancy. Mr. Collinson is a remarkably fine man. He is quite a linguist & very earnest. I wish the Bishop was more like some of his clergy & yet he is a very fine man in many respects.

To go back to our trip up the Skeena we found the river exceedingly high & very swift. Our second day from Essington we reached a rapid which the Captain declined to attempt at that stage of water, this was only 8 miles below the Canyon. We waited one day hoping the water might fall so as to enable us to ascend to the Canyon but it failed to fall sufficiently so the next day we started in a canoe manned with 4 men.

We had to make a portage over the rapid & after a hard day's work to make 8 miles we reached the foot of the Canyon, where we camped at an Indian house.

Next morning we got another man & changed our canoe for a better & bigger one. It took us all morning to get over the "Canyon", a terribly wild place. The men had to portage the canoe & of course we had to help them.

We remained in camp on Sunday during which time the water began to rise again.

Monday we pushed out, and fought against the terrible current all day. Both Willie & I had to help to pole or paddle & sometimes we took to the woods while the men got the canoe past very bad places.

One of the men fell overboard & would have been drowned no doubt seeing that he could not swim, but one of his companions grasped him by the hair as he was swept past the stern of the canoe. He was most unmercifully chaffed by the others for the whole trip. They seemed to consider it a great joke.

The water rose day after day, our progress was very slow, and we were in constant danger. Fortunately the wind was favourable so that our sail helped us considerably but was a constant source of danger as it was too large & the men careless.

Willie was very nervous at first but he got quite accustomed to the canoe & gave good help with his pole.

Our fifth day from the Canyon we reached an Indian village called Kitmangah where we decided to leave our canoe & foot it to Hazelton the distance being said to be 40 miles. We packed all our stuff in bundles giving the men loads of from 60 to 80 lbs each & off we started at 11 AM.

The trail was good and we got along famously that evening only that it rained hard for the last hour before camping time and as the trail was quite overhung with underbrush we were thoroughly soaked.

We were looking for a good place to camp when we were pleased to find and old Indian [community] house which altho decidedly out of repair gave us excellent shelter & enabled us to dry our clothes.

Next morning we started at 5 having risen at 4.

The brushes were very wet and soon we were in the same condition but our men thought we would reach H- for dinner. Soon we came to a fork in the trail & the men did not know which was the right one & of course took the wrong one, which we followed for two hours & which ended abruptly at an Indian garden. We then tried to force our way along the river bank but the underbrush was so thick that we could make no headway—especially the men carrying heavy loads.

Here we got separated. We (W & I) heard two of the men calling on top of a mountain above us; so we scrambled up as best we could through the thick underbrush & "Devils Crooks" but when we got to the top could get no answer altho we called till we were hoarse & Willie fired his pistol. I knew that the road we had left must be above us & decided upon striking out till we reached it but after walking for miles we had to give it up.

Willie was afraid we were lost but I could see the Hazelton mountain on our right, but ahead of us so on we plodded up one hill & down it to a gully & up the other side hanging onto the bushes & through "Brules". At last about 2 PM we came to a mountain stream at high flood with a current like a mill race which we could not cross, & a high mountain right ahead on the other side. We then decided to follow this stream back to the river. We reached the river (Skeena) at 3 PM & found a trail & best of all we heard our men calling away down the river. Here we waited for them, as we were hungry having eaten nothing since 4.30.

When they came up we found that they had left very little for us. We had a snack of a 1 lb can of Oysters & a few crumbs of biscuit. The men said it was two hours walk to Hazelton, but we walked hard for six hours and only reached the crossing opposite to Hazelton at 9.30 after about 14 hours of as hard walking as I ever put in in my life.

I was quite proud of Willie, as he stood it like a man, but he was very tired as you can imagine.

On reaching the river we called for a canoe to cross us, but no one came. I got a big fire made & prepared to have a cup of coffee when all of a sudden a canoe arrived. Mr. Clifford hearing there were white men across sent a crew for us.

Mrs. Clifford bustled round & got an excellent supper for us of ham & eggs & other good things to which we did ample justice.

Next morning the Cliffords who had everything packed for their departure for Simpson took advantage of the return of my men to embark for that place.

We passed Sunday at Hazelton & on Monday morning continued our journey on foot to Babine which we reached on Tuesday evening very footsore, but here our troubles were over as we got a canoe & three men. We were unfortunate in having head wind most of the time but made good time reaching home on Sunday morning about 9.

I will not attempt to describe the excitement & joy of Harriet & the children on the arrival of the canoe. Willie would not show himself but lay in the bottom of the canoe until we arrived at the beach. I had been so long away & not seeing anyone H- was in a great fear lest something should have happened to Willie, but her fears were soon dissipated & joy reigned in the Traill family.

The girls are all delighted with Willie & are all very fond of him as they well may be. Baby & Hattie were very shy of him at first, but now baby is as fond of him as of me.

Now my dear sister I must really close this as I have spent several hours writing & must look after other things. I will see that Willie writes to make up for my laziness.

With much love & again thanking you both for your care of Willie Believe me dear Annie Your loving brother

W.E. Traill

[FORT ST. JAMES *Spring, 1892*]

Dear Kate

[beginning missing] 25th. I have been off to Williams Lake with Mr. Borland our packer, where we passed the night. Mr. Pinchbeck, the rancher we went to see, is an old Englishman who came out here early in the Sixties. He made a fortune in the balmy days of Caribou, but is now in difficulties as the mines appear to be giving out & produce of all kinds is in very little demand and fetches low prices. He has a very fine house but unfinished. The situation is one of the most beautiful I have ever seen. He is surrounded by hills from one to two thousand feet in height, which hills are wood like a park. The lake is very beautiful and [there] is a small river that runs in front of the house which turns his mill. The old fellow has a young wife also English & three very handsome boys. She is educated but he is not & drops his h's in the most approved fashion.

We had a very pleasant evening. One or two of the neighbours dropped in and all were musical excepting myself. Mrs. P. played the piano & sang very well altho her voice is a little sharp. A nephew played the violin & they all sang. Borland is a good singer.

We came home yesterday & I found that the wire is working well both ways, which enabled me to wire for my portmanteau by stage & to Willie to wait for me at Ashcroft. I am sure he will find three days waiting there intolerable. It is the dullest place imaginable.

Had I known how things would turn out I should have written for Willie instead of telegraphing for him. [...]

We had a snowstorm yesterday after we got home from Pinchbecks. The night was cold, but this is a glorious morning. I think we will have fine weather now.

I am impatient to get off from here now that I have done my business here, which was the arranging of a freight contract, the purchase of 27 head of cattle & of 30,000 lbs flour.

If I had my gun I could have swan shooting but as it is I can only write. [...]

Your loving brother
WE Traill
[...]

Dear Annie

It is a shame that your most interesting letter of 26th June should have lain so long unanswered, but the fact is altho the spirit is willing I find but little time to indulge in correspondence. The reason is that they have reduced my staff of [an] assistant so that I have much more to do than formerly. Of course I do not work night & day but am generally pretty tired when night comes, and as for pen, ink, & paper I get enough of them, so that I am glad to get a rest.

All you tell me concerning the last hours of dear Mary [Willie's sister] is of the deepest interest to me.

You know how much more we were thrown together as playmates than any of the others. I little thought when I parted in 86 that I should never behold her on earth again and yet life is so uncertain that when we part for even a few hours we know not but it may be forever on Earth.

It is such comfort to know that she died so happy. Our prayer should always be 'Let me die the death of the righteous' but to that end we should not neglect to live the life of the righteous. [...]

I am on the other hand somewhat anxious about dear Kate [another of Willie's sisters] who you all seem to say is but poorly. No doubt it has been a very severe tax on her strength & nerves. [...]

It must have seemed hard for Clin to have to leave the bank when he was getting along so famously, but I was very glad to learn that he was not long out of a billet & that he is getting along so well & that his health is so much improved. I believe myself any young man with fair education & abilities can get along if so be that they are steady. You have much to be thankful for in your sons who are a pattern to all young men. Walter gives me the greatest cause of satisfaction. I think that he & his cousin Clin resemble each other greatly in character. [...]

After all we shall not be able to have a governess, so I have made up my mind to take the two eldest girls to Victoria. I believe it would pay me to send them to Ont as everything is so high in Victoria & no friends to look after them during holidays. It must be frightfully dull for girls who have no friends & who have to remain at school during vacations when all the others go to their homes. [...]

All the servants are away here and there & Murray off on a shooting excursion. [...]

Believe me dear Annie Your loving brother
W E Traill

Dear Mother

[...] Your most welcome letter of 6th November came to hand on the 3rd Instant—Less than a month which is unusual. I need not say how glad we were to hear from you and to learn that you were well & able to visit in Peterborough. It is really wonderful my dear mother how you manage to get about at your age. You complain of waning powers & faculties, but I see very little difference in your hand writing and except that you occasionally repeat yourself I perceive no change. I am sure I repeat myself just as much—especially if I have to put by my writing for a day or two.

We are now (that is to say the children) full of Christmas making ready for a Christmas tree. We have not much this year to put on it but that makes no difference with them. There will be very little but what they make themselves and we will have fewer people. We will miss our dear Willie very much, but at the same time cannot be too thankful that he is now doing for himself & that his employment is congenial. It is so pleasant to know that he is with his worthy cousin & to know that they are such friends. [...]

Harriet is quite well but rather overworked. The children too are all well & happy. Little Barbara[18] is almost walking. She is a sweet tempered pet & the sisters are all very fond of her. She has no teeth yet but they are coming. [...]

Hattie is not quite so fat as she used to be, but still she is very plump. She is a great chatterbox. Her hair altho very fine is not so curly as formerly She is very amicable.

Yum Yum objects to that name now & insists on being called Maria. She is very dull to learn but I do not think it is from any want of intellect. She too is a great chatterbox at times. She reminds me very much of what her cousin Carrie was at her age. Mary is I think going to be the clever one of the family. She is rather lazy to assist in house work, but always has a book in her hand. She knows lots of hymns & pieces of poetry which she has learned herself without being taught. She can read almost as well as her two elder sisters. I think she would be grandmama's favourite & yet I do not know.

Jessie is very tall for her age. She too will be quick to learn if she is among strangers. I think she will learn to draw readily. She is always trying to draw something or other particularly flowers. Some of her attempts are not at all bad. She is rather too open saying whatever comes to her mind, something like her brother Willie. She has very little tact.

Ethel more resembles her brother Walter. She is not clever, but has no difficulty in learning. She is very thoughtful of others & very seldom offends with her tongue. She is a great help to her mother in all kinds of work. They are all very careless, but were they to see more of the ways & manners of others they would I think mend some of their faults.

I have quite made up my mind to take them out to Victoria next summer (the two eldest) & if I cannot find a suitable institution there I shall have to send them east either to London or Toronto. [...]

We did not hear from Walter by last chance & Willie wrote that Walter was not very well when he heard last. This makes the mother a little anxious.

Walter continues to give us cause to be pleased with him. He is much thought of in the HB Office. I doubt however if they will give him wages at all in proportion to his deserts.

I too have not heard from W.J.S. for a long time. I do not think you should fret or find it so strange that he has not written since the death of dear Mary. You know he is frequently from home for months at a time. He may be somewhere in the far west. [...]

It may be very hard on Tom having to part with Norman & the others, but then on the other hand he must be thankful to see him so well when he expected that he would lose him altogether.

I am deeply grieved to hear of the sad news of my worthy cousin Rowland. I sincerely hope & pray that he may be restored to a sound mind. The loss of property is very sad, but death itself is preferable to loss of the faculties. The whole family have my hearty sympathy, but particularly poor Elenor. It must be so hard to have to break up her household & part with her children & them so young.

You need not be troubled my dear mother because you cannot send anything to your numerous grandchildren. They do not expect presents, and are happy & contented, nor are they in want for anything. If they never know greater want than they have done hitherto they will be better off than most children.

I do not think it probable that I shall remain long at Stuarts Lake or indeed in the service. This district was a forlorn hope for years before I took charge of it. Had furs only been numerous as in past years I should have made something of it, but the country is cleaned out of fur bearing animals & so year by year they are getting scarcer. It is not likely that it will be kept up much longer, besides which nearly all the old hands are leaving & I fully expect I will not long remain in what I consider a sinking ship. Should I leave they will give me a pension for a few years. [...]

We had a very cold spell in November, but of late we have had very fine bright weather and not at all cold. [...] [end missing]

W.E. Traill

My dear Annie

I am your debtor for a letter that I regret to say I have someway mislaid, and I am so busy that I have not time to spend looking for it but will not let the Express go with out a line in acknowledgment.

I need not say how pleased we were to learn that Willie had got employment, and that he & Evan are rooming together.

I have written to Evan [Annie and Clinton Atwood's third eldest son] thanking him for his kindness to Willie.

I hope & trust that Willie will work hard, and do credit to us all. [...]

This is the last letter I intend writing just now. Tomorrow we start the Packet directly after breakfast. You cannot understand the sense of relief to me when I see the Packet closed. I dread Packet time above everything.

I have told the girls that I intend taking the two eldest girls out next summer and placing them at some school in Victoria, or perhaps sending them further east.

It is hard for us to part with them but we can no longer put off the evil hour. They will soon be full grown, and as yet know nothing.

If I can find suitable schooling for them in Victoria it will be very pleasant for both Walter & for them. The trouble will be to find suitable lodgings for them during the long vacations.

I am rather out of temper with the Company and were it not for the education of my family I would soon leave. As it is I may do so very soon. [...]

Ethel has just sat down to write to Emily. She has allowed a letter of hers to remain for a long time unanswered.

I leave them to express themselves as they like that you may know what they can do of themselves. I made an attempt to teach them for a while this fall but soon found that I had not the necessary time. After the Packet is off I will make another attempt—as for their mother she has really more than she can do and to tell the truth the girls have more to do than is good for them & we never could give them time to study their lessons.

I have no doubt but that when they are among strangers and can give their lessons [their full attention] they will learn rapidly.

Harriet has been in very good health this winter, but as I have said has too much to do. She will miss the girls when she has to part with them—more perhaps than I will as I am not much in the house during the day. [...]

Dear mother's health is wonderful for her age. If she could only be persuaded to take better care of herself she might live several years yet. [...]

Believe me dear Annie Your loving brother
WE Traill

EPILOGUE

PRINCE ALBERT *June 18, 1893*

My dear Mother

You are no doubt surprised that you have not heard from me before.
When I last wrote I expected to be going out immediately. The fact is
I was delayed waiting for Mr Hall who was about a month late putting
in an appearance.

As soon as he arrived we made ready, as we had had nearly everything packed up for several weeks.

On the 29th May we bid good by to our very good friends Murray &
McKenzie & embarked on an old used up boat bound for Quesnel. Murray, Hall & McKenzie came a few miles with us and we all had supper
together after which they went back very downcast & we dropped a few
miles further down stream. The next day we had a favourable wind &
made a long distance, running several of the numerous rapids which are
a characteristic of the Stuarts River.

The next day we nearly reached Fort George, running all the rapids
without accident. Next morning we reached Fort George & found Char-
ley Ogden who has also left the service waiting for a passage down on
our boat.

Portaging goods at the foot of some rapids. (Edgelow Family Collection)
Edgelow 20

Fortunately he is rather a coward about rapids so when we reached the canyon he & Harriet with all the children walked over the portage, about 1½ miles through a very rough piece of ground.

We were rather short loaded so I had to stay on board & pull an oar. It was a difficult & dangerous rapid so H was very much afraid that we might come to grief.

As it was, in the worst part of the rapid our steersman was knocked overboard & at once disappeared but fortunately came up close to the boat. He threw up one hand as he was again disappearing. One of the men tried to grab him but failed but another was more successful & succeeded in catching him & four men hauled him in—in the meantime I [missing] to my oar and another held the [illegible] & so held her straight & so we managed to bring her into a [landing] but below the regular landing.

In running the Cottonwood the family were put ashore. Our steers-man—unnerved by the accident at F G Canyon—did not manage the boat well, keeping too far out, so that we could not make the usual landing. We with great difficulty got her ashore about ½ mile further down in an almost inaccessible place. This necessitated H & the children climbing a big hill & then climbing down the face of a almost inaccessible cliff some 500 feet high. However we got down in safety & reached Quesnel on the evening of 2nd Instant.

As it would have cost us almost a fortune to go by stage I got our packer to send a waggon & buggy to meet us at Soda Creek 55 miles below Quesnel. On Sunday morning we again embarked & floated down to S.C. The stage left Quesnel 3 hours before us [but] we overtook it at S.C., but we allowed it to proceed. We lay over until Monday morning. We made the 60 miles by River in 6½ hours including a stoppage for dinner.

We were delayed nearly 3 days at 150 Mile House by rain. From that place we came up stream to Ashcroft. I drove the buggy & a 6 horse team with the baggage followed us.

I am now going to stop as the children are going to Sunday school and I wish to accompany them.

I will add a few lines before closing this evening. The train goes out at 7 AM so I have not much time. Just home from Sunday School but have only time for a few lines as the train goes out early & I have something to look after.

Will write to Kate during the week giving her an account of the rest of our journey & our arrival in P.A. last evening at 9. We are all well & Harriet looks happier & younger than I have seen her look for a long time.

I got a letter from Annie today which I will reply to in a few days.

I wrote to Katie Atwood from Q to try & meet us at the Station but I suppose that she either did not get my letter or could not get out so early in the day. I shall write her shortly.

We met Walter at Ashcroft. He looked overworked. He could only stay one day but being there before us we only saw him a few hours.

I have not time to write Willie by this mail. We found all our friends here well.

We are just now stopping with the old lady Kate & James, but as soon as our luggage comes to hand we will move into a rented house for the present.

I met Darcy Strickland at the station. He tells me that his father is very well.

I must now close. Hoping to be able to write shortly & trusting that you & Kate are well. With much love to Kate & Katie believe me my dear mother in much haste.

Your loving son
W E Traill

PRINCE ALBERT *July 16, 1893*

Dear Annie

It is a great shame that your kind & most interesting letter of 24th May should have remained so long unanswered. I fear you will hardly be inclined to excuse me on the ground of my unsettled state, but really I find it very hard to sit down and write while my plans are so immature & my time is so much broken up by running hither & thither & people running in to see us. We are now a little more settled in our plans, altho not quite.

I have bought a place out of town about seven miles. It is an im-proved property. That is to say there [are] about 50 acres which have been broken & cropped, but which I must get ploughed again before cropping. There is but a small poor house on it, into which we shall have hard work to squeeze for the winter. The out buildings on the other hand are excellent. A stable big enough for a dairy with a loft which will hold as much as a good sized barn. There is also a low byre of equal size. A hen house & milk house—the latter is small. I have paid or am to pay for this property (267 acres) $1500 in three annual instalments of $500. The buildings alone cost double what I pay for the whole.

Chief Trader Willie Traill, who retired in 1893, in his home at Meskanaw,
Saskatchewan, c. 1914. GAA NA-2617-77

I have bought a double waggon & harness & a [democrat] (double)
and a span of horses which I drove yesterday for the first time.

I have not heard from the Commissioner but there is no doubt but
that they will grant me my pension Niz 2 years full pay + 5 years half pay
or about $700.

We (H & I) are going up to the house tomorrow to whitewash, etc.
and will move up in about a week's time.

It is as you say hard for me at my age to turn round & work hard but
if I have health (the greatest earthly blessing) I have no fear but I shall
be able to scratch along.

In reply to a very kind letter to Evan, I have written him that I will
only remove Willie when I am forced to do so. I cannot express my
thanks to your son for his generosity towards Willie & his most disin-
terested interest in his welfare.

I heard from Katie since her arrival at Kelowna but have not had time to reply. I should so much like to see her & we are all so disappointed that she did not get my letter in time enough to enable her to drive in & see us at Moose Jaw. [...]

It is as you say strange that so many of your children have to wear glasses. My own sight is not so good as it was, but it is only at night that I have any difficulty in reading.

We thank you very much for the pinafores you sent, which however have not yet come to hand. Perhaps Katie is keeping them in case she comes to see us. The drawers too will be very acceptable when they reach us. [...]

William, Harriet's brother, arrived with his family from Fort Pitt. He too has left [the HBC]. He has lots of horses & 16 head of horned cattle. We are just close neighbours just now. He will take a farm in the neighbourhood.

We will have a school within two miles of us. If we can manage it, we will keep all our daughters at home. If not I shall send them East. Kate would take one & I would have to make other arrangements for the other, but I think we can manage without parting with them at all.

Our horses are Dick & Dora. The children have already settled the ownership of all the colts Dora may have for the next seven years.

I am happy you say that my girls do not seem behind those of the same age who have been at school & who may have had many advantages that they have been deprived of. [...]

Tell Clinton I am going to go into raising pigs. There is more money in that than in any other form of stock raising. We are overstocked with all kinds of meat except pork in all its shapes & that is imported & fetches high prices.

Harriet joins me in kind love to all. Believe me dearest sister your loving brother

WE Traill

Dearest Kitten Katten

I fear you have quite given me up in despair, it is so long since you wrote me. Like everything else I cannot now lay my hands on your letter. Living in a tent as we have done for the last two months is horrible. We cannot lay our hands on anything we want. My ink just now is a composition hard to describe, but the principle constituent is flies.

I am afraid you may have started for home before this reaches Kelowna. My hand is so stiff with work & so unused to the pen that I cannot write at all just now. [...]

We as I said before are still in the tent but the house is almost ready. Two or three days carpenters work & then some painting & then we can move in, but it will be pretty cramped for us until I can put up a Kitchen which I must do this fall.

Today is cold & blustery & driving mist, so we have put up a stove in one of the bedrooms upstairs which is quite comfortable.

The four eldest girls go to a day school & have to walk more than two miles night & morning. In fine weather it is all right, but in bad weather we will have to drive them or they must stay home. The teacher is a young woman from the village & does very well. [...]

We will all be so disappointed that you cannot come & see us. Were it not that I have hard work to pay my bills just now I would gladly have paid your fare from Regina. The train service is much more convenient than when we came through. There is a sleeper attached & instead of staying over in Regina the train comes straight through & [will be] arriving in P.A. at 9 AM instead of at night as previously.

Aunt Kate drove Walter out & would drive anyone who was coming to see us. She lives about a quarter of a mile from the station. [...]

We hear frequently from Willie who seems happy & contented. He had been unwell [with] a bad cold—but was getting all right again. He always speaks with great affection of Evan who has been so extremely kind to him.

Walter takes the gun occasionally & has brought home several ducks & chickens each time he has gone out, which is an agreeable addition to our somewhat limited bill of fare. I have killed quite a few fish of late too.

Now dearest of nieces I must close.

With love from your aunt & all your cousins believe me your Affct Uncle

WE Traill

21st I was downtown on Tuesday but forgot to take this to post.

I got the two parcels from our Annie for which convey to your mother our united thanks. The things are very nice & equally acceptable. Little Annie goes about telling everyone that Aunt Annie send her some pinnies & daws.

I will write to your mother shortly to thank her myself. Darcy Strickland called the other day to say that he had just heard from his father who said that Grandmamma Traill was up the lakes & particularly well.

We have moved into our house altho it is still unfinished. We will have to leave the painting till next summer.

At the age of 49, Willie began a new life. As is clear from his letters, he resigned from the HBC in 1893 and settled on a farm near Prince Albert, Saskatchewan. In 1900, he and Harriet purchased a homestead near the present day village of Meskanaw, Saskatchewan. Not only did this estimable gentleman continue to be a source of great pride to his family—with his intelligence, dignity, and honesty, he soon became the patriarch of the community. The village Meskanaw was named in his honour (Meskanaw is the Cree word for "trail"), and the nearby hamlet of Ethelton was named for his eldest daughter.

Mary McKay had moved in with Willie and Harriet after the untimely death of her husband William in 1883, and she remained with

Willie and Harriet Traill's abandoned homestead near Meskanaw, Saskatch-ewan. Daughters Annie, Mary, Harriet, and Barbara farmed the land until the early 1950s after their mother's death in 1920. (Willie Traill Family Collection)
Willie Traill 6

them until her death in 1917. Their house swarmed with cousins, nephews, and nieces. Many family members in need found solace and comfort in their home—it was a safe and cherished haven.

William (Willie) Traill died at Meskanaw, Saskatchewan, January 14, 1917. He and his beloved Harriet are buried side by side in the Traill Family graveyard on the northeast corner of their homestead, immediately adjacent to the '44 Trail. They lie surrounded by much-loved family members. Two hundred yards west of their resting place stands a cairn that commemorates their impact on, and contribution to, the community.

Willie and Harriet's eldest son, Walter, married Harriet Ann McKay at Prince Albert, Saskatchewan, on January 9, 1895. They had four sons and five daughters. In 1925, Walter's strange odyssey involved the family in a lengthy, troubling, and never-solved mystery. His saga is described by Marion Hage (neé McKay), one of his granddaughters, in "Ken Munro thinks he has found your father":

First silence, then tears and questions. I don't know why I was home from school but this was the day in about 1951 that I learned I had a grandfather. Until then I had believed a rather thin story that he had fallen off his horse and been killed on his way home from a summer's work.

At first, Katie and mother decided to let sleeping dogs lie, but Ken said "If you don't go to find him, I will." With that, Ken and Winnie Munro (neé Bigg) took Katie (Traill) Totty, and my parents Jessie (Traill) and Percy McKay to Kelvington, SK, where Ken had seen him at a Saskatchewan Wheat Pool meeting. When his daughters saw and heard him, Katie walked over, put her arms around him and said, "Twenty-six years is a long time, Dad."

Short visits were followed by longer visits, and eventually he saw all his children and spent time with them before he died at Katie's May 10, 1957.

The mystery of his long disappearance will never be solved, but his account was to the effect that he had started for home with his summer's wages, and stayed over in Melfort. The hotel was overcrowded and he had shared a room with a stranger. Next morning, the stranger was gone and so was his money. Shattered, he suffered a blackout, a condition that had happened before. When he recovered his mind, he had some furs, and people were calling him "Mac." Again he started for home, but met an acquaintance who told him "You can't go home. Your family has disowned you." Not knowing what else to do, he assumed the name "Macdonald" and went on with his life after a fashion. He was more or less adopted by the Willard Hall family of Kelvington. He worked at their mill and was serving as a caretaker when the family found him. Mrs. Hall knew he had a family as when he was very ill, he talked about them and his "little dark girl," my mother. She had been in school in Prince Albert and when she asked her mother what had happened, Grandma said, "Oh, he's had a memory lapse. He's had them before."[1]

There is no record of alcohol, other women, or other vices. Walter's oldest son, Dougal, had been killed in World War I—that had been a deep blow to him, and the challenge of providing for a wife and eight children had worn him down. Aunt Annie also told me that Walter had had typhoid when he was young and had never been the same after that. Being the eldest child and losing three younger siblings would also have put a strain on him.

During all those years of estrangement, he was never very far from his family, but apparently no one made a great effort to find him. He mentioned a kind letter from his, Barbara Morrow, but maybe that was after he was found.

Willie's second eldest son, William (also called Willie) married Nellie Fortescue in 1909, in a union blessed with a daughter and a son.

Ethel, the eldest surviving daughter of Willie and Harriet, married Jack Bigg, a former member of the North West Mounted Police, in 1901. They were the proud parents of three girls and five boys. A lifelong nomad, Jack moved his family to a variety of Saskatchewan locations including Maple Creek, Tisdale, and Meskanaw. When Ethel died, leaving Jack a widower with seven small children, Annie and Mary informally adopted her youngest son Hugh.

Jessie married Bill Drever in 1900. They had two daughters and four sons, and became successful ranchers near Hardisty, Alberta.

Maria (known all her life as Yummie, so named by her father after The Mikado's Yum Yum) married John McCloy, a Boer War veteran, in 1903. On a farm a few miles south of Kinistino, Saskatchewan, they

Kate Clarke (neé McKay) standing, and seated left to right are Harriet Traill (neé McKay) and Mary McKay (neé Cook). This photograph was probably taken on the family farm at Maskanaw in the early 1900s. Traill family collection.

raised their two daughters and four sons—one of whom was Pat McCloy, to whom this book is dedicated. With their usual generosity, Annie and Mary provided Pat with financial support, which enabled him to obtain a degree in Library Sciences.

Hattie never married. Like Annie and Mary, she unselfishly provided warm and loving care to many members of her extended clan. For a brief period after her sister Ethel's untimely death, she helped her brother-in-law raise his seven children.

Barbara, the baby of the family, married Harold Morrow in 1914, and raised two sons and one daughter.

After the death of their parents, Mary and Annie (fondly dubbed "the Aunts") took over the operation of the family farm. No one in need was ever turned away from their door, regardless of race or creed. The Aunts continued their father's practice of extending a warm and sincere welcome to the local Indian band. They were pillars of the Anglican Church and Christians in the best sense of the word. They practiced and epitomized the many personal virtues they had assimilated from their parents. And they ensured that these virtues and the Traill family history, in which they took considerable and understandable pride, were passed to their many younger family members.

Mary, a registered nurse, operated a small community medical clinic in their home. She was the Commander-in-Chief of the family—an intelligent, dynamic woman who never married, she must have scared any potential Meskanaw swain right out of his wits. She managed a bottomless job jar with skill, wit, and endless zeal. She performed—or ensured that someone else performed—all domestic tasks commensurate with a well organized household.

Annie was a gentle soul. The third woman in the family to forego marriage, she took on the outside chores: feeding, watering, and caring for the animals, sowing and harvesting the crops, and generally tending to all aspects of a farm operation. The farm continued to attract a plethora of nieces and nephews like a welcoming magnet. An affectionate hug and a kind word were always available.

It was a source of family pride that Mary could, well into her nineties, complete *The New York Times* crossword. She died a few months short of her 101st birthday—she had been determined to live as long as her cousin Annie Atwood, who had also celebrated her 100th birthday. Sadly, Annie was taken, before her time, in her eighty-eighth year.

GENEALOGY

William Edward Traill
(1844–1917)

married
Harriet McKay
(1847–1920)

Walter
(1870–1957)
— *married*
Harriet Ann McKay
(1872–1948)

- Allan Dougal (1896–1918)
- Henry Magnus (Harry) (1898–1976)
- Evelyn (1901–1990)
- Catharine Parr (Katie) (1903–1990)
- Edna (1906–)
- William Edward (Bill) (1907–1985)
- Jessie (1910–1999)
- Florence Marion (1912–1974)
- Roland McKay (1914–1977)

Catharine Parr (Katie)
(1871–1878)

Mary (Mollie)
(1873–1874)

William McKay (Bill)
(1875–1969)
— *married*
Eleanor Frances Fortescue (Nellie)
(d. 15 Dec 1928)

- Evadne Frances Gertrude (1910–2004)
- William Fortescue (1913–1913)

Henry
(1877–1878)

Ethel
(1879–1919)
— *married*
Frederick Johnstone *Bigg* (Jack)
(1875–1967)

- Phyllis Margaret (1902–1991)
- Winifred Harriet (1904–1994)
- Harold Edmund (Ted) (1905–1978)

Jessie
(1881–1970)
— *married*
William Rothney *Drever* (Bill)
(1873–1961)

- Walter Lionel (1907–1986)
- Helen Mary (1910–1979)
- Frederick Johnstone (Jack) (1912–1975)
- Richard Grenville (1914–1915)
- Hugh Traill (1917–1973)

Mary
(1883–1984)

Maria (Yummie)
(1886–1969)
— *married*
John *McCloy*
(1875–1965)

- William Cyril (1901–1995)
- Albert Percival (Adam) (1903–1985)
- Richard Ernest (Dick) (1905–1982)
- Jessie Rothney (1915–)
- Eric Justus (1917–1919)
- Ethel Jean (1919–)

Harriet (Hattie)
(1888–1930)

Anne
(1889–1977)

Catharine Barbara
(1892–1990)
— *married*
Harold Kells *Morrow*
(1892–1924)

- William Richard (Dick) (1915–1968)
- Robert Fowler (Bob) (1917–)
- Edith Jean (1920–1982)

- Thomas Rennie (Pat) (1906–1996)
- Aileen Winifred (1909–1998)
- Kathleen Dorothy (1912–2002)
- John Kenneth (Jack) (1916–1997)
- Charles Dennis (1924–2003)

BIBLIOGRAPHY

Beaumont, Raymond, Ed. *Grand Rapids Stories: Vol. 2*. Winnipeg: Frontier
    School Division No. 48, 1996–97.

Beaver Magazine, March, 1935.

Beaver Magazine, August, 1923.

Beaver Magazine, September, 1931.

Beaver Magazine, Spring, 1956.

Butler, William Francis. *The Great Lone Land: A Narrative of Travel and
    Adventure in the North-west of America*. London: Low, Marston, Low,
    and Searle, 1872. Reprint, Edmonton: Hurtig, 1968.

Cowie, Isaac. *The Company of Adventurers on the Great Buffalo Plain*.
    Toronto: Briggs, 1913.

Glenbow Archives, Pat McCloy Fonds.

Glenbow Archives, Traill Family Collection.

Hargrave, Joseph James, *Red River*. Montreal: Lovell, 1871. Reprint, Altona,
    Manitoba: Friesen, 1977.

Hudson's Bay Company Archives, Provincial Archives of Manitoba.

Manitoba Historical Society website,
    http://www.mhs.mb.ca/docs/pageant/08/mckay_j.shtml

National Archives of Canada, Traill Family Collection.

Personal collection, Marion Hage.

Personal collection, W.M. Traill.

Public Archives of Canada, RG 381A, Vol. 106.

Saskatchewan Archives Board.

Traill, Catharine Parr. *Canadian Wild Flowers*. Montreal: Lovell, 1868.

————. *The Female Emigrant's Guide, and Hints on Canadian Housekeeping*.
    Toronto: Maclear, 1854.

————. *I Bless You In My Heart*. Edited by Carl Ballstadt, Elizabeth Hopkins, and Michael A. Peterman. Toronto: University of Toronto Press, c1996.

Traill, Walter John Strickland. *In Rupert's Land: Memoirs of Walter Traill*. Edited by Mae Atwood. Toronto: McClelland and Stewart, 1970.

NOTES

ONE: FORT GARRY, 1864

1   *Beaver*, 1956 Spring 44.
2   Lower Fort Garry is now a museum site northwest of Winnipeg, Manitoba.
3   Fortune City website, http://members.fortunecity.com/cptdad/45.html
4   *Beaver*, 1923 August 418; *Encyclopedia Canadiana*, 4: 217.
5   A faint note in the margin of the letter, written in pencil in Pat McCloy's handwriting, notes that this letter was "written between July 15 and 22nd 1864. Probably July 21/64—Letter copied by Mrs C.P. Traill."

TWO: FORT ELLICE, 1864–1867

1   Cowie, Isaac, *The Company of Adventurers on the Great Buffalo Plain*, (Toronto: Briggs), 1913.
2   *Saskatoon Star*, May 12, 1917.
3   Walter John Strickland Traill, *In Rupert's Land: Memoirs of Walter Traill*, ed. Mae Atwood (Toronto: McClelland and Stewart), 1970, 49. Walter Traill was Willie's brother.
4   Buffalo were plentiful in 1865, but by the late 1870s large herds were a fast-fading memory. Buffalo had been the Plains Indians' predominant staple, providing the vast bulk of their food, shelter, and clothing. Without a viable substitute, the Indian's traditional way of life was in jeopardy. Historians estimate that, by 1893, decimated by indiscriminate slaughter, less than 500 buffalo remained, a miniscule remnant of the vast herds—perhaps as many as 70 million—that had roamed the Great Plains before the arrival of the European.
5   The Moose Mountains are approximately 60 km west-southwest of present-day Virden, Manitoba; the Wood Mountains are approximately

300 km west-southwest of the Moose Mountain, SK, southwest of Twelve Mile Lake, SK, and astraddle the international boundary.

6   This letter is available from the SAB, NAC, and GAA.

7   The current month.

8   Rocky Mountain House is approximately 1200 km west of Fort Ellice.

9   Mr. McKay was born in 1819 at an HBC post "in the valley of the Assiniboine near the mouth of Beaver Creek, ...about 400 yards east of the site on which Fort Ellice was established in the autumn of 1831." Manitoba Historical Society website at http://www.mhs.mb.ca/docs/pageant/08/mckay_j.shtml

10 Buffalo and other dried meat.

11 Willie's youngest brother.

12 Although lacking a formal education, William McKay taught himself to read and write.

13 Grizzly bears are no longer indigenous to the Fort Ellice region.

14 Undoubtedly 40 pounds sterling.

15 Also called muskrats or musquash.

16 Possibly a derivative of "bobtail."

17 Probably in what is now Riding Mountain National Park.

18 Chief Trader (later Chief Factor) Robert Campbell.

19 "When the Hudson's Bay Company began trade with the First Nations, goods were bartered directly. Gradually, however, counters such as ivory discs, small wooden sticks and other objects were introduced to facilitate the transactions. About the middle of the 19th century, tokens with a stamped value replaced these counters. In northeastern Canada the tokens were generally valued in 'made beaver.' However, in the prairies and western Canada, where trading was not primarily in furs, the tokens had values based on the dollar." Government of Canada, *Canada's Digital Collections* at http://collections.ic.gc.ca/bank/english/edec83.htm

20 Walter Traill wrote similarly: "in addition to these items and the sugar each HBC employee receives annually, 20 lbs tea, 10 lbs raisins & currants, 5 lbs cocoa, and the following liquor ration—2 gallons Sherry, 2 Port, 2 Brandy & 2 Rum or whisky." Walter Traill, *In Rupert's Land*, 49–50.

21 In the Moose Mountains. Willie may be referring to the place he dubbed Fort Defiance.

22 The free traders' sale of liquor to the Indians diverted considerable business away from the HBC. Egg Lake Journal excerpts below show in 1853, liquor had been a major item of trade for the HBC. However, by the 1860s, its use was no longer encouraged by the Company: "Oct 21, 1853. We arrived at the Guard Post at last..., about an hour after our arrival we were visited by the old Sky Ruttler and his followers, we gave them each a plug of tobacco & a glass of Rum, and after a short conversation on different matters with regard to trade—two Quarts of Rum were given to them, as a token of goodwill & Friendship of my being the first time

among them, they went off quite contented with many fair promises that they would endeavour to please me too.[...]" / "Saturday, Nov 5, 1853. Our visitor of last Thursday Asaskookanaib, having received his gratuity of rum. Three quarts. Three quarts for his father, old Terrangeau, and two quarts for the Yellow Head. And one quart for Mecamass, took his departure from us very well pleased indeed. He made many fair promises that he would exert himself in collecting Fine Furs to pay his Debts." HBCA B.62/a/1.

23 "Fort Ellice, too, had its regular fur-trading outpost in the wooded Riding Mountains, from which it derived large quantities of fine furs trapped by the splendid hunters of the Saul-teaux tribe, of whom the family of Little Bone (Ouk-an-nay-sic) was the most expert." Cowie, *Company of Adventurers*, 187.

24 The McKay daughters, Harriet and Kate, "were enrolled in the school 'for young ladies' that Miss Matilda Davis operated at Red River from 1858 until 1873." GA-PMF M8486/182.

25 Wife of Chief Trader Robert Campbell.

26 Catharine Parr Traill, *The Female Emigrant's Guide, and Hints on Canadian Housekeeping*. First edition, Toronto: Maclear, 1854.

27 Willie may be referring to an area from Moose Mountain in the east to Cypress Hills in the west, and from Fort Benton in the south to the Qu'Appelle valley in the north.

28 Jerry McKay was one of William McKay's younger brothers and a fabulous character. "He could run foot and snowshoe races and with dog-trains for days and nights in succession with the best in that land of runners.... I don't know if there were any better buffalo hunter on the plains, for, mounted on an ordinary runner, and armed with a common Indian single barrel flint-lock (such as that used by Lamack), he would commence firing as soon as he came within range, often killing two selected buffalo before his companions considered it worthwhile to waste ammunition at such a distance, and continue the race till his mount was blown and he had slain thirteen choice animals." Cowie, *Company of Adventurers*, 216–17.

29 A copy of this letter was obtained from the SAB.

30 Willie's record of the location and date of writing are not on this letter. However, the text of the letter suggests he is writing from Fort Ellice, and the words "to Annie March 1865" have been written in the margin.

31 A method of transferring money. A cheque or other negotiable instrument.

32 An inflammation near a finger or toenail.

33 "Qu'Appelle (the Calling Valley of the Cree) post was erected in the 1850s. The first fort on the Qu'Appelle, Fort Esperance, was erected by the NWC 'two short days' march by canoe to the riviere qui Appelle from its mouth. The first HBC post was built 17 miles south of the present day

town of Fort Qu'Appelle. The Fort was re-sited between Echo and Mission Lakes by Peter Hourie, in 1864. The area near Qu'Appelle was the traditional scene of many skirmishes between the Cree and Saulteaux on one side and the Blackfoot Confederacy and their allies on the other. In 1869, Joseph McKay, another of William's younger brothers, built a post on Last Mountain Lake, some 80 kms West of Qu'Appelle." *Beaver*, 1935 March 20.

34   Walter joined the HBC on June 1, 1866. His twelve years with the HBC are described in the very interesting and entertaining book *In Rupert's Land: Memoirs of Walter Traill*, ed. Mae Atwood (Toronto: McClelland and Stewart), 1970.

35   Willie's reference to Harriet's mixed ancestry is not exactly correct. Both William and Mary McKay had Cree ancestors. William's maternal great grandfather John Favell, Jr. was married to Titameg, a Cree woman from the James Bay Region. Mary's paternal grandfather, Williams Hemmings Cook, was married to a Muskego Cree woman named Kahnapawanakan and her maternal grandfather William Sinclair's wife was Nahoway, a Cree from Fort Prince of Wales. Raymond Beaumont, ed., *Grand Rapids Stories: Vol .2* (Winnipeg: Frontier School Division No. 48) 1996–97.

36 · Willie's brother Walter described a cariole (a type of buggy) as "made of 2 oak boards 10 feet long, 10 inches wide and 1 inch thick. These are planed at one end and turned up so as to form a floor 20 inches wide with a front end to protect the traveler. This is covered with buffalo parchment stretched on a light frame and extended from the front to 4 feet back so as to form a shoe in which one can sleep. There is an upright back or heel in front of which is the opening by which the passenger enters the bag in which he can sit comfortably with back supported and when not sleeping. Behind this the floor extends 2 feet in order to provide room for the driver to stand if he cares to ride. Unless it is bitterly cold the cariole provides a delightful way to travel." Walter Traill, *In Rupert's Land*, 62.

37   There is no record of anyone else ever outshooting this very capable huntress. It is conceivable that Mrs. McKay quietly let Willie outshoot her due to his status as a favoured son-in-law to be. Mrs. McKay's eulogy told the following story: "Two Blackfeet...found themselves one morning in the vicinity of Fort Ellice. They were in hostile territory, so they hid themselves.... All day they lay among the trees watching the goings and comings at the fort. Towards evening Mrs. McKay came walking alone down towards the river looking for mallards, on which to test her new gun....Arrow was laid to bow, and scalping knives loosened in sheath, while Mrs. McKay unconsciously walked toward her danger. When almost within striking distance she paused. A crow was wheeling over a bluff sixty yards away. Thinking this a good opportunity to try the range of the new gun, she fired at the bird which fell. The noise of the shot startled a flock of mallards.... Quickly throwing out the empty cartridge

she reloaded, and with two quick shots brought down a pair of ducks to the astonishment of the watchers. After a whispered consultation they decided it would not be wise to meddle with a woman in possession of such a weapon. Many years afterwards when breech loaders had ceased to be a mystery, and the Blackfeet no longer road on war parties, one of the Indians related the incident to a missionary, and Mrs. McKay learned of the danger in which she had stood on that day on the banks of the Qu'Appelle." *Saskatoon Star*, May 12, 1917.

38   Probably 15 shillings.

39   Mary's husband.

40   Original letter owned by W.M. Traill of Victoria, BC.

41   The year 1867 was written in the margin of the transcribed letter.

THREE: TOUCHWOOD HILLS, 1867–1869

1   The name relates to the Cree Indians' practice, prior to the development of matches, of obtaining wood from the region. Dry wood from the locale was easily lit using flint and steel—it "lit to the touch," so to speak. Between 1849 and 1879, the Touchwood Hills post was located at four different sites. In approximately 1860, it was moved to Little Touchwood Hills about 30 miles away from the first location and amalgamated with Fort Qu'Appelle. In 1867, it returned to the original Touchwood Hills site. In 1879, buildings from the old post were relocated adjacent to the main trail north between the Indian Reserves. HBCA Post Records Section 25 Touchwood Hills Post Mark.

2   The post was abandoned in 1909. HBCA Post Mark B.357.

3   HBCA Post Mark B.62.

4   Sir William Francis Butler (1838–1910). William Butler was born in Ireland, and served for 47 years with great distinction in many of the major campaigns of the Victorian era, including the Red River expedition, the Ashanti Wars, the Zulu War, and the relief of Khartoum. In his last campaign he was, briefly, Commander-in-chief during the Boer War. In 1872, he wrote *The Great Lone Land: A Narrative of Travel and Adventure in the North-west of America*, Edmonton: Hurtig, 1968 (Original publisher: London: Low, Marston, Low, & Searle, 1872). The book documents his "mission to report on the need of troops, the fur trade, the Indian's etc., in Saskatchewan, following the course of the Saskatchewan River from Carlton to the Rocky Mountains." He retired in 1905 with the rank of Lieutenant General.

5   Butler, *Great Lone Land*.

6   Cowie, *Company of Adventurers*, 342–43.

7   Willie had proposed to Harriet McKay. They married at Fort Ellice, June 1, 1869.

8   James Fenimore Cooper, author of *The Last of the Mochicans*.

9   James George Traill, 1833–67.

10 This poem is a paraphrase of Job 5:6.

11 Née Amelia Keye Muchall.

12 Sometimes referred to as the Guard Post, the bleak Egg Lake post seems to have guarded little more than a sizable swamp and a horde of mosquitoes.

13 A "bull dog" is a Prairie nickname for a horse fly—a large biting insect with no redeeming features.

14 Westove, the Traills' home in Upper Canada, was named for the their ancestral home in the Orkney Islands.

15 Captain William F. Butler, told a similar tale. "Seven men in thirteen days consumed two buffalo bulls, seven cabrie, 40 lbs of pemmican, and a great many ducks and geese, and on the last day there was nothing to eat. I am perfectly aware that this enormous quantity could not have weighed less than 1600 lbs. At the very lowest estimate, which would give a daily ration to each man of 18 lbs.; but, incredible as this may appear, it is by no means impossible. During the entire time I remained at Fort Pitt the daily ration issued to each man was 10 lbs. of beef. Beef is so much richer and coarser food than buffalo meat, that 10 lbs. of the former would be equivalent to 15 lbs. or 16 lbs. of the later, and yet every scrap of that 10 lbs was eaten by the man who received it. The women got 5 lbs., and the children, no matter how small, 3 lbs. each." Butler, *Great Lone Land*, 310.

16 The Cypress Hills are located about 15 miles due south of present-day Maple Creek.

17 The enemy referred to was doubtless the Blackfoot Confederacy, composed of three tribes: the Piegan, the Blood, and the Siksika—collectively traditional enemies of the Cree, the Saulteaux, and the Stoney.

FOUR: SASKATCHEWAN RIVER POSTS, 1869–1874

1   Fort Pitt, midway between Carlton House and Edmonton House, was opened in 1829 and abandoned in 1890. HBCA-PAM Post Records: Post No: B.165.

2   Carlton House had been established in 1795 by James Sanderson. Before 1910, when it was established on its final site near Crossing Place on the south bank of the North Saskatchewan River, it had had three locations: near the confluence of the North and South Saskatchewan, at Upper Nipawin, and at South Branch House. During the North West Rebellion of 1885, the post accidentally caught fire while being abandoned and was torched by the rebels a few days later. The post never reopened. HBCA-PAM Post Records: Post No: B.27.

3   A grist mill, installed in 1880, was destroyed by fire in 1884 and soon replaced. The farm ceased operation in 1914. HBCA Prince Albert Post Records: Post Mark B.332.

4   Catherine Parr Traill to Frances Stewart, July 15, 1870, *I Bless You In My Heart*, eds. Carl Ballstadt, Elizabeth Hopkins, and Michael A. Peterman (Toronto: University of Toronto Press), c1996, 185.

5   On October 10th, 1870, The Honourable Adams G. Archibald, Lieutenant Governor of Manitoba, commissioned Captain William Francis Butler to report on a number of matters, including any requirement to send troops to the region, the status of the smallpox epidemic, the Indian population, their nations and tribes, between Red River and the Rocky Mountains, and the health of the fur trade. Butler's first-rate General Report, dated March 10th, 1871, has been reproduced as an appendix to his book, *The Great Lone Land*.

6   Butler, *Great Lone Land*, 371.

7   Willie and Harriet were married at Fort Ellice June 1, 1869.

8   This is apparently the only letter still in existence of those written by Willie in the period from October 1869 to November 1870.

9   While recovering from the assault described by Cowie, Willie learned that his brother Harry, a guard at the federal penitentiary in Kingston, Ontario, had been murdered by prison inmates.

10   Lawrence Clarke, later Chief Factor Clarke, subsequently married Harriet's younger sister Kate.

11   On February 26th, 1870, Harriet gave birth to a son; they named him Walter.

12   D.A. Smith was possibly the most remarkable of the many Scots whose intelligence, ambition, energy and drive helped forge the Canada we cherish today. At age eighteen, he joined the HBC. His first posts were in Quebec, (1841–48). He served in Labrador for the next twenty years. He was appointed chief trader in 1852 and chief factor in 1862. In 1870, he was appointed chief commissioner of the HBC in Canada and, in 1889, being the Company's largest shareholder, he was appointed governor. His meteoric rise in the Company arguably pales by comparison to his other endeavours. He was appointed to effect the transfer of Rupert's Land to Canada in 1869, elected to the Manitoba legislature in 1870 and to the federal House of Commons in 1871, appointed Canada's high commissioner to London in 1887, and substantially bankrolled the construction of the CPR—he drove the last spike at Craigellachie, BC. He was appointed president of the Bank of Montreal in 1887 and chancellor of McGill University in 1889. He equipped and maintained Lord Strathcona's Horse, one of the Canadian regiments that took part in the Boer War. He was raised to the peerage as 1st Baron Strathcona and Mount Royal in 1897. *Encyclopedia Canadiana*, 9: 337.

13   Harriet's round trip to Fort Ellice to bring her sister Kate to Carlton must have exceeded 600 miles. Harriet was seven months pregnant and had their twenty-month-old son Walter in tow. They were on the trail for 22

days in early winter, averaging roughly 27 miles per day. Willie would later write: "Again in the early seventies my wife paid a visit to her parents, then living at old Fort Ellice. I was then stationed at Prince Albert. She travelled with one man and several horses. On the Big Salt Plain they had the misfortune to lose their horses, they having strayed away during the night. [...] Providentially a couple of Sioux Indians arrived on the scene. [...] As soon as they heard [her father's] name they gave her to understand that it was all right. They told her that they would bring her horses back or die in the attempt. [...] I may say also the Mr. McKay 'Wa han' had been quite unknown to the Sioux tribe until 4 or 5 years before." An excerpt from the article "So the Poor Indian," written by Willie in the early 1900s. It is uncertain whether his article referred to the journey to fetch Kate or to another journey. PMF M8486/283.

14 The first of Harriet and Willie's nine daughters, Catharine Parr, was born November 29, 1871. Harriet's sister Kate came to lend a hand running the household.

15 Cole Falls is on the North Saskatchewan River, a few miles west of the junction of the North and South branches.

16 Joseph James Hargrave, *Red River*. Montreal: Lovell, 1871. Reprint, Altona, Manitoba: Friesen, 1977.

17 W.F. Butler, *The Great Lone Land: A Narrative of Travel and Adventure in the North-west of America*, (London: Low, Marston, Low, & Searle), 1872. Reprint, Edmonton: Hurtig, 1968.

18 Paid professional magistrates.

19 The Traills' second daughter, Mary (Mollie), was born November 12, 1873.

20 Two of Harriet's eight brothers.

FIVE: LAC LA BICHE, 1874–1881

1 In the 1850s, Notre-Dame-Des-Victories, a Roman Catholic mission inspired by Father Lacombe, opened at Lac la Biche. In 1862, the Oblate missionaries were joined by the Grey Nuns. These remarkable women operated a mission school and nursed the ill and the aged. They would be of immeasurable value to Willie and his family during their years at LLB.

2 A byre is a cowshed.

3 Their second son, William McKay (Bill) Traill, was born June 25, 1875. Bill grew into his hands and feet. When he joined the Strathcona's Horse, February 9, 1900, bound for the Boer War he was 6' 2" tall and weighed 181 pounds. He received the Queen's medal with three Clasps: Belfast, the Orange Free State, and Natal. When honourably discharged March 8, 1901, he had attained the rank of Sergeant. (Public Archives of Canada—RG 381A, Vol 106). Bill died in 1969.

4 After twelve long years of loyal service, Willie was finally granted his first furlough. He left Fort Pitt for Canada on May 20, 1876. It is likely that he travelled to his parental home at Rice Lake, then to Philadelphia, to

Montreal, back to Rice Lake, to Toronto and then to Fort Garry. When in Philadelphia, he attended the National Surgical Institute for treatment on his throat.

5 The youngest son of Susanna Moodie. Catharine Parr Traill, *I Bless You in My Heart*.

6 Willie is referring to a dispute between Catharine Parr Traill and one of her publishers. Catherine's elder sister Agnes, author of the series *Lives of the Queens of England*, died in 1874 and bequeathed the copyright to these volumes, in equal shares, to Catharine Parr Traill and Percy Strickland. Longmans (one of the co-publishers with Bell and Sons) demanded the beneficiaries pay part of the printing costs for a new edition, effectively avoiding paying Catharine and Percy their share of the profits of sale. In 1877, Bell and Sons purchased the copyright from Catharine and Percy on satisfactory terms. It appears that the situation would never have been resolved had Bell and Sons not so acted. Catharine Parr Traill, *I Bless You In My Heart*.

7 A horse-drawn vehicle with a body formed by a plank fixed between two axles.

8 The Traills' third son (fifth child) Henry was born November 20, 1877.

9 The HBC had two posts named Victoria—a minor post on the North Saskatchewan River located some 75 miles east of Edmonton and Fort Victoria on the southern tip of Vancouver Island.

10 The adverse market for furs in Europe was having a predictable impact on promotions. Willie had expected to reach officer status (Junior Chief Trader) before now—unfortunately he was destined to wait a bit longer.

11 Annie's son Henry died in 1864, at age four. Catharine Parr Traill, *I Bless You In My Heart*.

12 My maternal grandmother Ethel Traill, was born October 9, 1879. After the death of the two children in December 1878, her arrival was truly a blessed event.

SIX: LESSER SLAVE LAKE, 1881–1885

1 HBCA-PAM Post Records: Post B.115.

2 During seasons of open water, the York boat was the HBC's primary vehicle for transporting personnel and freight between Western posts. First used in the 1820s or 1830s, York boats "supplanted the birch bark canoe as a means of transport in the interior waterways of Rupert's Land....[after] the call went out from Sir George Simpson and his Council for a type of boat which would prove light enough to be taken on rollers over portages, strong enough to shoot the rapids, seaworthy enough to cross such stormy waters as Lake Winnipeg, and commodious enough to carry a cargo of eighty pieces, each of which weighed ninety to one hundred pounds, as well as a crew of eight voyageurs, and carry a sail when required....The dimensions of the York boat differed according to the

routes covered, and were from twenty-eight feet to forty feet in length, seven feet to eight feet in beam and three to four feet in depth.... The last two York boats for the service were built at Norway house by William and James Robertson, old boat builders for the Company. These boats were finished and launched in the spring of 1923." *Beaver*, 1931 September, 281–2.

3   In 1881, Willie's younger brother Walter married Mary Gilbert, a widow with two children. Walter Traill, *In Rupert's Land*, 23.

4   Willie may have been referring to the Emerson West Lynne border crossing south of Winnipeg, as Walter was living and working just south of there.

5   Possibly a local free trader.

6   Later Chief Factor Clarke.

7   Their eldest son Walter was enrolled in St John's College, Winnipeg— now St John's Ravenscourt.

8   No relation to Chief Factor William McKay.

9   It was rumoured that a rail line would be developed in the Peace River District—unfortunately a far distant dream.

10 Chief Factor McFarlane.

11 On Christmas Day, 1883, a great light went out in the West when William McKay died at Fort Edmonton, at age 65. His death was a terrible blow to his family, his friends, the Indians, and the HBC. This excerpt from his wife's memorial in the *Saskatoon Star* requires no elaboration: "The McKays have been for generations commissioned officers in the Hudson's Bay Company, wielding on occasion almost despotic power over Territories larger than European kingdoms, and using, always, the influence placed in their hands with discretion and wisdom.... Their influence with the Indians, their reputation for personal courage and integrity is well known to have been one of the chief factors in keeping the settlement of the North West so remarkably free from the sanguinary troubles with the native population, which has almost invariably characterized similar epochs in similar countries." *Saskatoon Star*, May 12, 1917.

12 Another daughter Mary was born November 26, 1883. She was given the same name as an earlier daughter, Mary (Mollie), who had died of scarlet fever.

13 The Northwest Rebellion took place in the spring and early summer of 1885. Willie and family were physically removed from the Rebellion, although in late April 1885 the Indians sacked their former post Lac la Biche.

14 Five of Harriet's brothers were actively involved in the uprising: James was a private in the 90th Regiment and attached to Colonel French's Scouts; Thomas was a scout and interpreter with Crozier; George served with Sam Steele's scouts at the Battle of Frenchman's Butte; and Thomas and Angus served as scouts and interpreters.

15 Willie later wrote in an article: "I honestly believe that it was solely owing to Mr. McKay's influence over the tribe in general & over Big Bear in particular that hostilities did not break out years before they did. I can state positively that Mr. McKay succeeded in extracting a promise from Big Bear that so long as he (Mr. McKay) lived that he would never take up arms against the whites." PMF M8486/283.

16 Willie found himself in a new and unpleasant relationship—he reported to a superior officer he neither respected nor trusted. Regarding the controversy with Dr. MacKay, Willie faced a dilemma. If he solicited support from Dr. MacKay's superiors, he might obtain relief. On the other hand, there is every possibility the HBC hierarchy would support MacKay. Even if they sided with Willie, his copybook would be blotted. It is probable that Willie elected to do what he deemed proper—regardless of the outcome.

SEVEN: FORT VERMILION, 1886–1889

1 The first Fort Vermilion was built by the NWC in 1800 on the south bank of the Peace River, 17 miles below Keg River. In 1828, the post was moved down the river, first to the south bank and finally to the north bank. HBCA-PAM Post Records B.224.

2 While in Ontario, Willie formed a great fondness for his niece, Katharine Stewart Atwood, the second eldest daughter of Willie's sister Annie and her husband Clinton. He addresses Katherine, then eighteen years old, as "Kitten Katten" or "Kit Kat."

3 Fort Chipewyan is located where Lake Athabasca empties into the Slave River. The journey to Fort Vermilion from Chipewyan, 300 miles by water and approximately 175 miles direct, is 20 miles down the Slave River to the confluence of the Peace and westward up the Peace to Vermilion.

4 The Traills' social life was immeasurably enhanced by the presence of the families of Bishop Young and Mr. Scott. Both families proved very compatible and contributed notably to the Traills' religious well-being.

5 The Traills' sixth daughter Maria was born February 8, 1886. Willie nicknamed her "Yummie" after Yum Yum in the Mikado.

6 Nan was a nickname for Willie's sister Annie.

7 *Canadian Wild Flowers*. Montreal: Lovell, 1868.

8 Harriet (Hattie), the Traill's seventh daughter, was born February 12, 1888.

9 Religion continued to play a central part in the Traills' day-to-day lives— supporting them in good times and bad. On many occasions Willie, in the absence of an ordained minister, conducted Sunday Service. He was also chosen as a lay delegate to one or more Anglican Synods.

10 Christmas of 1888 was the Traills' last at Fort Vermilion. Their stay there had been much more pleasant than anticipated. Based on many mutual interests and similar social backgrounds they had formed warm and lasting friendships with the Youngs and the Scotts.

1   Fort St. James was "about a mile from the mouth of Stuarts River on the north east shore of Stuarts Lake." ("Stewart" and "Stuart" are used interchangeably.) The fort had been "established by the North West Company (Simon Fraser and John Stuart) July, 1806 as headquarters of New Caledonia District" and then "acquired as a result of coalition with the North West Company. Fire destroyed the trading store and contents in 1919." HBCA Post Records: Post B.188.

2   Annie lived until 1977, and Barbara lived a remarkably long life; she died in 1990.

3   Harriet was five months pregnant.

4   150 Mile Station is 10 miles east of present-day Williams Lake.

5   A York boat.

6   Fort George was one of Fort St. James' satellite posts.

7   Mr. McFarlane, Willie's predecessor at the post, had extended excessive credit to the Indians, who had come to expect this as their right.

8   Soda Creek is approximately 25 kms north of Williams Lake.

9   Fort Alexandria is approximately 30 miles south of Williams Lake.

10   A Celestial is a subject of China (the Celestial Empire).

11   Candle-fish, native to the northwest coast of North America.

12   Most likely "Carrier."

13   Anne (Annie), the Traills' 11th child and 8th daughter, was born December 28, 1889.

14   A sedative.

15   McLeod's Lake was another of Fort St. James' satellite posts.

16   Connolly was another satellite post of Fort St. James.

17   Young Willie's health problem eventually resolved itself.

18   Willie and Harriet's last child, a daughter named Barbara, was born at Fort St. James on March 18, 1892.

EPILOGUE

1   1950. Personal collection of Marion Hage.

INDEX